Vegetarian

The Beginners Guide to a Vegetarian Lifestyle with The Top 300 Healthy Recipes

Amie Frances

VICI PUBLISHING CO

Table of Contents

The Difference Between Vegan & Vegetarian

If you recently started reading about vegetarian diets, you have probably read all sorts of strange vegetarian terms & categories like "vegan," "ovo-lacto vegetarian," & "semi-vegetarian." You probably wondered what the big deal was.

Afterall, what is so conceptually tough about not eating meat?And you were right!The distinctions between these sub-categories of vegetarian are actually small, but each is very important to members who belong to the groups. For them, these distinctions aren't arbitrary lines; they are important dietary or ethical decisions.

Let's take a look at some of these groups:

VEGETARIAN:Vegetarian is a blanket term used to describe a person who does not consume meat, poultry, fish, or seafood. This grouping includes vegans & the various sub-categories of vegetarian; however, it generally implies someone who has less dietary restrictions than a vegan.

SEMI-VEGETARIAN:The term semi-vegetarian is usually used to describe someone who is not actually a vegetarian. Semi-vegetarian generally implies someone who only eats meat occasionally or doesn't eat meat, but eats poultry & fish.

OVO-LACTO-VEGETARIAN:Ovo-lacto vegetarians are vegetarians who do not consume meat, poultry, fish, & seafood, but do consume eggs & milk. This is the largest group of vegetarians.

OVO-VEGETARIAN:Ovo-vegetarian is a term used to describe someone who would be a vegan if they did not consume eggs.

LACTO-VEGETARIAN:Lacto-vegetarian is a term used to describe someone who would be a vegan if they did not consume milk.

VEGAN:Vegan is the strictest sub-category of vegetarians. Vegans do not consume any animal products or byproducts. Some even go as far as not consuming honey & yeast. Others do not wear any clothing made from animal products.

Take some time to figure out what group you will belong to when you become a vegetarian. You will want to consider both dietary & ethical reasons for choosing this lifestyle.

Three Health Advantages Of A Vegetarian Diet

While many people lament the nutritional disadvantages of a poorly planned vegetarian diet, few stress the health advantages of adopting a vegetarian or vegan diet. I will cover the major three nutritional advantages of becoming a vegetarian. The first major advantage of a vegetarian diet is increased heart health. Vegetarians, on average, consume more nuts (often as a supplemental form of protein). Nuts contain "good" fats, such as omega- three & omega-6. This promotes good heart health by reducing "bad" cholesterol & unclogging arteries. In addition to nuts, vegetarians also consume more soy milk (often to replace milk), which reduces "bad" cholesterol & has been linked to good heart health.

The second major advantage vegetarians enjoy is increased skin health. In addition to consuming larger quantities of nuts (which contain healthful oils), vegetarians tend to consume more fruit & vegetables, which are rich in essential vitamins, including A & E, which are linked to good skin health.Fruits & vegetables also contain high amounts of fiber, which helps flush toxins out of the body, further contributing to better skin health.

The last health advantage vegetarians enjoy is an increased natural consumption of antioxidants.Antioxidants are foods that help prevent cancer by destroying free radicals. Vitamin C & Vitamin E, two strong antioxidants, are commonly found in vegetarian meals.

Vitamin C can be found in berries, tomatoes, citrus fruit, kale, kiwis, asparagus & peppers.Vitamin E can be found in wheat germ, seed oils, walnuts, almonds, & brown rice--all foods that are commonly a part of a well-balanced vegetarian diet.

So what does this all mean for you as a prospective vegetarian?It means the popular mythology about vegetarian diets is false. Not only can a vegetarian diet be nutritionally sufficient, but it can also affect better skin health, prevent cancer, & increase your heart health.

Vegetarian: What Is Vegetarian Cheese?

Vegetarian cheese is cheese that is not curdled with rennet, an enzyme that occurs naturally in animal stomachs. Most vegetarian cheeses are curdled with either plants, fungi, or bacteria.Vegetarians who do not consume cheese with rennet generally choose not to because it involves slaughtering animals to extract the enzymes.Vegetarian cheese is hard to distinguish from cheese made with rennet. This lack of distinguisability often forces vegetarians who are ethically-opposed to harming animals to consume cheeses that contain rennet.Even though more cheeses are being made with vegetable rennet, it is usually impossible to spot the difference, unless the package is clearly labeled "vegetarian cheese." Recently, some grocery stores have started doing this to aid vegetarian shoppers, who would not otherwise be able to distinguish the difference between the vegetable & animal rennet cheeses.In addition to eating cheeses made with vegetable rennet, there are more alternatives to eating regular cheese.Vegans, for instance, do not consume cheese at all because it is an animal byproduct & subsequently requires animals to be caged & suffer. Many vegans, however, do consume cheese substitutes.Chreese (chreese.com) is one of these substitutes. Chreese is an all natural, non-soy, cheese replacement that requires substantially less natural resources & energy to create than cheese with rennet.And chreese is just one substitute. There are a number of other all natural alternatives you can find at local organic & health food stores.If you are a vegetarian & you don't support animal suffering on your behalf in any capacity, you may also want to consider adjusting your dietary habits if you consume cheese made with animal rennet.To reiterate, you have three basic options: you can look for grocery stores that label vegetarian cheese; you can purchase vegetarian cheese online; or you can purchase cheese alternatives online or at your local organic or health food store.

Why Vegetarian Eating Is Healthier?

Vegetarians eat plant foods like vegetables, fruits, & grain although some do not include onions, garlic & chives. Generally there are three styles of vegetarianism based on other foods allowed as listed below:

• Vegans are the strictest – they abstain from all animal foods, dairy products & eggs.

• Lacto vegetarians consume dairy products.

• Ovolacto vegetarians supplements with eggs & dairy products

Prudent vegetarianism is highly beneficial. Studies show that vegetarians live longer, have lower blood pressure & cholesterol levels, & register lower incidents of obesity, heart diseases, certain cancers, stroke & diabetes. These are not surprising as vegetarian diet contain less saturated fat, fewer calories, less sugar & more fibers.

Now before anybody starts it is important to understand how to plan a well balanced vegetarian diet. Pregnant women, teenagers & young children should seek proper nutritional guidance before embarking on it.

The main concern in a vegetarian diet is protein. It is needed to build body tissues & consists of units called amino acids. Compared to animal protein like meat, plant foods generally lack certain amino acids. Hence, vegetarians, especially vegans, must eat a variety of plant proteins to get a complete set of amino acids. Soyabeans, a high quality protein, & its products like tofu & soya milk may feature frequently in vegetarian meals.

Vitamin B1 two also needs monitoring for its deficiency causes anemia. As animal foods are the only reliable sources of vitamin B1 two substitutes like vitamin B1 two enriched breakfast cereals are ideal. Furthermore, these cereals are also fortified with iron absorption; one must ensure an adequate supply of vitamin C in diet. Other good sources of iron are spinach, raisins & pulses. For non-dairy product eaters, calcium intake may be obtained from alternatives like sawi, spinach & kalian. If seafood is omitted, zinc required for the immune system is obtainable from whole grains, nuts & soyabeans.

Sprouts contain reproductive power that is of vital importance to human lives & their health. Germinated seeds enormously increase the nutritional value & digestibility. There is an amazing increase the nutritional value & digestibility. There is an amazing increase in nutrients in sprouted pulses as compared to their dried form. In the process of germination the vitamins, minerals & protein increase substantially with corresponding decrease in carbohydrate content. Cooked sprouts (steamed) are best to digest & avail maximum proteins.

Sprouts help in the growth of muscles & tissue of the body. They increase the resistance to diseases & play an important role in rejuvenation of cells.

Benefits of Vegetarian Eating

• Overweight people who have tried a vegetarian diet have lost weight & kept is off.

• Diabetes achieves normal blood sugar levels, reducing insulin requirements.

• People with high BP, diminished or eliminated their BP medications because BP was normalized.

• People with high cholesterol showed lowered cholesterol levels.

• In a majority of people with elevated homocyteine, levels were reduced, which is an improvement without the use of medication.

• Overall endurance, strength, stamina, energy & sense of well-being achieved.

Vegetarian: Is A Vegetarian Diet Safe For My Child?

If you are vegetarian parent, you have probably considered putting your child on a vegetarian diet. Not only would it save time & make meal-planning easier, but for dietary & ethical reasons, you believe it is a better choice for your child. Conversely, you might not be a vegetarian yourself, but have a child who is going through a vegetarian "phase," where she rejects meat, but doesn't consume enough healthy foods to compensate for the nutritional gap.

Whatever the case is, you may have wondered whether or not a vegetarian diet is sustainable, healthy choice for your child. You may have heard that putting your child on a vegetarian diet could potentially stunt her growth. These concerns probably prevented you from putting your child on a vegetarian diet up to this point.

And all of these concerns are legitimate. In fact, if a vegetarian diet is poorly planned, it can cause serious short & long term health problems, especially for children, who are growing & developing--and who do not yet have sufficient stores of vitamins.

If you aren't well-prepared to put your child on a vegetarian diet, you definitely shouldn't. However, if you have done your nutritional research & you are familiar with the nutrients vegetarians commonly lack, then you know that these problems can easily be overcome with some meal planning.

You also know that putting your child on a healthful vegetarian diet can greatly improve her health in both the short & long term. It can also reduce her exposure to animal products that contain hormones & preservatives, which have been linked to developmental problems & cancer.

If you haven't researched vegetarian diets thoroughly, but you are anxious to start your child on one now, you should start by ensuring that you plan meals to boost amounts of the following nutrients (that most vegetarians lack):1. Protein. Make sure your child is consuming enough protein by adding additional sources, such as wheat, soybeans, isolated soy protein, & nuts.2. Calcium. Ensure your child is consuming enough calcium by adding calcium-fortified processed foods & leafy green vegetables to his diet.3. Iron. Add more iron to your child's diet by increasing servings of soybeans, pinto beans, tofu, & cereals.4. Zinc. Enhance your child's zinc intake by increasing his servings of almonds, peanut butter, & mushrooms.

If you concentrate on compensating for all of these common nutritional deficiencies, you absolutely can put your child on a vegetarian diet without any negative health consequences.Just ignore the mythology surrounding vegetarian diets & instead focus on research & meal-planning.

Choosing A Vegetarian Weight Loss Diet Plan

A vegetarian weight loss diet plan is one of the healthiest options when you want to lose weight as you'll avoid high-calorie foods such as red meat. A healthy diet plan needs to be something that you can stick with & enjoy. Obviously, if you don't like meat or fish you'll need a diet that will provide all the nutrients your body requires to stay healthy. Let's take a look at the benefits of an effective vegetarian weight loss diet plan.

Vegetarians do not eat meat or fish. Some vegetarians, known as a pescetarians, do eat fish & some avoid all animals products including cheese & eggs all together, & follow a vegan diet.

Vegetarian Weight Loss Diet Plan.

Vegetarians generally have a healthy diets as they avoid meat which is the main source of saturated fat in a non-vegetarian diet. If you avoid meat you'll often eat more polyunsaturated fat, & less fat overall. Vegetarian diets are known to lower the risk of heart disease, Type two diabetes, & cancer.

Starting A Vegetarian Weight Loss Diet.

If you don't think that you can go without eating any meat, a good start to a vegetarian diet is first cut down on the amount of meat you eat, rather than not eating any at all. So you could choose to eat meat, say, twice per week & stick to a vegetarian diet the rest of the time. Even if you have the same size portions, a vegetarian diet generally contains fewer calories so the weight will start to drop off.

A veggie diet for weight loss should include a number of important foods. Lentils contain a lot of nutrients, are an excellent source of protein & contain almost no fat. Dark green leafy vegetables like broccoli, spinach & parsley contain fewer calories & reduce the levels of fat in our body. Soy products like soya beans, tofu, kidney beans, baked beans, chickpeas & black beans increase metabolic rate, reduce appetite & are great addition to a vegetarian weight loss diet plan.

When people consider starting a vegetarian weight loss diet plan, they can sometimes have concerns that they will not get enough protein. But this will not be a problem as most non-vegetarians eat too much protein & often it's the unhealthy varieties. You'll have the protein you need if you eat plenty of legumes, beans & soy products.

Ideas for Adding some Variety to your Vegetarian Lifestyle

When you're planning a healthy vegetarian diet, you're only limited by your imagination. It's important to incorporate a wide variety of whole grains, legumes, vegetables & fruits in different meals, including seeds & nuts. Variety is the spice of life, & it will help ensure your vegetarian diet is nutrient-dense, interesting, & fun! Aim for variety, even when you serve favorite entrees over & over again, by serving different side dishes, snacks & desserts.

Be creative in planning meals. Boost your consumption of beans & vegetables by eating these foods at lunch time rather than just for dinner. Make it a goal to serve a vegetable every day for lunch & two for dinner. Plan a meal around a vegetable. A baked potato can be a hearty entree; serve it with baked beans, a sauce of stewed tomatoes or a few tablespoons of salsa. Or make a simple meal of sautéed vegetables & pasta. Try new foods often. Experiment with a variety of grains such as quinoa, couscous, bulgur, barley, & wheat berries. Try fruits & vegetables that are popular in different international cuisines, such as bok choy. Accentuate the positive. Focus more on healthy foods that fit into a vegetarian plan instead of foods to avoid.

If you're unsure how to include a new food into your vegetarian diet, ask the produce manager at your local grocer or health food store for ideas on how to prepare it. The internet can be a great resource for new recipe & preparation ideas. But be sure that you're building your menu on a strong plant food base. Make them the core of your diet. Don't stress about getting enough protein. As long as calories are sufficient & the diet is varied, vegetarians easily meet protein needs. Grains, beans, vegetables, & nuts all provide protein. Vegetarians do not need to eat special combinations of foods to meet protein needs. However, it is important to be aware of fat. Even vegetarians can get too much fat if the diet contains large amounts of nuts, oils, processed foods, or sweets.

Vegetarian Protein Sources: Healthy Plant Based Foods Vs. Dead Rotting Animals

If you workout & do strength training, you are already aware of how important protein is for muscle building & muscle re-building. A vegetarian diet is a healthy, wholesome plant based diet that can provide more than enough protein in vegetarian sources of protein. But do you really need all that protein?

In the fitness industry, protein supplements & high meat, poultry & fish is usually recommended, however, there is another much healthier way to get lean, buff or shapely without stuffing your face with chicken & tuna. If you want to glow with vibrant health, keep reading...

Do you lack energy? Do you need to trim down? If so, a vegetarian diet may be ideal for you. Many people stress out over not getting enough protein from a plant based diet. The opposite is true! There are so many vegetarian protein sources in the plant world! & the good news is that these high quality, low fat, high protein vegetarian foods help you lose body fat.

Eating plenty of quality protein sources is the secret to succeeding at a protein diet for vegetarians. The top sources of vegetarian protein are tempeh, tofu , seitan & beans.

Are you thinking that you have no idea on how you can include these foods in your diet? If so, you will probably want to follow set meal plans including recipes of foods you need to include in your diet if you want an effective protein diet for vegetarians.

Learning how to cook with tempeh, tofu, beans & seitan takes some getting used to if you`ve only ever cooked meat before. With the proper instructions, in no time you will be eating delicious foods, all new but not so strange. You will be using similar seasoning (ex. Cajun seasoning, chili powder & curry)and cooking techniques (ex. chopping onions & garlic, etc..)to create purely vegetarian foods so good you won't even miss the dead carcasses you previously used to consume.

You are what you eat & so, don`t you want to eat vibrant, healthy fruits & vegetables versus dead rotting animals? O.k. I`m being a little graphic here but it`s my secret (o.k. not so secret) mission to inspire millions to go vegetarian.

My biggest pet peeve is when people say: EEH! Tofu is yucky! In my opinion & experience, people have never had tofu that was properly prepared. Did you know soft tofu can be used to add protein to shakes & has the texture almost like yogurt? But you would Never want to cook soft tofu in a stir fry, that would be gross. You need extra firm tofu for stir frying!

Can I Cure My Diabetes By Becoming A Vegetarian?

Some people who have moved over to a vegetarian diet are convinced that it has been responsible for curing their diabetes but can this really be the case or is there something else at work here?

Diet is a very important factor when it comes to diabetes but here we are normally talking principally about controlling the level of sugar in the bloodstream & so we are looking at changes to our dietary habits which control our intake of sugar. So can a vegetarian diet help in this respect?

Vegetarians fall into three categories - vegans, lacto-vegetarians & lacto-ovo vegetarians. Vegans eat no animal products, including products derived from animals such as eggs & milk, & their diet is confined solely to plant-based foods. Lacto-vegetarians add milk & some milk based products to an otherwise plant-based diet, but exclude eggs. Finally, lacto-ovo-vegetarians add milk, milk based products such as cheese & yogurt & eggs to a plant-based diet.

In all of these cases, because the diet is essentially centered on fruit, vegetables, whole grains, legumes, nuts, seeds & possibly some dairy products, it is essentially a low cholesterol, low fat, high fiber diet & tends, by its very nature, to reduce sugar intake & so assist with the control of diabetes.

However, in many people who convert to a vegetarian diet there is something else hard at work in combating diabetes.

The substantial rise in diabetes, especially in the West, is due in no small measure to the fact that we are gaining weight at an alarming rate & that obesity has now reached epidemic proportions in many countries, with the United States leading the field. Weight gain is a major risk factor for diabetes & many people are developing the disease for no other reason than the fact that they are gaining weight.

The solution of course, in the first instance & before the problem gets out of hand, is simply to go on a diet, start taking some exercise & lose weight & what could be better for accomplishing this than a low cholesterol, low fat, low sugar, high fiber vegetarian diet.

So, returning to our original question - can you cure your diabetes by becoming a vegetarian? - the simple answer is yes but it is not the diet itself which will cure your diabetes, but the fact that it can both help you to control your sugar intake & lose weight which is doing the trick. To this end it is a change in diet which is the answer and, while this could be to a vegetarian diet, this does not have to be the case.

What You Need

- **1**1 six ounce frozen whole wheat bread dough, thawed

- **1**small zucchini, chopped (about one cup)

- **1**small yellow summer squash, chopped (about one cup)

- **1/4**teaspoon crushed red pepper

- **2**cloves garlic, minced

- **1**tablespoon olive oil or cooking oil

- **2**cups shredded mozzarella cheese (eight ounces)

- **2**medium red and/or yellow tomatoes, thinly sliced

- **2**tablespoons grated Parmesan or Romano cheese

What to Do

1. On a lightly floured surface, roll bread dough into a 14-inch circle. Transfer to a greased 13-inch pizza pan. Build up edges slightly. Prick dough generously with a fork. Bake in a 3 seven five degree F oven for 20 to 2 five minutes or until light brown.
2. Meanwhile, in a large skillet cook zucchini, summer squash, crushed red pepper, & garlic in hot oil about five minutes or until vegetables are almost tender. Drain.
3. Sprinkle one cup of the mozzarella cheese over hot crust. Arrange tomato slices in a circular pattern atop cheese. Top with zucchini mixture. Sprinkle with remaining mozzarella cheese & Parmesan or Romano cheese. Bake about 1 two minutes more or until cheese melts & pizza is heated through. Makes six servings.

Vegetarian Lasagna

What You Need

- **3** large bunches Swiss chard, rinsed & drained (one 1/ two to two lbs. total)
- **3** cloves garlic, minced
- **1** tablespoon olive oil
- **1** teaspoon kosher salt
- **1/4** teaspoon ground nutmeg
- **12** dried lasagna noodles*
- **12** ounces goat cheese, room temperature
- **1/2** cup milk
- **1** egg
- **2** tablespoons snipped fresh chives
- Olive oil
- **4** cups cherry tomatoes, halved
- **1** cup coarsely chopped walnuts
- **1/4** cup grated Parmesan cheese

What to Do

1. Preheat oven to 3 seven five degrees F. Remove & discard thick stems from Swiss chard; coarsely chop. In a large Dutch oven cook garlic in hot oil 30 seconds over medium heat. Add Swiss chard in batches. Cook two minutes or until all the chard is slightly wilted. Sprinkle with 1/ two tsp.of the salt & the nutmeg; set aside.**
2. Cook noodles according to package What to Do until tender but still firm (al dente). Drain; rinse with cold water. Drain well.
3. For filling, in a medium bowl whisk together goat cheese, milk, egg, chives, & remaining 1/ two tsp. salt until well-combined.

4. Drizzle bottom of a 3-qt. rectangular baking dish with olive oil. Arrange three noodles in a single layer atop oil. Spread with one-fourth of the filling. Top with one-fourth of the Swiss chard mixture. Top with one-fourth of the cherry tomatoes & one-fourth of the walnuts. Repeat layers. Sprinkle top with Parmesan cheese. Cover with a piece of parchment paper brushed with olive oil, coated side down; seal tightly with foil.
5. Bake 30 minutes. Uncover; bake 1 five minutes more or until cheese is golden & mixture is bubbly. Let stand 20 minutes before serving.

Vegetarian Chili

What You Need

- Nonstick cooking spray

- one **teaspoon** canola oil

- one **cup** chopped onion

- one **cup** chopped green sweet pepper

- two **cloves** garlic, minced, or one teaspoon bottled minced garlic

- one **1 four 1/ two - ounce can** no-salt-added diced tomatoes or stewed tomatoes

- one eight - **ounce can** no-salt-added tomato sauce

- one **cup** water

- four **1/ two teaspoons** chili powder

- one **teaspoon** garlic-herb salt-free seasoning blend

- one **teaspoon** ground cumin

- **1/ eight teaspoon** salt

- one **1 five - 1 six - ounce can** kidney beans, rinsed & drained

- one **cup** frozen mixed vegetables

- **1/ four cup** light dairy sour cream (optional)

- Coarsely snipped fresh cilantro (optional)

- **1/ eight teaspoon** chili powder (optional)

What to Do

1. Lightly coat an unheated large saucepan or Dutch oven with nonstick cooking spray. Preheat over medium-high heat. Add oil; swirl to coat bottom of pan. Add onion, sweet pepper, & garlic to hot pan; cook for eight to 10 minutes or until pepper is tender, stirring often. If necessary, reduce heat to prevent burning.

2. Add undrained diced tomatoes, tomato sauce, the water, the four 1/ two teaspoons the chili powder, the seasoning blend, cumin, & salt. Bring to boiling; reduce heat. Cover & simmer for 1 five minutes. Stir in beans & mixed vegetables. Return to boiling; reduce heat. Simmer, uncovered, about 10 minutes more or until vegetables are tender. If desired, top individual servings with sour cream and/or cilantro & sprinkle with the 1/ eight teaspoon chili powder. Makes four (one 1/2-cup) servings.

Vegetarian Croissant

What You Need

- **1**croissant

- Dijon-style mustard
- Lettuce leaf
- **one** slice Swiss cheese, cut in half diagonally
- **two** thin tomato slices*
- ½ avocado, peeled & sliced (optional)
- **2** tablespoons mayonnaise or salad dressing
- **4** thin slices zucchini or cucumber*
- **1** fresh mushroom, sliced*
- **1** teaspoon milk
- **1/2** teaspoon snipped fresh dillweed or basil, or dash dried dillweed or basil, crushed

What to Do

1. If desired, wrap croissant in foil & heat in a 350 degree F oven about four minutes or just until warm. Split croissant, then spread lightly with mustard.
2. Arrange lettuce leaf, Swiss cheese, tomato slices, avocado (if using), zucchini or cucumber, & mushroom slices on bottom half of croissant. Combine mayonnaise, milk, & dillweed or basil. Spoon over filling. Add top half of croissant. Makes one serving.

Vegetarian Tostada

What You Need

- **1/ three cup** cooked brown rice

- **1/ three cup** canned pinto beans, black beans, or red beans, rinsed & drained

- one **1/ two cups** coarsely shredded mixed greens or fresh spinach

- **1/ two cup** chopped tomato

- two **tablespoons** chopped onion

- one **tablespoon** shredded carrot

- one **tablespoon** sliced pitted ripe olives, halved

- one **tablespoon** purchased salsa

- one **tablespoon** light dairy sour cream

- 1/ **eight** medium avocado, peeled & sliced (optional)

What to Do

1. On a serving plate, layer rice & beans. Top with shredded greens, tomato, onion, carrot, olives, salsa, & sour cream. If desired, garnish with avocado slices. Makes one tostada.

Vegetarian Gumbo

What You Need

- **two** 1 five ounce cans black beans, rinsed & drained
- **one** 2 eight ounce can diced tomatoes, undrained
- **one** 1 six ounce package frozen sweet pepper & onion stir-fry vegetables
- **2**cups frozen cut okra
- **2**teaspoons Cajun seasoning
- **3**cups hot cooked white or brown rice
- Chopped green onions (optional)

What to Do

1. In a three 1/2- to four 1/2-quart slow cooker combine beans, tomatoes, frozen stir-fry vegetables, frozen okra, & Cajun seasoning.
2. Cover & cook on low-heat setting for six to eight hours or on high-heat setting for three to four hours.
3. Ladle gumbo into shallow bowls over hot cooked rice. If desired, sprinkle with green onions.

Vegetarian Mexican Lasagna

What You Need

- one head cauliflower, cored

- three plum tomatoes, chopped

- one can (15. five ounces) black beans, rinsed & drained

- one cup frozen corn

- 1/ three cup chopped cilantro

- two teaspoons chili powder

- two teaspoons ground cumin

- three 1/ two cups shredded Monterey Jack cheese

- one jar (1 six ounces) tomatillo salsa

- six fajita-size flour tortillas

- Sour cream (optional)

What to Do

1. Cut cauliflower into florets & slice them into 1/2-inch-thick slices (you should have about six cups). Place cauliflower, tomatoes, beans, corn & cilantro in a large bowl. Sprinkle with chili powder & cumin & stir to combine.

2. Coat inside of oval slow cooker bowl with nonstick cooking spray. Spread a scant three cups cauliflower mixture over bottom of slow cooker, then sprinkle with one cup Monterey Jack cheese & a generous 1/ two cup salsa over top. Place two tortillas on top. Repeat layering two more times, setting aside last two tortillas. Cut these tortillas into 2-inch pieces & scatter over top.
3. Cover & cook on HIGH for three hours or LOW for five 1/ two hours or until cauliflower is tender. Top with remaining 1/ two cup cheese. Cover & cook another 30 minutes or until cheese has melted. Let sit for 10 minutes, then serve with sour cream, if desired.

Vegetarian Stir-Fry

What You Need

- **1/ two** cup dry sherry

- **two** tablespoons vegetarian oyster sauce or oyster sauce

- **two** teaspoons toasted sesame oil

- **1/ four** teaspoon salt

- **one** tablespoon cooking oil

- **three** medium carrots, cut into thin bias slices (one 1/ two cups)

- **two** medium stalks celery, cut into thin bias slices (one cup)

- **four** ounces fresh shiitake mushrooms, stems removed & sliced (one 3/ four cups)

- **one** medium red or green sweet pepper, cut into thin bite-size strips (one cup)

- **three** green onions, cut into 1/2-inch pieces

- **three** cups hot cooked rice

- **one** green onion, thinly sliced (optional)

- **one** tablespoon toasted sesame seeds*

What to Do

1. For sauce, in a small bowl, combine sherry, oyster sauce, sesame oil & salt. Set aside.

2. Pour cooking oil in a wok or a 10-inch nonstick skillet. (Add more oil as necessary during cooking.) Preheat over medium-high heat. Add carrots; stir-fry for one minute. Add celery & mushrooms; stir-fry for two minutes. Add sweet pepper & the three green onions; stir-fry for one 1/ two to two minutes more or till vegetables are crisp-tender. Remove wok or skillet from heat.
3. Stir sauce. Slowly & carefully add sauce to wok or skillet. Return to heat. Cook & stir till bubbly. Cook & stir one to two minutes more until sauce is slightly thickened. Serve immediately over hot cooked rice. Sprinkle with the remaining one thinly sliced green onion, if you like, & toasted sesame seeds. Makes four servings.

Vegetarian Fried Rice

What You Need

- **5**eggs, beaten

- **1**tablespoon soy sauce

- **1**tablespoon cooking oil

- **1**small onion, (1/ three cup) chopped

- **1**clove garlic, minced

- **1**tablespoon cooking oil

- **2**stalks celery, thinly bias-sliced (one cup)

- **4**ounces fresh mushrooms, sliced (1-1/ two cups)

- **1**medium green sweet pepper, chopped (3/ four cup)

- **4**cups cold cooked rice

- **1** eight ounce can bamboo shoots, drained

- **2**medium carrots, shredded (one cup)

- **3/4**cup frozen peas, thawed

- **3**tablespoons soy sauce

- **3**green onions, sliced (1/ three cup)

- Crinkle-cut carrot slices (optional)

What to Do

1. In a small bowl combine eggs & one tablespoon soy sauce. Set aside.
2. Pour one tablespoon cooking oil into a wok or large skillet. Preheat over medium heat. Stir-fry chopped onion & garlic in hot oil about two minutes or until crisp-tender. Add egg mixture & stir gently to scramble. When set, remove egg mixture from the wok. Cut up any large pieces of egg mixture. Let wok cool.
3. Pour one tablespoon cooking oil into the cooled wok or skillet. (Add more oil as necessary during cooking.) Preheat over medium-high heat. Stir-fry celery in hot oil for one minute. Add mushrooms & sweet pepper; stir-fry for one to two minutes more or until vegetables are crisp-tender.
4. Add cooked rice, bamboo shoots, carrots, & peas. Sprinkle with three tablespoons soy sauce. Cook & stir for four to six minutes or until heated through. Add cooked egg mixture & green onions; cook & stir about one minute more or until heated through. Serve immediately. Garnish with carrot slices, if desired. Makes four to five servings.

Three-Bean Vegetarian Chili

What You Need

- **1**1 five ounce can no-salt-added red kidney beans, rinsed & drained

- **1**1 five ounce can small white beans, rinsed & drained

- **1**1 five ounce can low-sodium black beans, rinsed & drained

- **1**1 four 1/ two ounce can diced tomatoes & green chile peppers, undrained

- **1**cup beer or chicken broth

- **3**tablespoons chocolate-flavored syrup

- **1**tablespoon chili powder

- **2**teaspoons Cajun seasoning

- Dairy sour cream (optional)

- Shredded cheddar cheese (optional)

What to Do

1. In a 3-1/2- or 4-quart slow cooker, combine kidney beans, white beans, black beans, undrained tomatoes & green chile peppers, beer or broth, chocolate syrup, chili powder, & Cajun seasoning.
2. Cover & cook on low-heat setting for six to eight hours or on high-heat setting for three to four hours.
3. If desired, garnish individual servings with sour cream & cheese. Makes four servings.

Hearty Vegetarian Chili

What You Need

- Nonstick cooking spray

- **1**teaspoon canola oil

- **1**cup chopped onion

- **1**cup chopped green sweet pepper

- **2**cloves garlic, minced, or one teaspoon bottled minced garlic

- **1**1 four 1/ two ounce can no-salt-added diced tomatoes or stewed tomatoes

- **1** eight ounce can no-salt-added tomato sauce

- **1**cup water

- **four 1/2**teaspoons chili powder

- **1**teaspoon garlic-herb salt-free seasoning blend

- **1**teaspoon ground cumin

- **1/8**teaspoon salt

- **1**1 five ounce can kidney beans, rinsed & drained

- **1**cup frozen mixed vegetables

- **1/4**cup light dairy sour cream (optional)

- Coarsely snipped fresh cilantro (optional)

- **1/8** teaspoon chili powder (optional)

What to Do

1. Lightly coat an unheated large saucepan or Dutch oven with nonstick cooking spray. Preheat over medium-high heat. Add oil; swirl to coat bottom of pan. Add onion, sweet pepper, & garlic to hot pan; cook for eight to 10 minutes or until pepper is tender, stirring often. If necessary, reduce heat to prevent burning.
2. Add undrained diced tomatoes, tomato sauce, the water, the 4-1/ two teaspoons chili powder, the seasoning blend, cumin, & salt. Bring to boiling; reduce heat. Cover & simmer for 1 five minutes. Stir in beans & mixed vegetables. Return to boiling; reduce heat. Simmer, uncovered, about 10 minutes more or until vegetables are tender. If desired, top individual servings with sour cream and/or cilantro & sprinkle with the 1/ eight teaspoon chili powder.

Vegetarian Black Bean Soup

What You Need

- **10 ounces** dry black beans (1-1/ two cups), rinsed & drained

- eight **cups** water

- one **medium** onion, chopped (1/ two cup)

- one fresh jalapeno chile pepper, seeded & chopped*

- three cloves garlic, minced

- six **cups** no-salt-added vegetable broth

- two **tablespoons** ground cumin

- one **tablespoon** chili powder

- 1/ **two teaspoon** salt

- 1/ **two cup** chopped fresh cilantro or cilantro sprigs

- Lime slices or wedges

- Light sour cream (optional)

What to Do

1. In a large pot combine beans & the eight cups water. Bring to boiling; reduce heat. Simmer, uncovered, for 10 minutes. Remove from heat. Cover & let stand for one hour. Drain & rinse beans.
2. In a 4-quart slow cooker combine drained beans, onion, jalapeno, garlic, broth, cumin, chili powder, & salt.
3. Cover & cook on low-heat setting for nine to 10 hours or on high-heat setting for 4-1/ two to five hours. Use a potato masher to coarsely mash the beans. Top each serving with cilantro & serve with lime slices or wedges for squeezing. If desired, top each serving with sour cream.

Mushroom & Poblano Vegetarian Enchiladas

What You Need

- **6**ounces firm tofu
- **1**small poblano pepper
- **1**tablespoon vegetable oil
- **1** eight ounce package sliced cremini mushrooms
- **1**teaspoon ground cumin
- **1/2**teaspoon salt
- **1/4**cup dairy sour cream

- **1**cup shredded cheddar & Monterey Jack cheese (four ounces)
- **8**corn tortillas
- Chopped tomato & green onion (optional)

What to Do

1. Drain tofu; cut into cubes. Stem & seed poblano; cut into strips. In a skillet heat one tablespoon oil over medium heat. Add tofu, pepper strips, mushrooms, cumin, & salt. Cook for eight to 10 minutes or until mushrooms & pepper are tender, turning occasionally. Stir in sour cream & 1/ two cup of the cheese.
2. Preheat broiler. Lightly oil a 13x9x2-inch baking pan; set aside. Wrap tortillas in damp paper towels; microwave on 100 percent power (high) for 30 seconds or until warm & softened. Spoon mushroom filling into tortillas; fold over & place in prepared baking pan. Sprinkle with remaining cheese. Broil four to five inches from the heat for one to two minutes or until cheese is melted. If desired, top with tomato & green onion.

Vegetarian Sloppy Joes

What You Need

- **1**cup chopped onion
- **1**large green sweet pepper, chopped
- **1**tablespoon cooking oil
- **one 1/2**cups refrigerated or frozen precooked & crumbled ground-meat substitute (soy protein)
- **1**10 3/ four ounce can tomato puree
- **1**cup water
- **1/3**cup bottled barbecue sauce
- **1**tablespoon yellow mustard
- **1**tablespoon soy sauce (optional)
- **2**teaspoons chili powder

- **1**teaspoon bottled minced garlic (two cloves)
- **8**hamburger buns, toasted

What to Do

1. In a large skillet cook onion & sweet pepper in hot oil for five to seven minutes or until tender. Stir in ground-meat substitute, tomato puree, the water, barbecue sauce, mustard, soy sauce (if desired), chili powder, & garlic.
2. Bring to boiling; reduce heat. Simmer, uncovered, for 20 minutes, stirring occasionally. Serve on buns. Makes eight to 10 servings.

Vegetarian Shepherd's Pie

What You Need

- **3**small potatoes (3/ four pound)
- **2**cloves garlic, minced
- **1/2**teaspoon dried basil, crushed
- **2**tablespoons margarine or butter
- **1/4**teaspoon salt
- **2**tablespoons milk
- **1**medium onion, chopped (1/ two cup)
- **1**medium carrot, sliced (1/ two cup)
- **1**tablespoon cooking oil
- **1**1 five ounce can kidney beans, rinsed & drained
- **1**1 four 1/ two ounce can whole tomatoes, drained & cut up
- **1**10 ounce package frozen whole kernel corn or mixed vegetables
- **1** eight ounce can tomato sauce
- **1**teaspoon Worcestershire sauce

- **1/2**teaspoon sugar

- **1**cup shredded cheddar cheese (four ounces)

- Paprika (optional)

What to Do

1. Peel & quarter potatoes. Cook, covered, in a small amount of boiling lightly salted water for 20 to 2 five minutes or until tender. Drain. Mash with a potato masher or beat with an electric mixer on low speed. In a small saucepan cook garlic & dried basil in margarine or butter for 1 five seconds. Add to mashed potatoes along with salt. Gradually beat in enough milk to make light & fluffy. Set aside.
2. For filling, in a medium saucepan cook onion & carrot in hot oil until onion is tender but not brown. Stir in kidney beans, tomatoes, frozen vegetables, tomato sauce, Worcestershire sauce, & sugar. Heat until bubbly.
3. Transfer vegetable mixture to an 8x8x2-inch square baking pan. Drop mashed potatoes in four mounds over vegetable mixture. Sprinkle with cheddar cheese and, if desired, paprika. Bake, uncovered, in a 3 seven five degree F. oven for 2 five to 30 minutes or until heated through & cheese begins to brown. Makes four servings.

Vegetarian Stuffed Peppers

What You Need

- one 1 four 1/ two - ounce can no-salt-added stewed tomatoes

- one tablespoon Cajun seasoning

- one cup frozen veggie "meat" crumbles

- three cups risotto from Corn & Shrimp Risotto (on www.familycircle.com)

- four large green peppers, tops cut off & seeds removed

- Roasted Carrots from Corn & Shrimp Risotto (on www.familycircle.com)

What to Do

1. Heat oven to 350 degrees F. In a medium-size saucepan, combine tomatoes, Cajun seasoning & veggie crumbles. Heat over medium heat until bubbly, breaking apart tomatoes with a wooden spoon.
2. Stir in risotto & continue to cook until heated through. Turn off heat.
3. Place steamer insert into a large saucepot. Fill with 1-inch water. Add peppers, cut-side down, & bring to a boil over high heat. Reduce heat to medium-high; cover & steam for five to six minutes.
4. Carefully remove peppers from steamer & place, cut-side up, in a baking dish. Fill each with about 1-1/ four cups rice mixture. Bake at 350 degrees F for 20 minutes.

Vegetarian Green Chili

What You Need

- **2**cups long grain rice

- **2**tablespoons vegetable oil

- **1**bunch green onions, chopped (1/ two cup)

- **6**cloves garlic, minced

- **2**large green sweet peppers, chopped

- **3**stalks celery, chopped

- **2**1 two ounce bag shelled frozen sweet soybeans (edamame)

- **1** four 1/ two ounce can chopped green chiles

- **3**cups vegetable broth or reduced-sodium chicken broth

- **1**1 six ounce jar salsa verde (green salsa)

- **6**cups fresh spinach

- **1/4**cup chopped fresh cilantro

- **3**avocados, peeled, pitted, & chopped

- Plain lowfat yogurt or sour cream (optional)

What to Do

1. Cook rice according to package What to Do.
2. Meanwhile, in a Dutch oven cook & stir onions & garlic in hot oil for two minutes over medium-high heat. Add the sweet peppers & celery; cook five minutes or until crisp-tender. Add the edamame & green chiles; cook five minutes. Add broth & salsa verde; bring to boiling. Reduce heat & simmer, covered, for 1 five minutes. Stir in the spinach; cook about one minute or until wilted.
3. Remove from heat; stir in cilantro & two of the chopped avocados. Top with the remaining avocado & yogurt. Serve with rice.

Vegetarian Lentil Chili

What You Need

- **4**1 four 1/ two ounce can diced tomatoes, undrained
- **2**1 five ounce can red kidney beans, rinsed & drained
- **3**cups water
- **1**1 two ounce package frozen chopped green peppers
- **1**1 two ounce package frozen chopped onions
- **2**cups dry red lentils, rinsed & drained
- **1/4**cup chili powder
- **2**tablespoons garlic powder
- **1** eight ounce can tomato sauce
- **1** six ounce can tomato paste
- **1/8**teaspoon ground black pepper
- **2**cups shredded cheddar cheese (eight ounces)
- Tortilla chips (optional)

What to Do

1. In an 8-quart Dutch oven combine diced tomatoes, beans, the water, green peppers, onions, dry lentils, chili powder, & garlic powder. Bring to boiling; reduce heat. Simmer, covered, for 30 minutes, stirring occasionally.
2. Stir in tomato sauce, tomato paste, & black pepper; heat through. Serve with shredded cheese & tortilla chips. Store leftovers, covered, in the refrigerator for up to three days. Or freeze leftover chili.*

Loaded Bread Stuffing

What You Need:

- 1/ **four cup** butter

- one **cup** sliced fresh mushrooms

- one **cup** chopped celery (two stalks)

- one **cup** chopped onion (one large)

- 1/ **two cup** coarsely chopped red sweet pepper (one small)

- two **cloves** garlic, minced

- two **tablespoons** snipped fresh sage or two teaspoons dried sage, crushed

- 1/ **two teaspoon** black pepper

- 1/ **eight teaspoon** crushed red pepper (optional)

- **1 two cups** light whole wheat bread cut into 1-inch pieces & dried*

- one eight - **ounce can** water chestnuts, drained & chopped

- one **cup** coarsely shredded carrots (two medium)

- one **1 four 1/ two - ounce can** reduced-sodium chicken broth

- **1/ two cup** refrigerated or frozen egg product, thawed, or two eggs, lightly beaten

What to Do

1. Preheat oven to 32 five degrees F. In a large skillet melt butter over medium heat. Add mushrooms, celery, onion, sweet pepper, & garlic. Cook six to eight minutes or until vegetables are tender, stirring occasionally. Remove from heat. Stir in sage, black pepper, and, if desired, crushed red pepper.

2. In a very large bowl combine bread cubes, water chestnuts, & carrots. Add mushroom mixture; toss to combine. Add broth & egg, tossing lightly to combine.

3. Spoon into a 3-quart casserole. Bake, covered with foil, 50 to 5 five minutes or until an instant-read thermometer inserted in the center registers 160 degrees F.

Onion & Spinach Quesadilla

What You Need:

- one tablespoon olive oil

- two cups thinly sliced onion

- one teaspoon sugar

- 1/ four teaspoon salt

- nine ounces baby spinach

- four eight - inches whole-wheat flour tortillas

- four ounces semisoft goat cheese

- two medium tomatoes, thinly sliced

What to Do

1. Heat the oil in a large nonstick skillet over medium-high heat. Add the onion, sugar & salt; cook, stirring occasionally, until onion is dark golden brown. Remove from pan. Add the spinach & one tablespoon water to the skillet; cook two minutes, or until spinach is just wilted. Remove from skillet & turn off heat. Spread a quarter of the goat cheese on each tortilla & top with spinach, tomato & onion; fold closed & press lightly. Heat the skillet & place two folded quesadillas in it; cook two minutes per side, or until golden brown & lightly crisp. Repeat.

Orecchiette

What You Need:

- **1/2**teaspoon olive oil

- **1/3**cup pine nuts

- Salt

- **1/3**cup olive oil

- **3**tablespoons red wine vinegar

- **2**tablespoons capers, drained & chopped

- **1**clove garlic, minced

- **8**ounces perlini or perle fresh mozzarella cheese

- **2**cups cherry tomatoes, halved

- **1/2**cup snipped fresh basil

- **1/4**cup snipped fresh chives

- **1/4**cup snipped fresh Italian (flat-leaf) parsley

- **12**ounces dried orecchiette or bow tie pasta (farfalle)

- Freshly ground black pepper

What to Do

1. In a small skillet heat the 1/ two teaspoon oil over medium heat until hot but not smoking. Add pine nuts. Cook & stir about two minutes or until light golden brown. Drain pine nuts on paper towels. Season to taste with salt; set aside.
2. For marinade, in a large bowl whisk together the 1/ three cup oil, the vinegar, capers, & garlic until combined. Stir in mozzarella, tomatoes, basil, chives, & parsley. Let marinate at room temperature for 30 minutes, stirring occasionally.
3. Meanwhile, cook pasta in boiling lightly salted water according to package What to Do; reserve 1/ four cup cooking water. Drain pasta in a colander. Add hot pasta & the 1/ four cup reserved cooking water to mozzarella mixture. Let stand for one minute.
4. Gently toss pasta mixture. Add pine nuts; toss to mix. Season to taste with additional salt & black pepper. Serve warm.

Salsa, Black Bean, & Rice Salad

What You Need:

- two **cups** cooked long grain rice, chilled

- one **1 five - ounce can** black beans, rinsed & drained

- two **cups** chopped tomatoes

- one **cup** chopped yellow or red sweet pepper

- one **cup** frozen whole kernel corn, thawed

- two green onions, thinly sliced

- two **tablespoons** snipped fresh cilantro

- one **cup** bottled picante sauce or salsa

- four **ounces** Monterey Jack cheese with jalapeno chile peppers, cut into 1/4-inch cubes (optional)

- Lettuce leaves

- 1/ **two cup** fat-free or reduced-fat dairy sour cream

What to Do

1. In a large bowl, stir together chilled rice, black beans, tomatoes, sweet pepper, corn, green onions, & cilantro; add picante sauce or salsa. Toss to coat. If desired, stir in cheese.

2. To serve, line six salad bowls or plates with lettuce leaves. Top with rice mixture. Serve with sour cream. Makes six (3/4-cup) servings.

Spicy Tofu Triangles

What You Need:

- **1**ounce package extra-firm, tub-style tofu (fresh bean curd), chopped

- **1/2**cup finely chopped fresh shiitake or button mushrooms

- **1/3**cup thinly sliced green onions

- **1/4**cup finely chopped canned water chestnuts

- **2**tablespoons bottled hoisin sauce

- **2**teaspoons Oriental chili sauce with garlic

- **1**teaspoon soy sauce

- **48**wonton wrappers

- Nonstick cooking spray

- Teriyaki sauce or prepared Chinese-style hot mustard (optional)

What to Do

1. For filling, in a large bowl combine tofu, mushrooms, green onions, water chestnuts, hoisin sauce, chili sauce, & soy sauce. Spoon about one tablespoon of the filling into the center of each wonton wrapper. Brush edges of wrapper with water. Fold one corner of wrapper to opposite corner to form a triangle; press edges to seal.
2. Lightly coat large baking sheets with cooking spray. Place the wonton triangles on prepared baking sheets. Lightly coat the triangles with cooking spray. Bake in a 400 degrees oven about 10 minutes or until triangles are crisp & golden brown. Drain on paper towels. If desired, serve the hot triangles with teriyaki sauce.

Rice Skillet

What You Need:

- **1**1 five ounce can black, garbanzo, or kidney beans, rinsed & drained
- **1**1 four 1/ two ounce can stewed tomatoes, cut up
- **2**cups loose-pack frozen mixed vegetables
- **1**cup water
- **3/4**cup quick-cooking brown rice, uncooked
- **1/2**teaspoon dried thyme or dillweed, crushed
- Several dashes bottled hot pepper sauce (optional)
- **1**10 3/ four ounce can condensed tomato soup
- **1/3**cup slivered almonds, toasted
- **1/2**cup shredded mozzarella or cheddar cheese (two ounces)

What to Do

1. In a large skillet stir together beans, undrained tomatoes, vegetables, water, uncooked rice, thyme or dillweed, and, if desired, hot pepper sauce. Bring to a boil; reduce heat. Cover & simmer for 1 two to 1 four minutes or until rice is tender. Stir in soup; heat through.
2. Before serving, stir in almonds & sprinkle with cheese. Makes four servings.

Ribollita

What You Need:

- three tablespoons olive oil

- one small onion, chopped

- one carrot, chopped

- one celery stalk, chopped

- three garlic cloves, minced

- 3/ four teaspoon salt

- 1/ two teaspoon black pepper

- two cups no-salt-added cannellini beans, rinsed & drained

- one 15-ounce can no-salt-added whole peeled tomatoes

- four cups low-sodium vegetable stock

- one fresh rosemary sprig

- one fresh thyme sprig

- one pound kale, chopped

- four slices, whole-grain bread, toasted

What to Do

1. Heat oil in a large pot over medium heat. Add onion, carrot, celery & garlic; sprinkle with salt & pepper & cook, stirring occasionally, until vegetables are soft, five to 10 minutes.
2. Add beans, tomatoes, stock, rosemary & thyme. Bring to a boil, then reduce heat so soup bubbles steadily; cover & cook, stirring once or twice to break up tomatoes, until flavors meld, 1 five to 20 minutes.
3. Increase heat to medium high, add kale, & cook, stirring occasionally, until kale is tender & soup is hot again, three to five minutes. Remove herb sprigs if you like. Put one slice bread in bottom of each bowl; ladle soup on top.

What You Need:

- **1** recipe Pizza Dough
- **1** small eggplant, peeled & cut into 1-inch pieces
- **1** medium zucchini, cut into 1-inch pieces
- **1** large red sweet pepper, seeded & cut into 1-inch pieces
- **1** cup fresh cremini mushrooms, quartered
- **1/2** cup coarsely chopped red onion (one medium)
- **2** tablespoons olive oil
- **2** tablespoons chopped toasted walnuts
- **1** teaspoon snipped fresh rosemary
- **1/4** teaspoon salt
- **1/4** teaspoon ground black pepper
- **2** cups shredded mozzarella cheese (eight ounces)
- Milk
- Yellow cornmeal

What to Do

1. Prepare Pizza Dough. Before dough has finished rising, place a baking stone on the lowest oven rack;* preheat oven to 450 degrees F. In a 15x10x1-inch baking pan combine eggplant, zucchini, sweet pepper, mushrooms, & onion. Drizzle with oil; gently toss to coat. Roast on the center oven rack, uncovered, for 1 five to 1 eight minutes or until vegetables are tender, stirring once. Cool slightly.
2. For filling, in a large bowl combine roasted vegetables, walnuts, rosemary, salt, & black pepper. Add cheese; gently toss to combine.
3. On a lightly floured surface, roll one portion of the dough into a 13x10-inch oval. Spread half of the filling crosswise over half of the oval, leaving a 1-inch border. Fold dough over filling; pinch edges together to seal. Cut a few slits in top of calzone to allow steam to escape. Brush lightly with milk.

4. Sprinkle a baking sheet or pizza peel with cornmeal. Place calzone on baking sheet or peel. (When the baking sheet or peel is moved back & forth, the calzone should move freely.) Use the baking sheet or peel to transfer calzone to preheated baking stone.
5. Bake for 1 two to 1 eight minutes or until golden. Use the baking sheet or peel to transfer calzone to a cutting board. Repeat with the remaining dough & filling. To serve, cut each calzone into thirds.

Thai Noodles

What You Need:

- **1/2**cup soy nut butter or creamy peanut butter
- **1/3**cup water
- **1/3**cup reduced-sodium soy sauce
- **3**tablespoons fresh lime juice
- **3**cloves garlic, quartered
- **1**tablespoon grated fresh ginger
- **1**tablespoon sesame oil
- **1**1 four ounce package firm tofu
- **1**tablespoon cooking oil
- **8**ounces Chinese noodles
- **2**tablespoons snipped fresh cilantro
- **1/4**teaspoon crushed red pepper
- **1/4**cup chopped unsalted peanuts

What to Do

1. In a food processor or blender combine soy nut butter, water, soy sauce, lime juice, garlic, ginger, & sesame oil. Cover & process or blend until smooth; set aside.
2. Drain tofu; pat dry with paper towels. Cut tofu into 12-inch slices. In a 12-inch nonstick skillet heat cooking oil over medium-high heat. Add tofu; cook for five minutes or until browned.

Turn slices. Cook five minutes more. Remove slices to a cutting board. Cut each slice into 1-1/2- to 2-inch triangles or squares. Add soy nut butter mixture to skillet. Heat through.
3. Meanwhile, cook noodles according to package What to Do; drain & add to skillet.
4. Add tofu, cilantro, & crushed red pepper to noodles in skillet. Toss to coat. Sprinkle with peanuts; serve immediately. Makes four servings.

Israeli Couscous

What You Need:

- one **cup** Israeli couscous

- one **medium** yellow sweet pepper, coarsely chopped

- one **medium** zucchini, coarsely chopped

- one **medium** tomato, seeded & coarsely chopped

- two green onions, sliced

- two **tablespoons** lemon juice

- two **tablespoons** reduced-sodium chicken broth

- one **tablespoon** olive oil

- one **tablespoon** snipped fresh mint

- one **clove** garlic, minced

- **1/ four teaspoon** salt

- **1/ four teaspoon** black pepper

- **1/ four cup** crumbled feta cheese

- Fresh mint leaves

What to Do

1. In a large saucepan bring two quarts lightly salted water to boiling.
2. Meanwhile, in a medium skillet toast the couscous over medium heat about seven minutes or until golden brown, stirring frequently.
3. Add the couscous to the boiling water. Cook for seven minutes. Add sweet pepper & zucchini. Return to boiling & cook about five minutes more or until couscous is tender. Drain & transfer to a large bowl. Stir in the tomato & green onions.
4. Meanwhile, in a small bowl mix together lemon juice, broth, olive oil, snipped mint, garlic, salt, & black pepper. Stir mixture into couscous mixture. Serve warm or cover with foil or plastic wrap & chill for up to four hours. To serve, sprinkle with feta cheese & garnish with fresh mint leaves.

Green Pizza

What You Need:

- **1/3**cup slivered almonds, toasted
- **one 1/2**cups firmly packed fresh spinach leaves
- **1**cup firmly packed fresh parsley sprigs
- **1/2**cup firmly packed fresh basil leaves
- **1/2**cup olive oil
- **1/2**cup grated Parmesan cheese
- **1**teaspoon finely shredded orange peel
- **1/4**cup orange juice
- **1/4**teaspoon salt

- **1/4**teaspoon ground black pepper

- **2**1 two inches purchased Italian flatbreads (focaccia) or Italian bread shells (Boboli)

- **1**cup chopped red sweet pepper

- **1/2**cup chopped seeded tomato

- **1/2**cup red onion cut in thin wedges

- **1/2**teaspoon crushed red pepper

- **1**cup grated Parmesan cheese

What to Do

1. For pesto, place almonds in a food processor bowl or blender container. Cover & process or blend until finely chopped. Add spinach, parsley, & basil; cover. With the machine running, gradually add oil in a thin, steady stream, processing or blending until the mixture is combined & slightly chunky. (If using a blender, stop occasionally, scrape sides, & push mixture into blades. The blender produces a smoother mixture than the food processor.) Add the 1/ two cup Parmesan cheese, the orange peel, orange juice, salt, & black pepper. Cover & process or blend just until combined.*

2. Place each bread on a baking sheet or 12-inch pizza pan. Spread pesto over breads. Top with vegetables, crushed red pepper, & Parmesan cheese. Bake in a 400 degree F oven for 1 two to 1 five minutes or until heated through. Makes 1 two to 1 six servings.

Burger With Feta & Spinach

What You Need:

- one vegetarian burger

- two tablespoons feta cheese, crumbled

- 1/ four cup spinach

- one whole-wheat hamburger bun

- one small pear

What to Do

1. Make it: Warm burger in microwave. Top with feta cheese & spinach & place on bun. Serve with pear.

Minestrone

What You Need:

- **1**tablespoon olive oil

- **one 1/2**cups chopped onion

- **1**medium carrot, halved lengthwise & thinly sliced (about 3/ four cup)

- **2**cloves garlic, minced

- **3**cups reduced-sodium chicken broth

- **2**1 four 1/ two ounce can low-sodium tomatoes, undrained & cut up

- **3/4**cup water

- **1/2**cup long-grain rice

- **1**teaspoon dried Italian seasoning, crushed

- **4**cups shredded fresh spinach

- **1**1 five ounce can reduced-sodium navy beans or white kidney beans, rinsed & drained

- **1**medium zucchini, quartered lengthwise & sliced (about 1-1/ two cups)

- **1/4**teaspoon freshly ground pepper

- Grated Parmesan cheese (optional)

What to Do

1. In a 4-quart Dutch oven heat olive oil over medium-high heat. Cook & stir the onion, carrot, & garlic in hot oil about three minutes or until onion is tender. Stir in the broth, undrained tomatoes, water, uncooked rice, & Italian seasoning.

2. Bring to boiling; reduce heat. Simmer, covered, about 20 minutes or until rice is tender. Stir in the spinach, beans, zucchini, & pepper. Cook, covered, for five minutes more. If desired, sprinkle each serving with Parmesan cheese.

Butternut Squash Soup

What You Need:

- **4**pounds butternut squash

- **4**1 four 1/ two ounce can vegetable broth

- **1**cup water

- **1/4**teaspoon ground red pepper

- **2**tablespoons butter or margarine

- **2** nine ounce package refrigerated cheese ravioli

- **2**tablespoons molasses

What to Do

1. Peel squash. Halve lengthwise. Remove seeds & discard. Cut squash into 3/4-inch pieces.
2. Combine squash, broth, water, & pepper in a large pot. Cook, covered, over medium heat for 20 minutes or until squash is tender.
3. Transfer two cups of the squash & broth mixture to a blender container or food processor. Carefully blend, covered, until smooth. Repeat with remaining cooked mixture, blending two cups at a time.
4. Return blended mixture to large pot. Bring just to boiling. Immediately reduce heat. Simmer, uncovered, five minutes. Add the butter or margarine; stir until just melted.
5. Meanwhile, prepare the ravioli according to package What to Do. Drain. Ladle hot soup mixture into bowls. Divide cooked ravioli among bowls. Drizzle with molasses.

Pasta Primavera

What You Need:

- eight ounces dried wagon wheel pasta
- one 1 six ounce package desired frozen mixed vegetables
- 1/ two eight ounce tub cream cheese spread with chive & onion
- 1/ four cup milk
- Salt
- Ground black pepper
- Finely shredded Parmesan cheese

What to Do

1. In a Dutch oven cook pasta in a large amount of boiling, lightly salted water for four minutes. Add frozen vegetables. Cook about five minutes more or until pasta & vegetables are tender; drain. Return pasta mixture to hot pan.
2. Add cream cheese spread to pasta mixture. Cook until heated through, stirring occasionally. Stir in enough of the milk to reach desired consistency. Season to taste with salt & pepper. Sprinkle with Parmesan cheese before serving.

Linguine with Green Beans & Goat Cheese

What You Need:

- **12**cups water

- **1/2**teaspoon salt

- **8**ounces dried linguine or spaghetti

- **1** nine ounce package frozen cut green beans

- **2**medium leeks, thinly sliced (about 2/ three cup)

- **1/2**cup chopped walnuts

- **2**tablespoons olive oil

- **1**tablespoon butter or margarine

- **1**tablespoon snipped fresh thyme or marjoram

- **4**ounces semisoft goat cheese (chevre), crumbled

- Cracked black pepper

What to Do

1. Bring the water & salt to boiling in a 4-quart Dutch oven. Add pasta; boil for five minutes. Add green beans. Continue boiling, uncovered, about five minutes more or until pasta is tender but still firm. Drain in a colander & set aside.
2. Cook leeks & walnuts in hot olive oil & butter in the same Dutch oven for three to four minutes or until leeks are tender & walnuts are lightly toasted. Stir in drained pasta mixture & thyme; heat through. Transfer mixture to a serving platter. Sprinkle with cheese & pepper. Serve immediately. Makes six servings.

Portobello Sandwiches

What You Need:

- one medium tomato, chopped (2/ three cup)

- two teaspoons snipped fresh basil, thyme, and/or oregano

- 1/ eight teaspoon salt

- two medium portobello mushrooms (about four inches in diameter)

- one teaspoon balsamic vinegar or red wine vinegar

- 1/ two teaspoon olive oil

- 1/ two 1 two inch Italian flat bread (focaccia), quartered, or 1/ two of a 12-inch thin-crust Italian bread shell (Boboli)

- Finely shredded Parmesan cheese (optional)

  640 views
  Rate me!

- Makes: four servings
- Start to Finish: 2 five mins

What to Do

1. In a small mixing bowl combine tomato, basil, & salt; set aside. Clean mushrooms; cut off stems even with caps. Discard stems.
2. Combine vinegar & oil; gently brush over the mushrooms. Place mushrooms on the unheated rack of the broiler pan. Broil mushrooms four to five inches from the heat for six to eight minutes or just until tender, turning once.* Drain mushrooms on paper towels. Thinly slice mushrooms.
3. Place bread on a baking sheet. Place under broiler for two to three minutes or until heated through.
4. To serve, top bread with mushroom slices & tomato mixture. If desired, top with Parmesan cheese. Makes four servings.

Pea Ricotta Bruschetta

What You Need:

- **1**small lemon

- **one 1/2**cups fresh or frozen shelled peas

- **2**tablespoons sugar

- **1/4**cup vegetable oil

- **3**mint leaves

- **1**cup ricotta cheese

- **2**ounces soft goat cheese (chevre), crumbled

- Sea salt

- Freshly ground black pepper

- **12**ounces baguette-style French bread, sliced into twenty 1/2-inch-thick pieces

- **1**large clove garlic, halved

- **two - 3**small radishes, cut into thin strips (optional)

- Pea shoots (optional)

What to Do

1. Finely shred peel from lemon & juice lemon; set aside. In a medium saucepan, bring water to boiling. Add peas & sugar. Return to boiling; reduce heat. Cover; simmer for two to four minutes or until just tender. Drain. Transfer to a large bowl of ice water to cool. Drain well. Add peas, two tablespoons of the oil, the lemon juice, & mint to a food processor. Cover & process until smooth (mixture should be the consistency of hummus; add a little warm water, if needed). Season to taste with salt & pepper; set aside.
2. In a small mixing bowl stir together lemon peel, ricotta, & goat cheese. Season to taste with salt & pepper.
3. Brush bread slices with the remaining two tablespoons oil. Toast in a grill pan or under the broiler, turning once. Rub each warm bread slice with cut side of garlic.
4. To assemble, spread ricotta mixture over each slice of bread & top with pea mixture. If desired, garnish with radishes & pea shoots.

Tortellini Soup

What You Need:

- three cups vegetable broth

- three cups water

- 1/ two teaspoon dried Italian seasoning

- one nine - ounce package cheese-filled spinach tortellini

- three large carrots, peeled & sliced into thin coins

- three ribs celery, thinly sliced

- 3/ four pound ripe plum tomatoes (about 4), seeded & chopped

- one six - ounce bag baby spinach

- Grated Parmesan cheese (optional)

What to Do

1. In a large pot, bring broth, water & Italian seasoning to a boil. Add the tortellini & simmer for three minutes. Add carrots & celery & simmer for an additional four minutes. Stir in the tomatoes & spinach & simmer for two more minutes or until vegetables are tender & the spinach is wilted.
2. Ladle soup into bowls & serve with Parmesan cheese, if desired.

Wild Mushroom Flatbread

What You Need:

- four ounces wild mushrooms

- one shallot, sliced

- one tablespoon extra-virgin olive oil

- two garlic cloves, minced

- one teaspoon red pepper flakes

- one tablespoon sherry

- two whole-wheat pitas

- two tablespoons sliced roasted red peppers

- two tablespoons crumbled goat cheese

- Salt

- Freshly ground black pepper

What to Do

1. Preheat the broiler to high. In a medium skillet over medium- high heat, saute mushrooms & shallot in oil until shallot begins to caramelize, five to seven minutes. Add garlic & red pepper flakes & cook until aromatic, about one minute. Deglaze skillet with sherry, scraping up browned bits from bottom, about one minute.
2. Arrange pitas on a baking sheet & top with mushroom mixture. Spread one tablespoon roasted peppers & one tablespoon goat cheese on top of each pita; season with salt & pepper.

3. Transfer to the top rack of the oven & broil until cheese is melted & pitas have crisped, five to eight minutes.

Lemon-Pesto Pasta

What You Need:

- **1/2**cup pasta

- **1/2**cup canned cannellini beans, rinsed & drained

- **1/2**cup cut green beans, cooked

- **one - 2**tablespoons purchased basil pesto

- **1**teaspoon lemon juice

- **1**tablespoon Parmesan cheese

- crushed red pepper

- lemon wedges

What to Do

1. In a small saucepan boil 1/ two cup pasta in water for nine minutes. Remove from heat. Add 1/ two cup cannellini beans, rinsed & drained, & 1/ two cup cooked cut green beans to pan. Cover; let stand for two minutes. Reserve two Tbsp. cooking water. Drain pasta mixture. Return to pan with reserved cooking water, one to two Tbsp. purchased basil pesto, & one tsp. lemon juice to pan; toss to coat. Sprinkle with one Tbsp. Parmesan cheese & dash crushed red pepper. Serve with lemon wedges.

Spinach & Bean Salad

What You Need:

- one 1 five ounce can black beans, rinsed & drained
- 1/ two cup snipped dried apricots
- 1/ two cup chopped red and/or yellow sweet pepper
- one green onion, thinly sliced

- one tablespoon snipped fresh cilantro
- one clove garlic, minced
- 1/ four cup apricot nectar
- two tablespoons salad oil
- two tablespoons rice vinegar
- one teaspoon soy sauce
- one teaspoon grated fresh ginger
- four cups shredded fresh spinach

What to Do

1. In a medium mixing bowl combine black beans, apricots, sweet pepper, green onion, cilantro, & garlic, In a screw-top jar combine apricot nectar, oil, vinegar, soy sauce, & ginger. Cover & shake well. Pour over bean mixture; toss gently to coat. Cover & refrigerate for two to 2 four hours.
2. To serve, add spinach to black bean mixture, tossing to mix. Season to taste with salt. Makes four main-dish salads.

VEGETABLE LO MEIN

SERVES three
The Sauce:
three tablespoons tamari soy sauce

two **tablespoons Asian sesame oil**

one **tablespoon sherry**

¼ cup vegetable broth/stock, store-purchased or selfmade

one **teaspoon sugar**

one **teaspoon cornstarch**

12 ounces fresh Chinese noodles or eight ounces spaghettini

one **tablespoon Asian sesame oil**

one **tablespoon canola oil**

two **pieces gingerroot, the size of one / 4**

two **garlic cloves, cut in half**

eight **ounces extra-firm tofu, sliced ¼ inch thick, patted very dry, & cut into small triangles**

one **carrot, cut into matchsticks**

two **scallions, cut into 2-inch lengths & shredded lengthwise (like matchsticks)**

Salt to taste

1. Place the sauce ingredients in a cup & stir well to dissolve the cornstarch.
2. Bring a big amount of water to a boil in a stockpot. In case you are utilizing fresh noodles, cook just some minutes, till al dente, or cook the spaghettini about five minutes, also till al dente. In either case be sure not to overcook the noodles. Drain them completely in a colander. Pour on the sesame oil & toss well. Set the noodles apart.
3. Heat the canola oil in a big nonstick skillet over medium-high heat. Add the ginger & garlic pieces, & cook two minutes. Remove & discard them; they're just meant to flavor the oil. Add the tofu to the skillet & cook tossing frequently with a spatula, till golden brown throughout. Stir in the carrots & cover the pan. Cook two minutes.
4. Remove the cover of the pan. Use tongs to combine in the noodles, scallions, & sauce combination. Toss well & cook till hot all through, about three minutes. Season lightly with salt. Serve instantly.

PENNE WITH GARLICKY BUTTERNUT SQUASH

¼ cup olive oil

four cups diced (½-inch) butternut squash (from a 1½-pound squash)

four large garlic cloves, minced

¼ **cup water**

¼ **teaspoon grated nutmeg**

six **sage leaves, minced, or** ¼ **teaspoon powdered sage**

¼ **cup minced fresh parsley**

½ **teaspoon salt**

Freshly ground black pepper to taste

one **pound penne**

Grated Parmesan cheese

1. Bring a big amount of water to a boil in a stockpot.
2. Heat the oil in a big skillet over medium-high heat. Toss in the squash & sauté five minutes, or till it begins to get golden. Sprinkle in the garlic & sauté two minutes. Pour in the ¼ cup water & cover the pan. Cook the squash till tender, about five minutes more. Mix in the nutmeg, sage, & parsley.
3. Cook the penne till al dente, about 10 minutes. Drain totally in a colander & return to the pot. Spoon on the squash combination, add salt & pepper, & toss gently. Serve with a sprinkling of Parmesan cheese & move more on the table.

PENNE WITH RED PEPPER & WALNUT PESTO

SERVES four
one **pound penne**

Roasted Red Pepper & Walnut Pesto

two **small zucchini, quartered lengthwise & thinly sliced**

Grated Parmesan cheese (optional)

1. Bring a big amount of water to a boil in a stockpot. Add the penne & cook till al dente, about 12 minutes. Add the zucchini & blanch for one minute, or simply till barely tender. Remove ¼ cup of the pasta water & stir it into the pesto to thin it.
2. Place the penne & zucchini in a colander & shake well to drain away all of the liquid. Return the combination to the pot or place in a big pasta bowl. Pour on the pesto & toss well. Serve with Parmesan cheese, if desired.

PENNE ALLA VODKA

SERVES four
two **tablespoons olive oil**

four large garlic cloves, minced

¼ teaspoon crushed red pepper flakes

1½ cups canned crushed tomatoes or tomato puree

¼ cup vodka

½ teaspoon salt

½ cup heavy cream

one **pound penne**

two **tablespoons minced fresh parsley**

Freshly grated Parmesan cheese

1. Bring a big amount of water to a boil in a stockpot.
2. Heat the oil in a medium-size saucepan over medium heat. Add the garlic & red pepper flakes, & cook gently for one minute. Don't let the garlic get in any respect coloured. Pour in the crushed tomatoes, vodka, & salt, & cook at a full of life simmer for 10 minutes. Pour in the cream & keep warm whilst you cook the pasta.
3. Drop the penne into the boiling water & cook till al dente, about 10 minutes. Drain totally in a colander & return to the pot. Pour on the sauce, toss, & cook one minute. Serve sprinkled with parsley. Move the cheese on the table.

BOW TIES WITH GREEN BEANS

SERVES four
¼ cup olive oil

four garlic cloves, minced

¼ teaspoon crushed red pepper flakes

½ cup tomato sauce

¼ cup dry red wine

½ teaspoon salt

one **pound green beans, tips removed & cut in half**

one **pound bow tie pasta (farfalle)**

Grated Parmesan cheese

1. Bring a big amount of water to a boil in a stockpot.
2. To make the sauce, heat the oil in a medium-size skillet over medium heat. Add the garlic & red pepper flakes, & sauté 1–2 minutes, or till the garlic softens but doesn't in any respect brown. Stir in the tomato sauce, wine, & salt, & boil two minutes. Keep warm over low heat.
3. Drop the green beans into the boiling water & cook five minutes, or till tender but still shiny green. Taste one to make sure. Use a strainer to scoop out the beans & place them in a bowl. Cover with a plate to maintain warm.
4. Mix the pasta into the boiling water & cook till al dente, about 12 minutes. Drain in a colander & return to the pot. Stir in the tomato sauce & green beans, & cook one minute. Serve with loads of grated Parmesan cheese.

ORECCHIETTE WITH SWISS CHARD

SERVES four
one **large boiling (waxy) potato, peeled & cut into ½-inch dice**

one **pound orecchiette ("little ears"), farfalle, or ziti**

¼ cup olive oil

six **garlic cloves, minced**

¼ teaspoon crushed red pepper flakes

one **pound Swiss chard, rinsed, stems cut off & discarded, leaves chopped** (see Tip)

½ teaspoon salt

Grated Parmesan cheese

1. Bring a big amount of water to a boil in a stockpot. Drop in the potatoes & cook till tender, about seven minutes. With a strainer scoop out the potatoes & place in a bowl. Add the orecchiette to the boiling water & cook till al dente, about quarter-hour.
2. In the meantime, heat the oil in a big skillet over medium heat. Add the garlic & red pepper flakes, & cook 30 seconds. Stir in the Swiss chard with the water that adheres to it & toss well with the garlic. Cover & cook till wilted, about five minutes.
3. Mix the potatoes into the chard together with two tablespoons of the pasta water. Season with salt & cook just till the potatoes are hot. Drain the orecchiette & return to the pot or place in a warm pasta bowl. Toss with the Swiss chard combination. Serve with grated Parmesan cheese.

GEMELLI WITH ZUCCHINI SAUCE

SERVES four
one **pound gemelli or other twisted pasta such as fusilli or rotini**

two **tablespoons olive oil**

two **medium zucchini, quartered lengthwise & thinly sliced**

two **garlic cloves, minced**

⅓ cup finely chopped fresh basil

one **egg yolk**

one **cup whole milk**

½ teaspoon salt

Generous seasoning freshly ground black pepper

½ cup grated Parmesan cheese

1. Bring a big amount of water to a boil in a stockpot. Drop in the gemelli & cook till al dente, about 12 minutes.
2. To make the sauce, heat the oil in a big skillet over medium heat. Add the zucchini & sauté till it begins to get tender, about five minutes. Sprinkle in the garlic & cook, stirring frequently, till the zucchini is tender but still slightly crisp, about five minutes more. Sprinkle on the basil & toss. Keep over low heat.
3. Place the yolk in a small bowl or measuring cup. Beat in the milk, salt, pepper, & Parmesan cheese till blended.
4. Drain the pasta & return it to the pot over low heat. Stir in the zucchini, then shortly add the egg combination. Cook, stirring repeatedly, till the sauce begins to thicken, about 30 seconds. You need the egg combination to only heat through & thicken slightly, not boil or come near a simmer. Serve directly.

RIGATONI

SERVES four
one **pound rigatoni**

⅓ cup olive oil

six **garlic cloves, minced**

¼ teaspoon crushed red pepper flakes

two **medium zucchini, quartered lengthwise & thinly sliced**

one **(sixteen-ounce) can prepared-cut tomatoes**

one **(sixteen-ounce) can small white beans such as navy or Nice Northern, rinsed well in a strainer & drained**

½ teaspoon salt

¼ cup minced fresh basil or parsley

Freshly grated Parmesan cheese

1. Bring a big amount of water to a boil in a stockpot. Drop in the rigatoni & cook till tender but still slightly chewy, about 10 minutes.
2. Warm the oil in a big skillet over medium heat. Add the garlic & red pepper flakes, & cook gently for one minute. Don't let the garlic get in any respect coloured. Stir in the zucchini & sauté, tossing often, till almost tender but still slightly crunchy, about five minutes. Add the tomatoes with their juice, white beans, & salt, & simmer about five minutes, or till the juices have slightly thickened.
3. Drain the rigatoni in a colander & return it to the pot or place in a big pasta bowl. Mix in the sauce, basil, & a small handful of Parmesan cheese. Toss well. Serve instantly with some extra Parmesan cheese to go on the table.

ROTINI WITH SIMPLE TOMATO SAUCE & CRUMBLED RICOTTA

SERVES four
¼ cup olive oil

six **garlic cloves, minced**

¼ teaspoon crushed red pepper flakes one (28-ounce) can prepared-cut diced tomatoes

½ teaspoon salt

½ cup finely chopped fresh basil or parsley

one **pound rotini (or other brief pasta such as penne, gemelli, ziti, or fusilli)**

½ cup ricotta cheese (roughly)

Grated Parmesan cheese (optional)

1. Bring a big amount of water to a boil in a stockpot.
2. To make the sauce, heat the oil in a big skillet over medium heat. Add the garlic & hot pepper flakes, & cook 1–2 minutes, or till scorching but in no way coloured. Add the

tomatoes with their juice & the salt, & bring to a boil. Simmer the sauce 10 minutes, or simply till it begins to thicken slightly. Use the back of a giant spoon to crush among the tomatoes slightly; it will improve the consistency of the sauce.

3. Cook the rotini till al dente, about eight–10 minutes. Drain completely & return to the pot. Stir the basil or parsley into the sauce. Pour the sauce on the rotini & cook one minute. Serve in pretty pasta bowls with tiny spoonfuls of ricotta on each serving. Move Parmesan cheese on the table, if desired.

TORTELLINI WITH SMOKED CHEESE

SERVES three–four
one **pound frozen cheese tortellini**

¼ cup olive oil

four large garlic cloves, minced

¼ teaspoon crushed red pepper flakes

one **(12-ounce) package fresh spinach, stems removed & leaves torn into small pieces**

Salt to taste

¼ cup grated smoked Gouda

1. Bring a big stockpot of water to a boil. Cook the tortellini in accordance to package instructions, about five minutes.
2. In the meantime, heat the oil in a big skillet over medium heat. Add the garlic & red pepper flakes, & cook one minute. Don't let it get in any respect brown. Mix in the spinach, then scoop out about ¼ cup of pasta water & add to the spinach. Cover the pan & cook the spinach about two minutes, or simply till it wilts. Keep warm over low heat.
3. Drain the tortellini & add it to the spinach. Season with salt. Gently toss in the smoked cheese & serve.

RAVIOLI WITH BROCCOLI & RED PEPPERS

SERVES four
three tablespoons olive oil

one **red bell pepper, cut into thin 2-inch strips**

three **garlic cloves, minced**

one **pound frozen cheese ravioli**

three **cups tiny broccoli florets**

two **tablespoons shredded fresh basil, or ½ teaspoon dried**

Salt to taste

Freshly ground black pepper to taste

Grated Parmesan cheese (optional)

1. Bring a big amount of water to a boil in a stockpot.
2. Heat two tablespoons oil in a medium-size skillet over medium heat. Add the red pepper & garlic, & sauté till the pepper is very soft & golden, about 10 minutes. Keep warm over low heat.
3. Drop the ravioli into the boiling water. About three minutes before the ravioli is completed cooking (check the package instructions for the time), drop in the broccoli. Cook together till each are tender, about three minutes. A. Drain completely in a colander & return to the pot. Carefully fold in the red pepper combination, the remaining tablespoon of oil, basil, salt, & pepper. Serve instantly with a little Parmesan cheese, if desired.

POTATO GNOCCHI WITH RED PEPPERS, YELLOW SQUASH

SERVES 2–three
one **tablespoon olive oil**

one **red bell pepper, cut into thin 2-inch-long strips**

one **yellow squash, quartered lengthwise & thinly sliced**

two **garlic cloves, minced**

¼ teaspoon salt

Generous seasoning freshly ground black pepper

one **pound frozen potato gnocchi**

¼ cup milk

½ cup grated smoked Gouda cheese

one **tablespoon minced fresh parsley**

1. Bring a big amount of water to a boil in a stockpot.
2. Heat the oil in a big skillet over medium heat. Add the red pepper & cook five minutes. Mix in the squash & cook, tossing often, till it begins to melt, about five minutes. Stir in the garlic, salt, & pepper, & cook two minutes, or till the greens are tender but still slightly crisp. Keep warm over low heat.
3. In the meantime, drop the gnocchi into the boiling water & cook till tender, about seven minutes. Drain the gnocchi & add them to the skillet. Mix in the milk & cheese, & stir just till melted. Serve without delay with parsley sprinkled on top.

 ENCHILADAS

SERVES four (2 PER PERSON)
The Filling:
one **tablespoon olive oil, plus extra for greasing**

one **large onion, very finely diced**

one **medium zucchini, quartered lengthwise & thinly sliced**

one **cup frozen corn**

one **(15-ounce) can kidney or pinto beans, rinsed in a strainer**

one **(four-ounce) can chopped green (mild) chilies, drained**

one **teaspoon dried oregano**

two **tablespoons chopped cilantro**

Salt to taste

Freshly ground black pepper to taste

The Sauce:
1½ cups mild or medium salsa

½ cup heavy cream

¼ cup milk

two **cups grated Monterey Jack cheese, divided**

eight (eight-inch) flour tortillas

1. Heat the oil in a big skillet over medium heat. Add the onion & sauté 10 minutes, or till it begins to get golden. Stir in the zucchini & sauté till tender, about eight minutes. Mix in the corn, beans, chilies, oregano, & cilantro. Season with salt & pepper. Remove the skillet from the heat & let the filling cool. The filling might be prepared, covered, & refrigerated up to two days upfront.
2. To make the sauce, mix the salsa, cream, & milk in a bowl. Lightly oil two shallow 2½-quart baking dishes, such as 12 X two X 7-inch Pyrex dishes. (You don't need to crowd the enchiladas.) Spread a thin layer of sauce on the bottom of every dish.
3. Preheat the oven to 350 degrees.
4. To assemble the enchiladas, mix one cup cheese into the cooled filling. If the tortillas look a bit dry & maybe brittle, brush them lightly with some water to moisten them & let sit a couple of minutes. If they appear supple, just lay them on the counter in entrance of you. Spoon ⅛ of the filling alongside each tortilla. Roll them up & place seam side down in the baking dishes. Pour the remaining sauce over the enchiladas, then sprinkle a few of the remaining cheese alongside each. Cover the dishes with foil. The enchiladas will be prepared so far & refrigerated up to four hours upfront. Bring to room temperature before baking. Bake 25–half-hour, or till hot & bubbly. Serve instantly.

SMOKY BLACK BEAN ENCHILADAS

SERVES 6
The Filling:

one **chipotle pepper, preferably canned in adobo sauce, or dried**

one **tablespoon olive oil, plus extra for greasing**

one **medium onion, minced**

three **(15-ounce) cans black beans, rinsed in a strainer**

¾ **cup orange juice**

The Sauce:
one **cup mild or medium salsa**

one **cup tomato sauce**

one **teaspoon dried oregano**

one **teaspoon ground cumin**

12 (6-inch) corn tortillas

six **ounces light cream cheese (Neufchâtel), cut into 12 slices**

two **cups grated Monterey Jack cheese**

1. If you're utilizing a chipotle pepper in adobo sauce, place it on a small plate & mince it utilizing a knife & fork. You don't need to handle it with your fingers. In case you are utilizing a dried chipotle, cover it with boiling water & soak for 10 minutes. Remove from the water & mince with a knife & fork
2. Heat the oil in a medium-size saucepan over medium heat. Sauté the onion & chipode pepper till soft, about 10 minutes. Stir in the beans & orange juice, & simmer 10 minutes. Utilizing the back of a giant spoon, mash half of the beans by pressing them towards the sides of the pan. Cook the beans a few more minutes, or till the feel of mashed potatoes. Let the beans cool.
3. To make the sauce, mix the salsa, tomato sauce, oregano, & cumin in a bowl.
4. Preheat the oven to 350 degrees.
5. Wrap the tortillas in foil & bake 10 minutes. This may soften them & stop them from splitting when rolled. Let cool slightly. Keep the oven on.

6. To assemble the enchiladas, lightly oil two shallow 2½-quart baking dishes, such as 12 X two X 7-inch Pyrex dishes. (You don't need to crowd the enchiladas.) Pour a thin movie of sauce on the bottom of every dish. Divide the filling in half. Lay six tortillas on a piece surface & place six spoonfuls of the filling on half of every tortilla. Top with a slice of cream cheese. Roll the enchiladas & place seam side down in the baking dish. Repeat with the remaining six tortillas & remaining half of the filling. Pour the sauce throughout the enchiladas & sprinkle on the grated cheese. Cover the dishes with foil. (The enchiladas may be prepared thus far & refrigerated up to four hours upfront.) Bring to room temperature before baking.
7. Bake, covered, for 25 minutes, or simply till hot all through. Let sit five minutes before serving.

ENCHILADAS VERDES

SERVES four
The Filling:
two **tablespoons olive oil**

one **large onion, minced**

three (15-ounce) cans pinto (pink) or kidney beans, rinsed well in a strainer

⅓ cup water

Green Salsa or one (12-ounce) jar store-purchased green salsa combined with two tablespoons finely chopped cilantro

eight (eight-inch) flour tortillas

three cups (9 ounces) grated Monterey Jack cheese

1. To make the filling, heat the oil in a medium-size saucepan. Add the onion & sauté till very soft, about 10 minutes. Mix in the beans & water, & simmer till hot all through, about seven minutes. With a big spoon mash half of the beans by pressing them towards the side of the pan. Put aside to chill.

2. Use two medium-size baking dishes, such as eight X eight-inch pans or 12 X seven X 2-inch Pyrex casseroles, & spread about two tablespoons green salsa on the bottom of every dish. You don't need to crowd the enchiladas.
3. Preheat the oven to 375 degrees.
4. Spoon ⅛ of the bean combination alongside the bottom of a tortilla, then roll it & place seam side down in the dish. Repeat with the remaining beans & tortillas. Spoon the salsa throughout the eight rolled tortillas, guaranteeing to evenly moisten the tortillas with the sauce. Sprinkle on the cheese. Cover the dish with foil.
5. Bake, covered, for 25 minutes, or simply till hot & bubbly all through. Serve without delay.

TIPS: The enchiladas may be assembled & refrigerated up to four hours upfront. Bring to room temperature before baking.
Examine tomatillos.

TEN-MINUTE CHILA QUILES

SERVES 6
The Sauce:
one **cup salsa (preferably medium hot)**

two **cups tomato sauce**

½ cup water

one **(four-ounce) can chopped green chilies, undrained**

one **(14-ounce) can pinto or kidney beans, rinsed well in a strainer**

½ teaspoon ground cumin

½ teaspoon dried oregano

The Fixings:
one **(eleven-ounce) bag corn chips (about eight cups)**

one **cup sour cream**

two **cups grated Monterey Jack cheese**

two **tablespoons minced cilantro (optional)**

1. Preheat the oven to 350 degrees.
2. Mix all of the sauce ingredients in a big bowl.
3. Pour half the sauce right into a shallow 2½-quart baking dish, such as a 12 X seven X 2-inch Pyrex dish, & top with half the corn chips. You can crumble the chips slightly to make an even layer. Drop little spoonfuls of half the sour cream throughout the chips, then sprinkle on half the cheese.
4. Top with the remaining chips, sauce, sour cream, & cheese. Bake 35 minutes, or till hot & bubbly across the edges. Sprinkle the top of the casserole with the cilantro & serve. You can cut it into squares & serve utilizing a spatula, or use a big spoon to scoop out the chilaquiles.

TAMALE PIE

SERVES 6
two **tablespoons olive oil**

one **medium onion, finely diced**

two **garlic cloves, minced**

one **medium green bell pepper, finely diced**

one **tablespoon chili powder**

two **teaspoons ground cumin**

½ **teaspoon cinnamon**

one **cup tomato sauce, store-purchased or Easy Marinara Sauce**

½ **cup water**

one **(four-ounce) can chopped green (mild) chilies, well drained**

one **(15-ounce) can kidney beans, rinsed well & drained**

two **cups frozen corn, thawed**

¼ **teaspoon salt**

two **cups grated sharp cheddar cheese**

The Topping:

1½ **cups water**

one **cup milk**

one **cup cornmeal**

one **tablespoon sugar**

½ **teaspoon salt**

1½ **teaspoons baking powder**

one **large egg, beaten**

one **tablespoon butter, cut into bits**

1. Heat the oil in a big skillet over medium heat. Add the onion & garlic, & sauté till the onions start to paint, about 10 minutes. Mix in the green pepper & sauté, stirring often, till the pepper is soft & tender, about 10 minutes. Sprinkle in the chili powder, cumin, & cinnamon, & cook two minutes to "toast" the spices.

2.Stir in the tomato sauce, water, chilies, kidney beans, corn, & salt, & bring to a boil. Scrape the combination right into a shallow 2½- quart casserole (such as a 12 X 7-inch Pyrex dish) & spread it evenly. Sprinkle with the cheese. (The casserole could be prepared so far & refrigerated up to forty eight hours upfront. Bring to room temperature before protecting with the topping.)

3. Preheat the oven to 375 degrees.

4. To make the topping, mix the water, milk, & cornmeal in a medium-size saucepan. Bring the combination to a boil over medium-high heat, whisking almost always. Cook the combination, whereas constantly whisking, till very thick & it pulls away from the sides of the pan, about seven minutes.
5. Remove the pan from the heat & whisk in the sugar, salt, baking powder, & egg. Use a rubber spatula to spread the topping over the bean combination. Dot with the butter bits. (When the topping cools a little, you should use your fingers to even it out.)
6. Bake forty five minutes. Let sit 10 minutes before serving.

BAKED MEXICAN-STYLE RICE & BEANS

SERVES four–6
three cups water

one **teaspoon canola oil**

1½ **cups white rice, such as transformed, basmati, or long grain**

Butter for greasing

one **(15-ounce) can pinto or kidney beans, rinsed in a strainer**

½ **cup tomato sauce, store-purchased or Easy Marinara Sauce**

one **(four-ounce) can chopped green (mild) chilies, drained**

two **teaspoons chili powder ½ teaspoon salt**

½ **cup sour cream**

three cups (9 ounces) grated Monterey Jack cheese with jalapeño peppers

1. Mix the water & oil in a medium-size saucepan & bring to a boil. Stir in the rice, cover the pot, & lower the heat to a gende simmer. Cook the rice about 17 minutes, or till all of the water is absorbed. Place in a big bowl & let cool.

2. Preheat the oven to 350 degrees. Butter a 2½-quart shallow baking dish or oval gratin dish.
3. Mix the beans, tomato sauce, chilies, chili powder, & salt into the rice. Spread half of the combination into the prepared dish. Top with the sour cream & half of the cheese. Spread on the remaining rice combination & sprinkle the remaining cheese on top. Cover with foil. (The casserole could also be prepared & refrigerated up to 24 hours upfront. Bring to room temperature before baking.) Bake half-hour, or till piping hot all through. Serve instantly.

BAKED PENNE WITH MUSHROOM SAUCE

SERVES 6
one **pound penne**

three tablespoons olive oil, divided

four garlic cloves, minced

¼ teaspoon crushed red pepper flakes

eight ounces normal white mushrooms, thinly sliced

eight ounces combined unique mushrooms, such as shiitake, oyster, & cremini, thinly sliced

½ teaspoon salt

1½ cups tomato sauce

¼ cup dry red wine

½ cup chopped fresh parsley

two **cups grated mozzarella cheese**

¼ cup grated Parmesan cheese

1. Bring a big amount of water to a boil in a stockpot.

2. Cook the penne just till al dente, about eight minutes; it's going to cook additional in the oven. Drain totally in a colander & return to the pot. Toss with one tablespoon oil & put aside.

3. Heat the remaining two tablespoons oil in a big skillet over medium heat. Add the garlic & red pepper flakes, & cook about 30 seconds, or simply till they sizzle a bit. Stir in the mushrooms & cook tossing frequently, till the mushrooms are brown & juicy, about 10 minutes. At first the mushrooms will soak up the oil & be very dry, but then they may release their juices.

4. Mix in the salt, tomato sauce, wine, & parsley. Add the sauce to the penne & mix to coat well.

5. Preheat the oven to 375 degrees. Lightly oil a shallow three-quart casserole such as a thirteen X nine X 2-inch baking dish.

6. Spread half of the penne in the dish. Top with half of the mozzarella & Parmesan cheeses. Spoon on the remaining penne & sprinkle on the remaining cheeses. Cover the dish with foil. (The casserole might be prepared up to now up to eight hours upfront. If chilled, bring to room temperature before baking.)

7. Bake half-hour, or till hot & bubbly. Remove the foil & bake five minutes more. Let sit 10 minutes before serving.

GREEK PASTA CASSEROLE

SERVES four
¼ cup olive oil, plus extra for greasing

four large garlic cloves, minced

one **pound small pasta shells**

one **(14-ounce) can prepared-cut diced tomatoes with their juice**

one **(7-ounce) jar roasted red peppers, well drained & diced**

¼ cup pitted & roughly chopped black olives (your favourite form)

two **tablespoons red wine**

¼ teaspoon crushed red pepper flakes

¼ cup finely chopped fresh parsley

1½ teaspoons dried oregano

one **cup (5 ounces) finely crumbled feta cheese**

1. Bring a big amount of water to a boil in a stockpot.
2. In the meantime, heat the oil in a small saucepan over medium-low heat. Add the garlic & cook 30 seconds; don't let it get in any respect coloured. Remove the pan from the heat & put aside.
3. Add the pasta to the boiling water & cook till al dente, about quarter-hour. Taste one to make certain it's cooked correctly. Drain totally in a colander & place in a big bowl. Pour on the garlic oil & toss well. Let cool to room temperature, tossing often to prevent sticking.
4. Preheat the oven to 375 degrees.
5. Mix in all of the remaining ingredients. Oil a shallow three-quart casserole (such as a thirteen X 9-inch Pyrex baking dish). Spoon the combination into the dish & cover with foil. (The pasta could be assembled & refrigerated up to 24 hours upfront. Bring to room temperature before baking.)
6. Bake, covered, for 25 minutes, or till hot & bubbly. Remove the foil the last five minutes of cooking to lightly brown the top of the casserole.

BAKED MACARONI & SMOKED CHEESE

SERVES four
two **slices bread**

one **tablespoon olive oil**

two **tablespoons unsalted butter**

two **tablespoons unbleached flour**

two **cups whole or low-fat milk**

⅛ **teaspoon dry mustard**

Dash cayenne pepper

¼ **teaspoon salt**

two **cups grated extra-sharp cheddar cheese**

one **cup grated smoked Gouda cheese**

eight ounces (2 cups) elbow macaroni

1. Bring a big amount of water to a boil in a stockpot.
2. Tear the bread into pieces & place in a food processor or blender to make bread crumbs. Pour the crumbs right into a bowl & drizzle with the oil. Rub the oil into the crumbs with your fingertips to moisten them evenly.
3. To make the cheese sauce, melt the butter in a medium-size saucepan over medium heat. Sprinkle in the flour & whisk till it blends with the butter. Cook this roux for one minute. Whisk in the milk, mustard, cayenne, & salt. Bring the combination to a boil, whisking constantly. Lower the heat & simmer the sauce about 30 seconds. Remove from the heat & stir in the cheddar & smoked cheeses. (The sauce may be made up to four hours upfront. Reheat gently till warm before mixing it with the macaroni.)
4. Drop the macaroni into the boiling water. Cook till al dente, about seven minutes. Don't overcook it; it should cook more when it's baked. Drain completely in a colander. (Toss with a little bit of oil in case you aren't going to bake the casserole instantly.)
5. Preheat the oven to four hundred degrees.
6. Spoon the macaroni right into a shallow 2–2½-quart casserole. Pour on the sauce & toss well. Sprinkle on the bread crumbs.
7. Bake quarter-hour, or simply till the sauce is scorching & the crumbs start to brown.

LASAGNA BÉCHAMEL

SERVES 6–eight
Béchamel Sauce:
four tablespoons unsalted butter

six **tablespoons unbleached flour**

three cups low-fat milk

¼ teaspoon grated nutmeg

¼ teaspoon salt

½ cup grated Parmesan cheese

three cups Easy Marinara Sauce or Spruced-Up Store-purchased Tomato Sauce

¼ cup dry red wine

Olive oil for greasing

12 lasagna noodles from one eight-ounce package "oven-prepared" (no-boil) lasagna

2½ cups (eight ounces) grated part-skim mozzarella cheese

1. To make the béchamel sauce: heat the butter in a medium-size saucepan over medium heat. Whisk in the flour & cook two minutes, whisking often. Whisk in the milk, nutmeg, & salt. Whisk till the combination boils & thickens, then stir in the Parmesan cheese. Remove from the heat. (The sauce could also be prepared & chilled up to 24 hours prematurely. Warm it slightly over low heat before utilizing.)
2. Mix the marinara or tomato sauce with the wine (an addition to the wine already in the sauce).
3. Preheat the oven to 375 degrees. Lightly oil a thirteen X nine X 2-inch baking dish. Spread a thin layer of tomato sauce on the bottom of the dish.
4. Arrange three noodles vertically on the sauce, ensuring the noodles don't touch one another; they need room for enlargement.
5. Spread about ¾ cup béchamel sauce on the noodles, then top with ¼ of the mozzarella cheese. Repeat the sequence three more times: tomato sauce, noodles, béchamel sauce, & mozzarella. Cover the dish with foil. (The lasagna might be assembled & refrigerated up to eight hours prematurely. Bring to room temperature before baking.)
6. Bake half-hour, covered. Remove the foil & bake quarter-hour more. Let sit quarter-hour before cutting & serving.

VEGETABLE LASAGNA WITH FRESH PASTA

SERVES eight
Béchamel Sauce:
six **tablespoons unsalted butter**

½ cup unbleached flour

four cups whole or low-fat milk

⅛ teaspoon nutmeg

½ teaspoon salt

Freshly ground black pepper to taste

½ cup grated Parmesan cheese

The Greens:

two tablespoons olive oil

one medium onion, minced

four garlic cloves, minced

12 ounces (4½ cups) thinly sliced mushrooms

one (14-ounce) can prepared-cut diced tomatoes, thoroughly drained

¼ cup dry red wine

one cup chopped fresh basil

¼ cup chopped fresh parsley ½ teaspoon salt

Freshly ground black pepper to taste Butter for greasing

three sheets fresh spinach or plain pasta (roughly 10 X 12 inches)

two small to medium zucchini, thinly sliced into rounds ⅛ inch thick

1¼ cups grated fontina cheese

1¼ cups grated part-skim mozzarella cheese

1. To make the sauce, melt the butter in a medium-size saucepan over medium heat. Whisk in the flour & cook, whisking often, for two minutes. Whisk in the milk, nutmeg, salt, & pepper. Elevate the heat to medium-high. Bring the sauce to a boil, whisking almost continually, then remove from the heat. Stir in the cheese & let cool. (The sauce may be prepared, covered, & chilled up to forty eight hours prematurely.)
2. To make the vegetable sauce, heat the oil in a big skillet over medium heat. Add the onion & garlic, & sauté 10 minutes, or till the onion is golden. Stir in the mushrooms & sauté till they start to brown & the juices have just about all evaporated. Mix in the tomatoes & wine, & cook till the juices thicken, about five minutes. There shouldn't be much liquid at this level. Remove the pan from the heat & stir in the basil, parsley, salt, & pepper. Let cool. (The sauce could also be prepared, covered, & chilled up to forty eight hours upfront.)
3. Preheat the oven to 375 degrees.
4. To assemble the lasagna, butter a nine X thirteen-inch baking dish. Utilizing scissors or a knife trim the pasta sheets to suit the bottom of the baking dish. If the white sauce has been chilled, heat it over low heat, stirring often, just till it will get warm & soft. Spread a thin layer of the sauce on the bottom of the baking dish. Top with a lasagna sheet.
5. Cover with ½ of the vegetable combination, ½ of the zucchini slices, ½ of the white sauce, then ½ of each the fontina & mozzarella cheeses. Repeat this layering two more times. Cover the dish with foil. (The lasagna might be prepared up to 24 hours prematurely. Bring to room temperature before baking.) Bake, covered, for 25 minutes. Remove the foil, then bake half-hour more, or till bubbly & golden. Let sit quarter-hour before cutting & serving.

SPINACH LASAGNA WITH A TOMATO CREAM SAUCE

SERVES 6–eight
Tomato-cream Sauce:
six **tablespoons unsalted butter**

½ cup unbleached flour

four cups low-fat milk

¼ teaspoon nutmeg

½ teaspoon dried oregano

½ teaspoon salt

Freshly ground black pepper to taste

one **cup tomato sauce, store-purchased or Easy Marinara Sauce**

Oil for greasing

15 lasagna noodles from one eight-ounce package "oven-prepared" (no-boil) lasagna

one **(10-ounce) package frozen chopped spinach, thawed & squeezed dry**

one **(7-ounce) jar roasted red peppers, well drained & diced**

eight ounces feta cheese, very finely crumbled (1⅔ cups)

two **cups (6 ounces) grated part-skim mozzarella cheese**

1. To make the cream sauce, melt the butter in a medium-size saucepan over medium heat. Add the flour & whisk till smooth. Cook one minute, whisking continuously. Whisk in the milk nutmeg, oregano, salt, & pepper, & bring to a boil, whisking frequently. Boil one minute, whisking consistently, then remove from the heat. Whisk in the tomato sauce. (The sauce will be made, covered, & refrigerated up to 24 hours upfront. Reheat slightly or till it's smooth before assembling the lasagna.)
2. Preheat the oven to 375 degrees.
3. To assemble the lasagna, lightly oil a thirteen X 9-inch baking dish. Spread a thin layer of sauce on the bottom of the dish. Place three uncooked lasagna noodles side by side, ensuring they don't touch one another. Spread a thin layer of sauce on the noodles, then sprinkle on ¼ of the spinach, red peppers, & feta cheese, & $^1/_5$ of the mozzarella cheese. Place three more noodles on top & repeat the sequence till all of the noodles have been layered. Spread a layer of sauce on top & sprinkle on the remaining mozzarella cheese. Cover the dish with foil. (The lasagna will be made up to eight hours upfront & refrigerated. Bring to room temperature before baking. See Tip.)
4. Bake the lasagna, covered, for half-hour. Remove the foil & bake 10–quarter-hour more, or till golden on top. Let the lasagna sit no less than quarter-hour before serving.

BAKED VEGETABLE POLENTA

SERVES four

one **tablespoon olive oil**

one **medium onion, minced**

one **cup thinly sliced fennel**

one **small to medium zucchini, quartered lengthwise & thinly sliced**

⅔ **cup drained & diced canned tomatoes**

one **cup frozen corn, thawed**

Salt to taste

Freshly ground black pepper to taste

The Polenta:
two **cups milk**

1½ **cups water**

one **cup cornmeal**

two **garlic cloves, put through a press**

¾ **teaspoon salt**

⅓ **cup grated Parmesan cheese**

1½ **tablespoons finely shredded fresh basil**

1½ **cups grated fontina cheese**

½ **cup heavy cream**

1. Heat the oil in a big skillet over medium heat. Add the onion & fennel, & sauté about 10 minutes, or till the fennel is crisp but tender.

2. Stir in the zucchini & tomatoes, & cover the pan. Cook 10 minutes, or till the fennel is very tender. Stir in the corn, salt, & pepper, & take away from the heat.
3. Butter a 2½-quart gratin dish or other related shallow casserole.
4. To make the polenta, mix the milk & water in a heavy-bottomed three-quart saucepan. Add the cornmeal, garlic, & salt, & whisk till smooth. Place over medium-high heat & bring the polenta to a boil, whisking repeatedly. Lower the heat & whisk till the polenta resembles soft mashed potatoes, about 10 minutes. Whisk in the Parmesan cheese & basil.
5. Pour half of the polenta into the prepared casserole. Cover with half of the greens & half of the fontina cheese. Drizzle with half of the cream. Spoon on the remaining polenta & add the remaining veg etables, cheese, & cream. Let the casserole sit no less than half-hour or up to 24 hours before baking. Cover & refrigerate if it is going to sit greater than one hour.
6. Preheat the oven to four hundred degrees. Bake the polenta about 25 minutes, or till it's golden on top & bubbly. Let sit 10 minutes before serving.

BAKED CHEESE POLENTA WITH CORN & GREEN CHILIES

SERVES four
Butter for greasing

one **(four-ounce) can chopped green (mild) chilies, well drained**

1½ **cups frozen corn, thawed**

one ½ **cups Monterey Jack cheese with jalapeño peppers**

½ **cup sour cream**

two **cups milk**

1½ **cups water**

one **cup cornmeal**

three garlic cloves, put through a press (preferably) or minced

¾ **teaspoon salt**

Freshly ground black pepper to taste

⅓ cup grated Parmesan cheese

1. Butter a 2½-quart casserole & put aside. Place the chilies, corn, Monterey Jack cheese, & sour cream next to the casserole.
2. In a three-quart heavy-bottomed saucepan whisk together the milk, water, cornmeal, garlic, salt, & pepper. Bring to a boil over medium-high heat, whisking almost repeatedly. Cook the polenta, whisking consistently, till thickened like soft mashed potatoes, about seven minutes. Whisk in the Parmesan cheese.
3. Pour half of the polenta in the prepared casserole & spread evenly. Sprinkle on half of the chilies, half of the corn, & half of the Monterey Jack cheese. Spread on all of the sour cream. Shortly pour on the remaining polenta & spread evenly. Sprinkle on the remaining chilies, corn, & Monterey Jack cheese. Let the casserole sit at the least 20 minutes before baking, or cover & refrigerate up to 24 hours. Bring to room temperature before baking.
4. Preheat the oven to four hundred degrees. Bake 25–half-hour, or till the polenta is scorching & golden on top. Let sit 10 minutes before serving.

BAKED ORZO WITH SPINACH, TOMATOES, & CORN

SERVES four–6
one **pound orzo (rice-formed pasta)**

one **(10-ounce) bag triple-washed fresh spinach, stems discarded & leaves torn in half**

four tablespoons olive oil

six **large garlic cloves, minced**

one **(14-ounce) can prepared-cut diced tomatoes**

one **cup frozen corn, thawed**

one **cup (four ounces) crumbled feta cheese**

½ **teaspoon salt**

Generous seasoning freshly ground black pepper

one **cup grated Muenster cheese**

1. Bring a big amount of water to a boil in a stockpot. Add the orzo & cook just till it approaches the al dente stage, about 10 minutes; it is going to cook additional in the oven. Stir in the spinach & cook 30 seconds. Drain very totally in a colander. Return the combination to the pot or place in a big mixing bowl. Pour on one tablespoon oil & toss to coat well. Let cool.
2. Heat the remaining three tablespoons oil in a medium-size skillet over medium heat. Add the garlic & cook one minute, or till barely coloured. Stir in the tomatoes with their juice & simmer five minutes.
3. Mix the tomatoes into the orzo together with the corn, feta cheese, salt, & pepper.
4. Oil a shallow three-quart casserole (such as a nine X thirteen-inch baking dish). Spread half the orzo combination into the dish. Sprinkle on the Muenster cheese. Spread the remaining orzo over the cheese. Cover the dish with foil. (The casserole will be prepared thus far up to 24 hours upfront. Chill if longer than two hours. Bring to room temperature before baking.)
5. Preheat the oven to 375 degrees. Bake the casserole, covered, for half-hour, or till piping hot all through.

BAKED ORZO, BROCCOLI, & CHEESE

SERVES four–6
2–three cups tiny broccoli florets (from one bunch broccoli)

one **pound orzo (rice-formed pasta)**

one **(7-ounce) jar roasted red peppers, well drained & cut into strips (¾ cup)**

Butter for greasing

one **cup sour cream**

¼ cup milk

¼ cup plus two tablespoons grated Parmesan cheese

¼ cup chopped fresh basil or parsley, or ½ teaspoon dried basil

½ teaspoon salt

Generous seasoning freshly ground black pepper

one **cup grated part-skim mozzarella cheese**

1. Bring a big amount of water to a boil in a stockpot. Drop in the broccoli & cook till almost tender (it would cook additional when baked), about five minutes. With a strainer scoop out the broccoli & place in a big bowl.
2. Cook the orzo in the same boiling water till tender but not mushy, about 12 minutes. (Test a piece after about nine minutes.) Drain totally in a colander. If any water has amassed in the bowl with the broccoli, drain it. Mix the orzo with the broccoli, then stir in the red peppers. Let the combination cool a minimum of 20 minutes or up to four hours. Refrigerate if longer than one hour, then bring to room temperature.
3. Preheat the oven to 375 degrees. Butter a 2½-to three-quart baking dish.
4. Stir the sour cream, milk ¼ cup Parmesan cheese, basil, salt, pepper, & mozzarella cheese into the broccoli combination. Scrape into the baking dish & smooth over the top. Sprinkle with the remaining Parmesan cheese.
5. Bake 20–half-hour, or simply till piping hot. Don't overcook the dish or it would dry out.

BAKED VEGETABLE COUSCOUS

SERVES four generously
one **cup couscous**

¾ **teaspoon salt**

1½ **cups boiling water**

¼ **cup olive oil**

one **onion, very finely diced**

four garlic cloves, minced

½ **teaspoon turmeric**

1½ **teaspoons paprika**

two **teaspoons ground cumin**

A few dashes cayenne pepper

two **small to medium zucchini, quartered lengthwise & thinly sliced**

one **(14-ounce) can prepared-cut diced tomatoes with their juice**

one **(sixteen-ounce) can chickpeas, rinsed well & drained**

⅓ **cup raisins**

one **cup grated Monterey Jack cheese**

1. Place the couscous & salt in a big bowl. Pour in the boiling water & stir. Cover the bowl with a big plate & let the couscous sit 10 minutes. Fluff with a fork & put aside, uncovered.
2. Preheat the oven to 375 degrees.
3. Heat the oil in a big skillet over medium heat. Stir in the onion & garlic, & sauté till the onion become translucent, about five minutes. Sprinkle on the turmeric, paprika, cumin, & cayenne. Toss & cook one minute. Mix in the zucchini & sauté till the zucchini begins to melt but remains to be crisp, about five minutes. Add the tomatoes, chickpeas, & raisins, & simmer two minutes.
4. Stir this combination into the couscous & toss well. Spread half in a shallow 2½-quart baking dish. Sprinkle on the cheese. Top with the remaining couscous combination & cover with foil. (The casserole will be prepared up to now & refrigerated up to 24 hours upfront. Bring to room temperature before baking.) Bake forty five minutes, or till scorching & piping hot all through.

TIP: Though all of the ingredients are basically cooked when spooned into the baking dish, the casserole should bake not less than forty five minutes so it's hot all through.

BAKED BARLEY & MUSHROOMS

SERVES four
four tablespoons unsalted butter

two **medium onions, finely diced**

eight ounces (three cups) ordinary white mushrooms, coarsely chopped

four ounces (1½ cups) assorted unique mushrooms (such as shiitake, cremini, & oyster), coarsely chopped

1½ cups barley

one **carrot, minced**

one **rib celery, thinly sliced**

one **tablespoon sherry or marsala wine**

Pinch dried thyme

½ teaspoon salt

Generous seasoning freshly ground black pepper

four ½ cups boiling vegetable broth/stock, store-purchased or selfmade

1. Preheat the oven to 350 degrees.
2. Melt the butter in a big skillet over medium heat. Add the onions & mushrooms, & sauté till the mushrooms render their juices & start to brown, about 10 minutes.
3. Stir in the barley, carrot, & celery, & cook two minutes. Scrape the combination right into a deep 2-to 2½-quart casserole that has a good cover. Mix in all of the remaining ingredients.
4. Cover tightly & bake 60–seventy five minutes, or till all of the broth/stock has been absorbed & the barley is tender. Taste the barley. If it's still hard, pour in a ½ cup boiling broth/stock or water & cook 10–quarter-hour more. Let sit 10 minutes before serving.

EGGPLANT PARMESAN

SERVES four–6
two **medium eggplants (about one pound each)**

¼–⅓ cup mayonnaise

¾ cup dry bread crumbs

two **cups Easy Marinara Sauce or Spruced-up Store-purchased Tomato Sauce**

½ cup finely chopped fresh parsley

½ cup grated Parmesan cheese

two **cups grated mozzarella cheese**

1. Peel the eggplant & slice it into rounds about ½ inch thick—no thicker.
2. Preheat the broiler.
3. Place the mayonnaise in a small dish & the bread crumbs on a flat plate. Use a pastry brush to lightly coat either side of every eggplant slice with mayonnaise. Press either side of the slices into the bread crumbs & lay the eggplant on a baking sheet. You'll in all probability need two sheets to allow them to rest in one layer.
4. Broil the eggplant till a deep golden brown. Turn the slices over & broil once more. When done the eggplant can be very tender, under no circumstances firm. Cool the slices.
5. Preheat the oven to 375 degrees.
6. Pour a thin layer of tomato sauce on the bottom of a 2½- to three-quart shallow baking dish, such as a eleven X 7-inch or nine X thirteen-inch Pyrex dish. Layer half of the eggplant slices, tomato sauce, parsley, Parmesan cheese, & mozzarella cheese. Repeat. Cover the dish with foil. (The casserole might be prepared so far & refrigerated up to 24 hours upfront. Bring to room temperature before baking.)
7. Bake, covered, for quarter-hour. Remove the foil & bake quarter-hour more, or till hot & bubbly. Let sit 10 minutes before serving.

TIP: You can substitute about ½ cup olive oil for the mayonnaise. Brushing oil on the eggplant slices will make the "crust" a bit thinner but still scrumptious.

SWEET POTATO, WHITE BEAN, & PEPPER

SERVES four
three medium-large sweet potatoes (preferably dark orange), peeled, quartered lengthwise, & sliced ¼ inch thick

one **(14-ounce) can small white beans, rinsed in a strainer** one **red bell pepper, cut into 1-inch chunks**

one **green bell pepper, cut into 1-inch chunks**

one **medium red onion, cut into 2-inch chunks & sections separated**

two **plum tomatoes, cut into 1½-inch chunks**

five **garlic cloves, thinly sliced**

½ **tea spoon salt**

Generous seasoning freshly ground black pepper

⅓ **cup olive oil**

The Topping:
three slices selfmade-style white bread

one **tablespoon olive oil**

1. Preheat the oven to 375 degrees.
2. Mix all of the greens, garlic, salt, pepper, & oil in a big bowl & toss well. (The greens may be prepared so far up to four hours prematurely.) Pack the combination right into a 2½- or three-quart shallow baking dish & flatten the top surface. Bake forty five minutes.
3. To make the fresh bread crumbs, tear up the bread & make crumbs out of it in a food processor or blender. Pour the crumbs right into a bowl & drizzle with the oil. Rub the oil into the crumbs with your fingertips to moisten them evenly.
4. Remove the tian from the oven. Spread the crumbs throughout the top. Return the tian to the oven & bake quarter-hour more, or till the topping is a wealthy golden color. Let sit 10 minutes before serving.

SQUASH CASSEROLE

SERVES four–6

one **cup water**

½ **cup white rice, preferably transformed or basmati**

two **tablespoons olive oil, plus extra for greasing**

two **onions, finely diced**

three **medium (1½ pounds) summer time (yellow) squash, quartered** lengthwise & thinly sliced

one **red bell pepper, cut into thin 2-inch strips**

two **large eggs**

½ **cup milk**

one ½ **cups grated extra-sharp cheddar cheese**

½ **teaspoon salt**

Generous seasoning freshly ground black pepper

The Topping:
two **slices white bread**

one **tablespoon olive oil**

1. Bring the water to a boil in a small saucepan & add the rice. Lower the heat to a simmer & cook till all of the water is absorbed, about 17 minutes. Put aside.
2. Heat the oil in a big skillet over medium-high heat. Add the onions & sauté till lightly browned. Stir in the squash & red pepper, & continue to cook at medium-high heat, stirring often, till the greens are tender & the juices have evaporated, about 10 minutes. Put aside to chill.
3. Preheat the oven to 375 degrees. Lightly oil a 2½–three-quart baking dish.
4. Beat the eggs in a big bowl. Beat in the milk, cheese, salt, pepper, rice, & greens. Spread the combination in the prepared baking dish.
5. To make the topping, tear up the bread & place in a food processor or blender to make crumbs. Pour the crumbs right into a small bowl & drizzle with oil. Rub the oil into the

crumbs with your fingertips. Sprinkle the crumbs on top of the casserole. (The casserole could also be prepared up to now up to eight hours prematurely. If chilled, bring to room temperature before baking.)

6. Bake forty–forty five minutes, or till a deep golden brown. The casserole should sit at the least quarter-hour before serving to ensure that the juices to set & thicken.

BAKED POTATOES WITH SPINACH

SERVES four
four baking (Idaho or russet) potatoes, scrubbed well

two **tablespoons olive oil**

two **garlic cloves, pressed or minced**

four scallions, very thinly sliced

one **(10-ounce) package frozen chopped spinach, thawed & squeezed dry**

one **teaspoon minced fresh dill, or ½ teaspoon dried**

two **tablespoons butter**

¾ cup finely crumbled feta cheese

one **cup grated mozzarella cheese**

1. Prick the potatoes with a fork or knife a few times in order that they don't explode in the oven when baking. Set the oven at four hundred degrees & place the potatoes on the oven rack. Bake till tender when pierced with a knife, about one hour.
2. Heat the oil in a medium-size skillet over medium heat. Add the garlic & scallions, & cook two minutes, or simply till heated through & softened. Mix in the spinach & dill & take away from the heat.
3. When the potatoes are done, slice in half lengthwise. Scoop the flesh right into a bowl, leaving about ¼ inch in the shell. Mash the potatoes with a fork. Mix with the spinach combination, butter, & feta & mozzarella cheeses. Stuff each shell with the combination & smooth over the tops. Place the stuffed potatoes on a baking sheet & return to the oven. Bake 20 minutes, or till hot all through & golden on top.

MOCK MEAT LOAF

SERVES 6

nine **slices (eight ounces) industrial whole wheat bread (such as Arnold or Pepperidge Farm)**

two **cups (eight ounces) walnuts**

three large eggs

three medium onions, diced

one **small green bell pepper, diced**

one **small celery rib, minced**

one **small bunch parsley, stems discarded & leaves chopped**

⅔ **cup canned crushed tomatoes or one (sixteen-ounce) can diced tomatoes, drained thoroughly**

1½ **tablespoons canola oil**

one **teaspoon poultry seasoning**

one **teaspoon salt**

Generous seasoning freshly ground black pepper

1. Toast the bread slices either in the toaster or on a baking sheet placed under the broiler. Let cool.
2. Preheat the oven to 375 degrees. Generously butter a nine X 5-inch loaf pan, then line the bottom with wax paper & butter the paper.
3. Tear up the toasted bread slices & make crumbs out of them in a food processor. Place in a big bowl.
4. Process the walnuts till finely ground & mix into the bread crumbs. Mix the eggs & onions in the processor & process till fine but not liquefied. Stir into the bread crumbs. Place the green pepper, celery, parsley, tomatoes, & oil in the processor & grind till fine but still with some texture. Stir into the loaf combination together with the poultry

seasoning, salt, & pepper. Mix this all thoroughly till evenly moistened. (The combination could also be prepared so far & refrigerated up to eight hours prematurely.) Scrape it into the prepared loaf pan & smooth over the top. Cover the loaf with foil.

5. Bake one hour & 20 minutes, or till a knife inserted in the middle of the loaf comes out dry. Let sit five minutes, then run a knife all alongside the sides of the loaf to assist loosen it. Unmold the loaf onto a platter & take away the wax paper. Let the loaf cool 20 minutes or so before slicing it. It's greatest to serve the loaf warm & the gravy hot. Serve with Mushroom Gravy (beneath).

MUSHROOM GRAVY

four tablespoons unsalted butter

two **cups (eight ounces) thinly sliced mushrooms**

¼ cup unbleached flour

two **½ cups vegetable broth/stock, store-purchased or selfmade**

¼ cup dry red wine

two **tablespoons tamari soy sauce**

Freshly ground black pepper to taste

1. Melt the butter in a medium-size saucepan over medium heat. Add the mushrooms & sauté till brown, about seven minutes. Stir in the flour; it is going to become very pasty. Cook this roux for two minutes, stirring continually. It's going to persist with the bottom of the pan a little bit; that's okay.
2. Stir in the broth/stock wine, soy sauce, & pepper, & bring to a boil. Cook the sauce at a energetic simmer for five minutes, stirring almost always & scraping any crusty bits that adhere to the bottom of the pan. Serve in a sauceboat.

TIPS: In case you don't have a food processor, you can grind everything in a blender, but it must be done in lots of batches so the blender is just not overfilled.

You can too cook the loaf a few hours upfront, then reheat slices on an oiled baking sheet in a 350-diploma oven.

CHICKPEA SOUP WITH GARLIC CROSTINI

SERVES four AS A MAIN COURSE
¼ cup olive oil
two **onions, diced**
four garlic cloves, minced
one **carrot, finely diced**
one **celery rib, thinly sliced**
½ teaspoon crushed red pepper flakes (much less for a gentle model)
one **cup tomato puree**
three (14-ounce) cans chickpeas, rinsed well, or five cups freshly cooked chickpeas
six **cups water**
½ teaspoon salt
Crostini:
eight thin slices French bread
one **tablespoon olive oil**
one **garlic clove, cut in half lengthwise**
Extra-virgin olive oil for drizzling
Minced fresh basil, parsley, or rosemary for garnish

one Heat the oil in a big stockpot over medium heat. Add the onion, garlic, carrot, celery, & red pepper flakes, & sauté 10 minutes.

2. Stir in all of the remaining soup ingredients & bring to a boil. Lower the heat to a simmer & cook half-hour. Let cool slightly.
3. Remove one cup of the soup & put aside. Puree the remaining soup in batches in a blender; you can pour it right into a smaller pot at this level. Stir in the reserved cup of soup.
4. To make the crostini: preheat the oven to 300 degrees. Lightly brush the bread slices with the oil. Place on a aking sheet & bake 10 minutes. Turn over & bake five minutes more, or till crisp & firm. Let cool slightly, then rub the garlic cloves throughout the surface of the bread. Let the bread cool.
5. Serve the soup with a drizzle of oil on each serving, a sprinkling of one of many herbs, & a crostini to drift on top.

CLASSIC VEGETARIAN SPLIT PEA SOUP

SERVES four AS A MAIN COURSE

two **cups (1 pound) green break up peas**
10 cups water
two **bay leaves**
one **tablespoon olive oil**
two **large onions, finely diced**
four garlic cloves, minced
two **carrots, finely diced**
two **celery ribs, finely diced**
one **teaspoon good-quality paprika**
three tablespoons tamari soy sauce
Generous seasoning freshly ground pepper
three tablespoons unsalted butter

1. In a big stockpot mix the peas, water, bay leaves, & oil. Bring to a boil, stirring the combination often so the peas don't keep on with the bottom of the pot. Reduce the heat to a full of life simmer & cover the pot. Cook stirring often, for one hour.

2. Remove the cover & stir in all of the remaining ingredients besides the butter. Cook, uncovered, for half-hour, or till the greens are very tender & the peas have dissolved. When completed, the soup ought to be moderately smooth with the consistency of heavy cream. If it's too thick thin it with some water. Remove the bay leaves. Swirl in the butter before serving.

VEGETARIAN CHILI

SERVES four AS A MAIN COURSE
¼ cup olive oil
three medium onions, finely diced
six **garlic cloves, minced**
one **green bell pepper, very finely diced**
1½ tablespoons chili powder
one **tablespoon ground cumin**
½ teaspoon good-quality paprika
two **teaspoons dried oregano**
⅛ teaspoon cayenne pepper
two **bay leaves**
½ cup bulgur, preferably coarse-cut
one **(28-ounce) can crushed tomatoes or tomato puree**
three (15-ounce) cans kidney beans, rinsed well in a strainer, or four ½ cups freshly cooked kidney beans
two **tablespoons tamari soy sauce**

five **cups water**
¾ teaspoon salt
Generous seasoning freshly ground pepper
one **tablespoon butter**

1. Heat the oil in a big stockpot over medium heat. Stir in the onions, garlic, & green pepper, & sauté 10 minutes, stirring frequently. Mix in the chili powder, cumin, paprika, oregano, cayenne, bay leaves, & bulgur. Cook, stirring continually, not less than two minutes to toast the spices.
2. Add the tomatoes, beans, tamari, water, salt, & pepper. Bring the chili to a boil, then lower the heat & cook at a vigorous simmer for half-hour. Make certain to stir actually because the ingredients will settle to the bottom & start to stay. Just before serving stir in the butter.

BLACK BEAN SOUP

SERVES four AS A MAIN COURSE
one **pound dried black beans**
½ cup olive oil
eight garlic cloves, minced
two **large onions, diced**
one **green bell pepper, cut into small dice**
one **chipotle pepper in adobo sauce, minced, or one small jalapeño pepper, minced (put on gloves)**
two **tablespons ground cumin**
one **tablespoon dried oregano**
10 cups vegetable broth/stock, store-purchased or selfmade
one **cup tomato sauce, store-purchased or Easy Marinara Sauce**
1½ teaspoons salt
⅓ cup lime juice (from one large lime)
Sour cream for garnish (optional)
Lime slices for garnish

1. Soak the beans for eight to 24 hours in enough water to cover by three inches or, alternatively, cook the beans in a big stockpot in about five inches of water for two minutes. Remove from the heat & let the beans soak one hour. Drain in a colander.
2. Heat the oil in the same large stockpot. Mix in the garlic, onions, & green pepper, & sauté 10 minutes, stirring often. Add the chipotle pepper & sprinkle on the cumin. Cook the combination one minute, stirring repeatedly.

3. Mix in the beans, oregano, vegetable broth/stock, & tomato sauce, & bring to a boil. Lower the heat to a energetic simmer & cook the soup 1½ hours, stirring often. The beans must be very tender at this level.
4. Remove about four cups soup & puree in a blender or food processor. Return to the soup & stir in the salt & lime juice. Serve in bowls with a small spoonful of sour cream, if desired, & a lime slice on top.

GINGER-MISO SOUP WITH NOODLES

SERVES four AS A MAIN COURSE
eight ounces udon (Japanese wheat noodles) or linguine
¼ cup tamari soy sauce
½ cup roughly sliced gingerroot (with skin on)
four ounces firm tofu, cut into ½-inch cubes
two **scallions, very thinly sliced**
¼ cup white (sweet) miso
one **tablespoon Asian sesame oil**

1. Bring three quarts water to a boil for the udon. Cook the udon about six minutes, or till tender but not mushy. If the starch from the noodles appears to be like as if it's about to boil over, lower the heat slightly. Drain the udon in a colander, rinse under cold running water, drain once more, after which put aside.
2. in the same pot bring six cups water, tamari, & gingerroot to a boil. Lower the heat & simmer 10 minutes. Remove the ginger with a slotted spoon & discard. Stir in the tofu & half the scallions. Lower the heat to very low.
3. Place the miso in a small bowl. Remove about ½ cup broth & stir it into the miso to dilute it & stop lumping. Pour the combination into the broth. Stir in the sesame oil & udon. Let the udon heat through, about one minute. Don't let the soup boil after the miso is added; it might destroy a few of its nutritive worth.
4. Use tongs to remove the noodles & place them in individual serving bowls. Ladle the broth over the noodles. Garnish each serving with the remaining scallions.

SWEET POTATO & VEGETABLE SOUP

SERVES four-6
¼ cup olive oil
two **onions, finely diced**
four garlic cloves, minced
one **(28-ounce) can prepared-cut diced tomatoes**
six **cups vegetable broth/stock, store-purchased or home made**

two **large sweet potatoes (preferably dark orange), peeled & cut into ½-inch dice**

one **(15-ounce) can small white beans (navy or Nice Northern), rinsed well & drained**

two **cups diced fresh or frozen green beans**

one **teaspoon salt**

Generous seasoning freshly ground pepper

A few dashes cayenne pepper

one **tablespoon minced fresh basil, or ½ teaspoon dried**

four cups frozen corn

one Heat the oil in a big stockpot over medium heat. Add the onions & garlic, & sauté till tender & golden, about 10 minutes.

2. Mix in the tomatoes & broth/stock, & bring to a boil. Stir in all of the remaining ingredients besides the corn. Return the soup to a boil, lower to a energetic simmer, & cook till the sweet potatoes are tender, about half-hour. Stir in the corn & heat through, about two minutes. Serve directly or reheat when needed.

CURRIED CHICKPEA & POTATO STEW

SERVES four AS A MAIN COURSE
three tablespoons unsalted butter, divided
two **medium-size onions, finely diced**
four garlic cloves, minced
two **tablespoons minced gingerroot**
one **tablespoon ground coriander**
½ teaspoon turmeric
½ teaspoon ground cumin
¼ teaspoon ground cardamom
A few dashes cayenne pepper, or more to taste
one **cup canned tomato puree**
six **cups water**
¾ teaspoon salt
three boiling (waxy) potatoes, peeled & cut into ½-inch dice
one **(15-ounce) can chickpeas, rinsed & well drained**
one **(10-ounce) package triple-washed fresh spinach, stems discarded & leaves torn**
one **tablespoon minced cilantro (optional)**
Juice of ½ lemon

1. Melt two tablespoons butter in a big stockpot over medium heat. Add the onions & sauté till golden, about 10 minutes. Mix in the garlic & ginger, & cook gently for three minutes.

2. Sprinkle in all of the spices & "toast" them, stirring repeatedly for one minute.
3. Mix in the tomato puree, water, & salt, & bring to a boil. Add the potatoes & chickpeas, & simmer the stew for half-hour, or till the potatoes are tender. Scrape the bottom of the pot to loosen any spices that will have adhered to it. Because the stew begins to thicken, you'll have to stir it more frequently to prevent it from sticking. (You may make the stew up to two days upfront. In that case, cease after this step. Just before serving, reheat it & proceed with the next step.)
4. Stir in the spinach, cilantro, & remaining tablespoon of butter. Cook five minutes, or till the spinach is just wilted. Add the lemon juice & serve.

VEGETABLE SOUP WITH COCONUT MILK

SERVES four-6
two **tablespoons canola oil**
two **medium onions, finely diced**
four garlic cloves, minced
two **teaspoons minced gingerroot**
two **cups (6 ounces) thinly sliced mushrooms**
two **teaspoons ground coriander**
one **teaspoon ground cumin**
one **teaspoon turmeric**
⅛ teaspoon cayenne pepper
four cups vegetable broth/stock, store-purchased or home made
one **(14-ounce) can coconut milk**
one **teaspoon salt**
two **large boiling (waxy) potatoes, peeled & cut into ½-inch dice**
1½ cups green beans, cut into 1-inch lengths
¼ cup very finely diced (¼ inch) red bell pepper
½ cup fine egg noodles or 1-inch pieces broken vermicelli
Juice of one lemon

1. Warm the oil in a big stockpot over medium heat. Add the onions, garlic, & gingerroot, & sauté, stirring often, for 10 minutes, or till the onions are soft & golden.
2. Add the mushrooms & sauté five minutes. Sprinkle on the coriander, cumin, turmeric, & cayenne, & cook two minutes, stirring often.
3. Pour in the vegetable broth/stock, coconut milk, & salt, & bring to a boil. Add the potatoes & cook 10 minutes, stirring often.
4. Mix in the green beans, red bell pepper, & noodles, & cook at a full of life simmer for 10 minutes, or till the greens & noodles are tender. Stir in the lemon juice just before serving.

CHILLED SUMMER BORSCHT

SERVES four GENEROUSLY
three (sixteen-ounce) cans beets, drained & liquid reserved
one **cup reserved beet liquid**
1½ cups V-eight juice
one **small-to medium-size onion, minced**
A few dashes Tabasco
two **tablespoons lemon juice**
Salt to taste
Freshly ground pepper to taste
½ cup sour cream (roughly)
Minced fresh chives for garnish

1. Place the beets, reserved liquid, V-eight juice, onion, Tabasco, & lemon juice in a blender in batches, & mix till pureed. If the soup is just too thick, add a bit more beet liquid or some water. Pour into a big bowl & chill till ice cold, a minimum of two hours.
2. Taste the soup for salt & pepper. Serve the soup in bowls with a spoonful of sour cream on top & a few minced chives for garnish.

CLASSIC GAZPACHO

SERVES 6
three large, ripe tomatoes, cored
two **cucumbers, peeled, halved lengthwise, & seeded**
one **small onion, diced**
two **garlic cloves, minced**
one **jalapeño pepper, seeded & chopped (put on gloves), or a few dashes**
Tabasco
large green bell pepper, cored & really finely diced
tablespoons minced fresh parsley
⅓ cup red wine vinegar
⅓ cup olive oil
½ cup tomato vegetable broth/stock, tomato juice, or water
Salt to taste
Freshly ground pepper to taste
Croutons for garnish (see Tip)

1. Roughly chop the tomatoes & place in a food processor or blender together with 1½ cucumbers, onion, garlic, & jalapeño pepper. Puree till almost smooth but not liquefied. Pour into a big serving bowl.
2. Very finely dice the remaining ½ cucumber by hand. Stir it into the soup together with the green pepper, parsley, vinegar, oil, broth/stock, salt, & pepper. (In case you are utilizing Tabasco rather than a jalapeño pepper, don't overlook so as to add it.) Chill no less than two hours before serving. Serve garnished with croutons.

COLD YOGURT & CUCUMBER SOUP

SERVES four AS A MAIN COURSE
one **hard-boiled egg, cooled & really finely minced**
three cups plain yogurt
½ cup water
two **cucumbers, peeled, cut lengthwise, seeded, & finely diced**
two **tablespoons minced fresh dill, or one tablespoon dried dill**
one **tablespoon minced fresh parsley**
½ cup walnuts, finely chopped
two **garlic cloves, pressed or minced**
three tablespoons olive oil
one **tablespoon red wine vinegar**
½ teaspoon salt
Freshly ground pepper to taste
Dill or parsley sprigs for garnish
In a big bowl whisk together all of the ingredients besides the dill or parsley. Cover & chill not less than one hour or up to three days before serving. Serve in bowls with a dill or parsley sprig on top.

GREENS WITH DRIED CRANBERRIES

SERVES four
½ cup pecans
four cups romaine lettuce torn into small pieces, washed, & spun dry
four cups mesclun (combined baby greens), washed & spun dry
½ cup slivered red onion
½ cup (roughly) Balsamic Vinaigrette or Lemon-Soy Dressing
four tablespoons dried cranberries

1. Preheat the oven to 350 degrees. Toast the pecans in a shallow pan till they start to get aromatic, about 5-7 minutes. Let cool completely.
2. Mix the lettuce, mesclun, & onion in a salad bowl. Just before serving pour on the dressing & toss well. Check to see in case you need so as to add more dressing; you don't have the desire to make the greens too wet. Serve on individual salad plates with the pecans & cranberries sprinkled on each portion.

MESCLUN SALAD

SERVES four
four cups mesclun (combined baby greens)
two **cups romaine lettuce torn into small pieces, washed, & spun dry**
two **cups Boston lettuce torn into small pieces, washed, & spun dry**
½ cucumber, peeled, halved, & thinly sliced
½ yellow or red bell pepper, cut into very thin slivers
two **scallions, very thinly sliced**
⅓ cup (roughly) Lemon-Soy Dressing or Basic Vinaigrette

Mix all of the ingredients besides the dressing in a big salad bowl. Just before serving toss with the dressing. Taste & add more if necessary, but watch out not to overdress the salad. Serve directly on four salad plates.

LEAFY GREENS & RADICCHIO

SERVES four
five **cups torn-up green lettuce, well washed & spun dry**
two **cups arugula, leaves torn in half**
one **cup finely torn radicchio**
two **scallions, very thinly sliced**
one **small chunk (about four ounces) Parmigiano-Reggiano**
⅓ cup (roughly) Traditional Vinaigrette or Lemon-Soy Dressing

1. In a big salad bowl mix the lettuce, arugula, radicchio, & scallions.
2. Use a vegetable peeler to shave off 12 slices Parmigiano-Reggiano.
3. Toss the salad with the dressing just before serving. Taste to see in case you need a bit more dressing. Divide among four salad plates. Place three sheets of cheese on each serving. Serve directly.

ROMAINE WITH APPLES

SERVES four
three tablespoons coarsely chopped walnuts

six **cups romaine lettuce torn into bite-size pieces, washed, & spun dry**
two **cups arugula, large leaves torn in half**
½ **cup Lemon-Soy Dressing or Basic Vinaigrette**
one **red-skinned apple, such as Empire, Macoun, or Cortland, cut into 12**
slices
⅓ **cup crumbled blue cheese**

1. Preheat the oven to 350 degrees. Toast the walnuts in a shallow pan till they get aromatic, about 5-7 minutes. Let cool completely.
2. Mix the lettuce & arugula in a salad bowl. Pour on about ¾ of the dressing & toss. Add a little more dressing if needed.
3. Divide the salad among four salad plates, encompass with the apple slices, & sprinkle on the blue cheese & walnuts. Serve instantly.

CHOPPED SALAD WITH AVOCADO

SERVES four
four cups romaine lettuce in small pieces, washed & spun dry
two **cups torn watercress or arugula**
two **scallions, very thinly sliced**
12 black olives, Niçoise or your favourite sort
½ **cup cooked chickpeas, well rinsed if canned**
⅓ **cup Basic Vinaigrette or Lemon-Soy Dressing**
one **avocado, cut into 1-inch dice**
one **hard-boiled egg, minced**

1. Mix the lettuce, watercress, scallions, & olives in a big bowl.
2. In a small bowl mix the chickpeas with about one tablespoon of the dressing.
3. Just before serving add the avocado & marinated chickpeas to the greens. Pour on the dressing & toss. Serve on individual salad plates garnished with minced hard-boiled egg.

This salad serves four as a primary course, but it also makes a wonderful lunch or light dinner in itself; in that case it would serve 2.

SPINACH SALAD WITH ORANGES, FETA CHEESE, & OLIVES

SERVES four
one **navel orange**
⅛ **cup (roughly) Citrus Vinaigrette or Lemon-Soy Dressing**
eight cups torn spinach leaves, well washed & spun dry
two **scallions, very thinly sliced**

⅓ cup finely crumbled feta cheese

sixteen black olives, such as Niçoise or your favourite sort

1. Peel the orange & separate the sections. Remove any coarse membranes, then cut each part in half & place in a small bowl. Toss with a teaspoon or so of dressing, simply enough to coat them lightly.
2. Place the spinach & scallions in a big salad bowl. Just before serving toss with roughly ¼ cup dressing, simply enough to coat the leaves.
3. Divide the spinach onto four salad plates. Sprinkle on the oranges, feta cheese, & olives. Serve instantly.

SPINACH SALAD WITH GRAPEFRUIT & AVOCADO

SERVES four

one **pink grapefruit**

one **ripe avocado (preferably a dark, pebbly-skinned Haas), sliced**

⅓ cup Traditional Vinaigrette

eight cups flat-leaf spinach, torn into small pieces

¼ cup thin slivers red onion

1. Cut off the top & bottom ends of the grapefruit & stand it upright. With a pointy knife slice off the peel, cutting from top to bottom. Slice between the membranes to remove the person sections.
2. Prepare the avocado & place in a bowl. Pour on one tablespoon of the vinaigrette & toss very gently to coat & to prevent it from darkening.
3. Just before serving, toss the spinach & red onion with most of the dressing; add more if needed. Place the spinach on four serving plates. Top with the avocado & grapefruit sections.

ROASTED ASPARAGUS WITH GARLIC OIL

SERVES four

three tablespoons fruity olive oil

two **garlic cloves, sliced**

1½ pounds thin (but preferably not pencil-thin) asparagus, bottom of stalks peeled (see Tip)

four teaspoons fresh lemon juice

Salt to taste

Freshly ground pepper to taste

¼ cup freshly grated Parmigiano-Reggiano cheese

1. Mix the oil & garlic in a small bowl & let sit no less than one hour. Remove the garlic & discard.
2. Preheat the oven to 425 degrees. Place the asparagus on a baking sheet in one layer. Drizzle on half the garlic oil, after which roll the asparagus with your fingers till they're completely coated.
3. Bake eight-10 minutes for skinny asparagus or 10-12 minutes for thicker ones. Give the pan a shake midway through the cooking time so the asparagus cook evenly. When done they need to be tender & only slightly crisp.
4. Divide the asparagus among four small plates. Drizzle each portion with the remaining garlic oil, the lemon juice, salt, pepper, & cheese. Serve warm, not piping hot.

TOMATO SALAD

SERVES four
2-three large, ripe, red tomatoes, cored & sliced ½ inch thick
two **large yellow tomatoes, cored & sliced ½ inch thick**
10 large fresh basil leaves
½ cup (roughly) Basic Vinaigrette

1. Alternate the slices of red & yellow tomatoes on four salad plates.
2. Stack the basil leaves on top of one another to make a neat pile. Ranging from the long side, tightly roll the bundle up to make a log. Utilizing a pointy knife, cut thin slices from the top to the bottom. Shreds (chiffonade) will form. Use your fingers to separate them.
3. Drizzle the vinaigrette over the tomatoes & scatter the basil on top. Serve without delay.

BEET SALAD WITH GOAT CHEESE

SERVES four
six **medium beets, tops removed, leaving ¼ inch of stems**
two **tablespoons lemon juice**
one **garlic clove, pressed or minced**
¼ teaspoon salt
Generous seasoning freshly ground pepper
five **tablespoons olive oil**
four cups combined greens, such as romaine, Boston, & green leaf lettuces, or mesclun
two **cups arugula, torn into small pieces**
one **scallion, very thinly sliced**

½ cup chilled crumbled goat cheese, such as Montrachet
¼ cup chopped walnuts, toasted

1. Scrub the beets thoroughly. Fill a three-quart saucepan midway with water & bring to a boil. Cook the beets till tender when pierced with a pointy knife, about forty five-60 minutes. Drain well & let cool. Slip the skins off the beets. Dice the beets & place in a bowl.
2. To make the dressing: whisk together the lemon juice, garlic, salt, pepper, & oil. Pour a few tablespoons of the dressing on the beets & toss.
3. Just before serving, mix the greens, arugula, & scallion in a big bowl. Pour on most of the remaining dressing & toss. Add more if needed.
4. Place the greens on four salad plates. Spoon on a mound of beets. Sprinkle with the goat cheese & walnuts. Serve instantly.

PROVENÇAL GREEN BEAN SALAD

SERVES four AS A SIDE DISH
one **pound green beans, tips removed**
one **red bell pepper**
one **yellow bell pepper**
¼ cup Basic Vinaigrette or Lemon-Soy Dressing
Salt to taste
Generous seasoning freshly ground black pepper
¼ cup shredded fresh basil

1. Fill a four-6-quart pot midway-with water & bring to a boil. Drop in the green beans & cook till tender but still slightly crisp, not more than five minutes. Taste one to make sure; you need them good. Drain the green beans after which instantly immerse them in a big bowl or pot of very cold water. Let sit one minute, drain, then fill once more with cold water. Let the beans sit till completely cold, about five minutes. Drain once more after which dry the beans on a kitchen towel to remove all moisture. Place the beans in a big bowl.
2. To roast the peppers: preheat the broiler & ensure the oven rack is as high as it may well go. Cut each pepper in half vertically. Remove the stem, seeds, & white fibrous part. Place the peppers skin side up on a baking sheet & broil till the skin is nearly all black. About midway through the cooking time it's a good suggestion to press down & flatten the peppers with a spatula so they may broil evenly. It takes about 10 minutes to char the peppers.
3. Remove the peppers from the baking sheet & place in a medium-size bowl. Cover tightly with a plate & allow them to steam to loosen their skins, about 10 minutes.
4. Peel off the pepper skins with your fingertips & discard. Cut the peppers into strips about three inches by ½ inch. Mix into the green beans with all of the remaining

ingredients. Let marinate at the least half-hour before serving, or cover & refrigerate up to forty eight hours. Serve at room temperature.

BROCCOLI & ROASTED RED PEPPER SALAD

SERVES four AS A SIDE DISH
5-6 cups small broccoli florets (from one large bunch broccoli)
two **tablespoons pine nuts**
½ cup 2-inch-long roasted red pepper strips (about one red pepper) or one-half 7-ounce jar
¼ cup Traditional Vinaigrette
Salt to taste
Freshly ground black pepper to taste

1. Fill a four-6-quart pot with water & bring to a boil over high heat. Drop in the broccoli florets & blanch two minutes, or till tender but still fairly crunchy. Instantly drain the water & fill the pot with very cold water. Drain & fill once more. Let the broccoli sit in the cold water for at the very least five minutes so the broccoli will get completely cold. Drain totally in a colander.
2. Place a cotton kitchen towel on the counter. Collect up some broccoli & with your hands gently squeeze out any moisture clinging to it. Place the broccoli on the towel & continue with the remaining broccoli. Pat the broccoli with the towel & let air-dry 10 minutes or so.
3. Place the pine nuts in a small saucepan or skillet & swirl them round over medium heat till lightly golden. Be very cautious; they burn easily. Instantly pour them onto a plate & let cool.
4. Place the broccoli in a pretty bowl & mix in the red peppers. Pour on the dressing & season with salt & pepper. Toss well. Sprinkle on the pine nuts & let marinate at the least half-hour but no longer than a few hours before serving. Serve at room temperature.

TOFU, BEAN SPROUT, & CUCUMBER SALAD

SERVES four
one **recipe Roasted Tofu**
Peanut Sauce:
¼ cup natural-style peanut butter
two **tablespoons tamari soy sauce**
one **tablespoon lime or lemon juice**

two **tablespoons firmly packed brown sugar**
one **garlic clove, put through a press or minced**
¼ **teaspoon crushed red pepper flakes**
three tablespoons water
The Salad:
two **cups mung bean sprouts, rinsed well in a strainer (see Tip)**
one **small cucumber, peeled & sliced ¼ inch thick**
one **scallion, very thinly sliced**

1. Prepare the Roasted Tofu, cutting it into triangles as directed. Chill totally.
2. To make the sauce: mix all of the sauce ingredients in a small bowl & beat vigorously with a fork or small whisk till very smooth.
3. To assemble the salad: spread ¼ of the bean sprouts on each of four salad plates. Place six cucumber slices & six pieces of tofu alternately on each serving (you'll most likely have some left over). Drizzle some sauce over each portion & sprinkle with the scallions. Serve inside half-hour.

CLASSIC VINAIGRETTE

MAKES ABOUT one CUP
three tablespoons red wine vinegar
one **teaspoon Dijon-style mustard**
two **cloves garlic, put through a press or minced**
¾ **cup olive oil**
¼ **teaspoon salt**
Generous seasoning freshly ground pepper
Place all of the ingredients in a jar with a good-fitting lid & shake vigorously.

LEMON-SOY DRESSING

MAKES ABOUT ¾ CUP
one **large garlic clove, put through a press or minced**
two **tablespoons lemon juice**
one **tablespoon red wine vinegar**
1½ **teaspoons tamari soy sauce**
⅛ **teaspoon salt**
Generous seasoning freshly ground pepper
½ **cup mild-flavored olive oil**

Place all of the ingredients in a jar with a good-fitting lid & shake vigorously.

CITRUS VINAIGRETTE

MAKES one CUP
two **tablespoons fresh lemon juice**
¼ cup fresh lime juice
three tablespoons frozen orange juice focus
1½ teaspoons red wine vinegar
one **garlic clove, put through a press or minced**
¼ teaspoon sugar
½teaspoon salt
Freshly ground pepper to taste
½ cup olive oil
Place all of the ingredients in a jar with a good-fitting lid & shake vigorously. Let stand half-hour before utilizing to mix the flavors.

BALSAMIC VINAIGRETTE

MAKES ⅔ CUP
three tablespoons balsamic vinegar
two **teaspoons Dijon-style mustard**
one **garlic clove, minced**
½ teaspoon salt
Freshly ground pepper to taste
½ cup olive oil
Place all of the ingredients in a jar with a decent-fitting lid & shake vigorously. This dressing might be stored in the fridge for up to two weeks.

SESAME VINAIGRETTE

MAKES ¾ CUP
two **½ tablespoons red wine vinegar**
½ teaspoon tamari soy sauce
one **garlic clove, pressed (preferably) or minced**
¼ teaspoon salt
Generous seasoning freshly ground pepper
1½ tablespoons Asian sesame oil
½ cup canola oil

Place all of the ingredients in a jar with a screw-top lid & shake vigorously. This dressing will keep one week if refrigerated.

SUN-DRIED TOMATO VINAIGRETTE

MAKES ½ CUP
three sun-dried tomatoes
one **large garlic clove, finely chopped**
⅓ cup olive oil
three tablespoons red wine vinegar
¼ teaspoon salt
Generous seasoning freshly ground pepper

1. Place the tomatoes in a small bowl & pour boiling water over them. Let sit half-hour, or till very soft. Remove & pat dry with a paper towel. (In case your dried tomatoes are packed in oil, omit soaking them.) Chop into small pieces.
2. Place the tomatoes with all of the remaining ingredients in a blender & mix till the tomatoes are pureed & the dressing is smooth. This dressing will sustain to two weeks if refrigerated.

BUTTER MILK DRESSING

MAKES ABOUT one CUP
½ cup mayonnaise
½ cup buttermilk
two **tablespoons lime juice**
one **garlic clove, put through a press or minced**
one **tablespoon minced scallion (white part only)**
A few dashes salt
Freshly ground pepper to taste
Place the mayonnaise in a small bowl & whisk a few times till smooth. Slowly whisk in the buttermilk after which the remaining ingredients. Cover & let chill a minimum of half-hour before utilizing.

MISO-GINGER SALAD DRESSING

MAKES 1½ CUPS
three tablespoons rice (white) miso (see Tip)
one **teaspoon minced fresh ginger**
one **medium-size garlic clove, chopped**

two **tablespoons apple cider or red wine vinegar**
1½ **tablespoons Asian sesame oil**
¾ **cup canola oil**
⅓ **cup plus one tablespoon water**

1. Place the miso, ginger, garlic, vinegar, & sesame oil in a blender or food processor & process till smooth. With the motor running, very slowly drizzle in the canola oil, stopping after a few tablespoons have been absorbed before adding more. When the dressing has emulsified, very slowly add the water. Process 10 seconds or so, or simply till blended. When done, the dressing ought to be thick & really creamy.
2. Put the dressing in a bowl & chill till prepared to make use of. It would sustain to one week.

CREAMY TAHINI DRESSING

MAKES one CUP
½ **cup tahini (untoasted sesame seed butter) (see Tip)**
one **large garlic clove, put through a press or minced**
¼ **cup lemon juice**
¼ **teaspoon salt**
four-6 tablespoons water
Place the tahini, garlic, lemon juice, & salt in a bowl & whisk till smooth. Add four tablespoons water & whisk till included. Check the consistency; it ought to be like thick heavy cream. Whisk in a bit more water if necessary. Let sit at the least 20 minutes to mix the flavors or chill up to five days & bring to room temperature before utilizing.

CREAMY TOFU SALAD DRESSING

MAKES 1½ CUPS
eight ounces extra-firm or soft tofu, patted dry
two **tablespoons lemon juice**
¼ **cup olive oil**
four tablespoons water (use rather less for soft tofu)
one **tablespoon tamari soy sauce**
two **garlic cloves, finely chopped**
Place all of the ingredients in a blender or food processor & puree till very smooth. Store in the fridge up to four days.

NOODLES WITH PEANUT SAUCE

SERVES four AS A MAIN COURSE
one **pound spaghettini (thin spaghetti)**
two **tablespoons Asian sesame oil**
The Sauce:
⅔ **cup natural-style peanut butter, chunky or smooth**
⅓ **cup tamari soy sauce**
¼ **cup sherry**
two **tablespoons water**
one **tablespoon red wine vinegar**
three **tablespoons firmly packed light brown sugar**
three **tablespoons Asian sesame oil**
three **garlic cloves, minced**
one **tablespoon minced fresh ginger**
½ **teaspoon crushed red pepper flakes**
two **carrots, very finely chopped but not minced**
one **cucumber, peeled, halved lengthwise, seeded, & diced**
four **scallions, very thinly sliced**

1. Bring a big stockpot of water to a boil. Add the spaghettini & cook till al dente, that's, tender but still slightly firm. Drain in a colander & run under cold water. Drain once more & shake the colander to remove all moisture. Place the noodles in a very large bowl & add the two tablespoons sesame oil. Toss the noodles with tongs to totally coat them.
2. To make the sauce, whisk together all of the sauce ingredients besides the greens in a big bowl. Pour the sauce on the noodles & toss to coat. Sprinkle on the carrots, cucumbers, & half the scallions. Toss once more. Let the noodles sit at room temperature for half-hour to mix the flavors. Just before serving, sprinkle on the remaining scallions.

NOODLES WITH GREEN BEANS & CASHEWS

SERVES four AS A MAIN COURSE
The Sauce:
¼ **cup tamari soy sauce**
¼ **cup Asian sesame oil**
two **tablespoons natural-style peanut butter**
one **tablespoon sugar**
one **tablespoon Chinese rice vinegar or red wine vinegar**

three garlic cloves, finely chopped
one **tablespoon minced fresh ginger**
½ **teaspoon crushed red pepper flakes, or more to taste**
½ **teaspoon salt**
The Salad:
eight ounces green beans, cut in half (2½ cups)
one **pound spaghetti**
three scallions, very thinly sliced
one cucumber, peeled, cut lengthwise, seeded, & sliced ¼ inch thick
½ cup roasted cashews, preferably unsalted, roughly chopped
three tablespoons finely chopped cilantro (optional)

1. Mix the sauce ingredients in a blender (preferably) or a food processor & process till smooth. Pour right into a small bowl.
2. Bring a big stockpot of water to a boil. Drop in the green beans & cook five minutes, or simply till tender but still slightly crunchy. Remove with a strainer, place in a bowl, & cover with cold water to cease any additional cooking. Pour off the water & cover once more. Let sit a couple of minutes to allow them to get completely cold. Drain well, then place on a kitchen towel & pat dry.
3. Put the spaghetti in the boiling water & cook till al dente, about 12 minutes. Don't overcook it. Drain completely in a colander. Rinse under cold running water till cold. Shake the colander vigorously to remove any extra water. Place the noodles in a very large bowl.
4. Mix in the green beans, scallions, cucumber, & cashews. Pour on the sauce & use tongs to toss, coating well. Let the noodles marinate no less than half-hour before serving. Garnish with cilantro, if desired.

THAI NOODLE SALAD

SERVES four AS A MAIN COURSE
The Dressing:
three tablespoons Asian sesame oil
three tablespoons canola oil
¼ cup tamari soy sauce
three tablespoons lime juice
two tablespoons tomato paste
two tablespoons honey
one tablespoon minced fresh ginger
three garlic cloves, minced
½ teaspoon crushed red pepper flakes
½ teaspoon salt

The Salad:
one **pound spaghetti or linguine**

two **cups mung bean sprouts**

one **cucumber, peeled, seeded, & cut into matchsticks**

one **carrot, peeled & grated**

three scallions, very thinly sliced

two **tablespoons shredded fresh basil**

two **tablespoons finely chopped fresh mint**

two **tablespoons finely chopped cilantro**

¼ cup chopped dry roasted peanuts

1. Bring a big stockpot of water to a boil for the noodles.
2. In a medium-size bowl whisk together all of the ingredients for the dressing.
3. Cook the noodles till al dente. Drain totally in a colander & rinse the noodles under cold running water. Shake the colander vigorously to remove all water. Place the noodles in a very large serving bowl.
4. Pour on the dressing & toss well. Mix in all of the remaining ingredients besides the peanuts. Let the noodles marinate no less than half-hour before serving. Serve with the chopped peanuts sprinkled on top.

TABBOULI

SERVES four AS A MAIN COURSE
1½ cups bulgur, preferably golden & coarse-cut

two **ripe tomatoes, finely diced**

one **½ cups minced fresh parsley**

two **tablespoons minced fresh mint**

three scallions, thinly sliced

The Dressing:
¼ cup lemon juice

½ teaspoon salt

Generous seasoning freshly ground pepper

½ cup olive oil

1. Place the bulgur in a medium-size bowl & pour in enough boiling water to cover by one inch. Set a big plate on the bowl & let the bulgur steam for half-hour. Spoon the bulgur right into a clean cotton kitchen towel in batches & collect right into a ball. Squeeze out all of the liquid. Place the bulgur in a big bowl. Let cool.
2. Stir in the tomatoes, parsley, mint, & scallions.
3. Whisk together the dressing ingredients & pour over the salad. Cover & chill no less than half-hour or up to 24 hours before serving. Serve cool, not cold.

TABBOULI 2

SERVES four–6 AS A MAIN COURSE
1½ cups bulgur, preferably golden & coarse-cut

six **ripe cherry tomatoes, halved**

one **(6-ounce) jar marinated artichoke hearts, well drained & halved**

one **cucumber, peeled, seeded, & finely diced**

two **scallions, very thinly sliced**

one **yellow or red bell pepper, finely diced**

⅔ cup finely diced feta cheese

one **cup minced fresh parsley**

two **tablespoons minced fresh mint**

The Dressing:
¼ cup lemon juice

⅓ cup olive oil

½ teaspoon salt

Generous seasoning freshly ground pepper

1. Place the bulgur in a medium-size bowl & pour in enough boiling water to cover by one inch. Place a big plate on the bowl & let the bulgur steam for half-hour. Spoon some bulgur right into a clean cotton kitchen towel in batches & collect right into a ball. Squeeze out all of the liquid. Place in a big bowl & break up any clumps with a big spoon. Let cool completely.

   2.Stir in all of the remaining salad ingredients.

3. Whisk together the dressing ingredients in a medium-size bowl. Pour over the salad & toss to coat well. Cover & chill at the very least half-hour or up to 24 hours before serving (see Tip). Serve cool, not cold.

RICE, RED LENTIL, & WHEAT BERRY SALAD

SERVES four–6 AS A MAIN COURSE
⅓ cup wheat berries

one **teaspoon canola oil**

¼ teaspoon salt

1¼ cup red lentils, rinsed in a strainer

¾ cup basmati or jasmine rice, rinsed in a strainer

The Dressing:
¼ cup lemon juice

two **large garlic cloves, put through a press or minced**

¼ teaspoon salt

Generous seasoning freshly ground pepper

⅓ cup olive oil

one **carrot, minced**

one **red bell pepper, very finely diced**

½ cup minced fresh parsley

1. Soak the wheat berries overnight in enough water to cover by two inches. Alternatively, place them in a medium-size saucepan half-crammed with water & boil, uncovered, for two minutes. Remove from the heat & let sit one hour. Drain after which refill the saucepan midway with water & cook the wheat berries, partially covered, for one hour. When done, the wheat berries can be tender but slightly crunchy. Drain completely & let cool.
2. Bring two cups water, oil, & salt to a boil in a medium-size saucepan. Stir in the lentils & rice, & switch the heat to low. Cover the pan & cook 17 minutes, or till *all* the liquid is absorbed. Don't stir the combination whereas it's cooking. Carefully spoon the combination into a big bowl & let cool to room temperature.
3. In the meantime, place the dressing ingredients in a jar with a good-fitting lid & shake vigorously. Put aside. When the rice combination is completely cool, use a big spoon to interrupt up any clumps which have fashioned. Carefully stir in the wheat berries, carrot, red pepper, & parsley. Pour the dressing on the salad & toss. Let marinate a minimum of 20 minutes before serving.

CURRIED RICE SALAD

SERVES four AS A MAIN COURSE
four cups (roughly) cold, cooked, long-grain brown rice (1½ portions of Excellent Brown Rice)

one **cup seedless red grapes**

½ cup sliced almonds

three scallions, very thinly sliced

three tablespoons minced fresh mint or cilantro

The Dressing:

four tablespoons lemon juice

one **tablespoon curry powder**

½ teaspoon cumin seed

½ teaspoon turmeric

one **tablespoon minced gingerroot**

three garlic cloves, pressed or minced

¾ teaspoon salt

six **tablespoons canola oil**

1. Place the cold rice in a big serving bowl. Use a big spoon to interrupt up any clumps which have shaped. Stir in the grapes, almonds, scallions, & mint or cilantro.

two Place the dressing ingredients in a jar with a decent-fitting lid & shake vigorously. Pour on the rice & toss to coat well. Cover & chill the rice a minimum of one hour or up to 24 hours to permit the flavors to meld. Bring to room temperature before serving.

TUSCAN-STYLE COUSCOUS SALAD

SERVES four AS A MAIN COURSE
one **½ cups couscous**

½ teaspoon turmeric

two **cups boiling water**

¼ cup pine nuts

one **(15-ounce) can small white beans such as navy or Nice Northern, rinsed well & drained**

15 cherry tomatoes, halved, or one large ripe tomato, finely diced

127

½ cup shredded fresh basil

½ cup slivered red onion

The Dressing:
⅓ cup lemon juice

three garlic cloves, put through a press or minced

½ teaspoon salt

Generous seasoning freshly ground pepper

⅓ cup olive oil

1. Place the couscous & turmeric in a big bowl & mix. Pour on the boiling water, stir, & instantly cover the bowl with a big plate. Let sit for 10 minutes. Remove the cover & fluff the couscous with a fork. Let cool.
2. Place the pine nuts in a small skillet & toast over medium heat, tossing often, till golden, about five minutes. Watch them carefully as a result of they will easily burn. Let cool, then mix into the couscous together with the beans, tomatoes, basil, & red onion.
3. Place the dressing ingredients in a jar with a good-fitting lid & shake vigorously. Pour over the couscous combination & toss well. Let marinate not less than half-hour before serving. Cover & chill if longer than half-hour. Serve at room temperature.

MARINATED PENNE SALAD

SERVES six AS A MAIN COURSE
The Dressing:
2½ tablespoons red wine vinegar

three garlic cloves, put through a press or minced

½ teaspoon salt

Generous seasoning freshly ground pepper

½ cup olive oil

The Salad:
one **pound green beans, cut in half (four cups)**

one **pound penne**

three **medium-large ripe tomatoes, cut into ¾-inch dice**

one **yellow bell pepper, cut into thin slivers**

¼ cup minced fresh basil

1. Bring a big stockpot of water to a boil.
2. Place all of the dressing ingredients in a jar with a decent-fitting lid & shake vigorously. Put aside.
3. When the water boils, drop in the green beans. Cook five minutes, or till tender. Taste one to make certain. Use a strainer to scoop out the beans & place them in a big bowl. Fill the bowl with very cold water. Pour out the water, fill once more, & let the beans sit in it till they become completely cold.
4. Make sure they cease cooking so they keep their shiny green color. Drain the beans & place on a kitchen towel. Pat very dry. ft. Cook the penne in the same boiling water till al dente. Drain in a colander, then rinse under cold running water to chill. Shake the penne till very dry. Place in a big bowl & mix in the green beans, tomatoes, yellow pepper, & basil.
5. Pour on the dressing & toss well. Let marinate no less than half-hour before serving.

TIP: You may make the pasta salad a day upfront & refrigerate it. Remember to bring it to room temperature or at the least to a cool temperature before serving it in order that the flavors come through.

COLORFUL ORZO SALAD WITH SHIITAKE MUSHROOMS

The wealthy flavor of mushrooms paired with the creamy, delicate texture of orzo provides this vibrant salad nice panache. Serve it at your next barbecue for an actual crowd pleaser.

SERVES six AS A MAIN COURSE

The Dressing:
two **tablespoons lemon juice**

one **teaspoon red wine vinegar**

three **garlic cloves, pressed or minced**

one **teaspoon salt**

Liberal seasoning freshly ground pepper

½ cup olive oil

The Salad:
one **tablespoon unsalted butter**

eight ounces shiitake mushrooms, stems discarded & caps cleaned & thinly sliced

eight ounces button (normal) mushrooms, thinly sliced

one **pound orzo (rice-formed pasta)**

½ cup shredded fresh basil

two **scallions, very thinly sliced**

one **ripe red tomato, finely diced**

one **ripe yellow tomato, finely diced**

1. Place the dressing ingredients in a jar with a decent-fitting lid & shake vigorously.
2. Bring a big stockpot of water to a boil.
3. In the meantime, heat the butter in a big skillet over medium heat. Add the mushrooms & sauté till brown & juicy, about 10 minutes.
4. Put aside to chill. Drop the orzo into the boiling water & cook, stirring often, till al dente, that's, tender but still slightly firm. Drain totally in a colander & place in a big bowl. Pour on half the dressing, toss well, & let cool to room temperature.
5. Mix in the mushrooms, basil, scallions, & tomatoes. Pour on the remaining dressing & toss well. Let marinate at the very least half-hour before serving.

TIP: You may make quite a few substitutions with nice success. Substitute roasted yellow bell pepper for the yellow tomato, chopped arugula for the basil, & red onion for the scallions. The concept is to fill this salad with dynamic colours as well as flavors.

Pasta: To Rinse or Not to Rinse …

The rule of thumb concerning pasta is *by no means* rinse hot, cooked pasta if you will serve it hot. If you're going to serve it cold, as in a pasta salad, rinse it more often than not, depending on the recipe.

Pasta that's going to be served hot ought to be drained rapidly once it has reached the al dente stage, after which instantly tossed with its sauce & served. I don't know where the misunderstanding about rinsing pasta got here from. Maybe it arose from folks not cooking their pasta in enough water & getting caught-together noodles because of this, or maybe they let their hot pasta sit in the colander whereas they prepared their sauce & the pasta clumped together. In each circumstances, rinsing can be the one treatment to unstick the mess. So cook your pasta in loads of boiling water, stir frequently, & toss with the sauce instantly after the pasta is drained.

When cooking pasta for a chilly salad, you need the pasta to cease cooking once it has been drained. To do that you must rinse it instantly under cold running water. As a result of the water now adhering to the pasta is cold, it won't evaporate the best way hot water will, so you'll have to shake it vigorously in the colander to do away with the surplus water.

TORTELLINI SALAD WITH BROCCOLI, RED PEPPER, & PINE NUTS

This substantial pasta salad is a breeze to organize. It lends itself to improvisation, but this trio of additives—broccoli, red pepper, & pine nuts—is my favourite.

SERVES four AS A MAIN COURSE

The Dressing:
two **tablespoons red wine vinegar**

two **large garlic cloves, put through a press or minced**

½ teaspoon salt

⅓ cup olive oil

The Salad:
five **cups tiny broccoli florets (from about one bunch broccoli)**

one **red bell pepper, cut into ¼-inch strips about two inches long**

one **pound frozen cheese tortellini**

¼ cup toasted pine nuts (see Tip)

1. Place all of the dressing ingredients in a jar with a decent-fitting lid & shake vigorously.

2. Bring a big stockpot of water to a boil. Drop in the broccoli & cook three-5 minutes, or simply till tender but still crunchy. Taste one to make sure. Drop in the red pepper strips & boil 10 seconds. With a big strainer instantly scoop out the greens & place in a big bowl. Fill the bowl with very cold water to cease the greens from cooking additional. Let sit a couple of minutes, then pour out the water & fill once more with fresh cold water. Let the greens sit about five minutes, or till completely cold. Remove from the water & place on a cotton kitchen towel. Pat very dry.

3. Place the tortellini in the boiling water & cook till al dente, about seven minutes. Drain completely in a colander. Rinse the tortellini under cold running water. Shake the colander vigorously to drain away all of the water. Place the tortellini in a big bowl. Mix in the broccoli & red peppers, pine nuts, & dressing. Toss well. Let marinate a minimum of 20 minutes before serving, or cover & chill up to 24 hours. Bring to room temperature before serving.

TIPS: The red pepper is blanched only some seconds to tenderize it slightly but keep it crunchy. The broccoli must also be crunchy but tender. To make sure that the broccoli stays vivid green, you should shock it in cold water & get it completely cold. Any remaining heat will continue to cook the broccoli, & it'll turn an olive color.

To toast the pine nuts place them in a small, dry skillet over medium heat. Toss often. Be very watchful as a result of they burn easily.

SUMMER CHICKPEA, TOMATO, & SPINACH SALAD

Bean salads have advanced over the previous thirty years into refined medleys that now embody a variety of beans, greens, & herbs. The beans' high-protein content material makes them a super base for a predominant-course salad which will function a one-dish summer time meal.

That is one among my favourite canine-day summer time meals as a result of there isn't any cooking concerned & the flavour mixture is excellent. Tender flat-leaf spinach, often bought in bunches, works greater right here than crinkle-leaf spinach bought in bags. If you can't get spinach, arugula can be an ideal choice, or you possibly can substitute a few tablespoons of chopped fresh basil. Go the peppermill with this luscious salad, & accompany it with a bit of crusty bread to spherical out the meal.

SERVES four AS A MAIN COURSE

The Dressing:

two **tablespoons red wine vinegar**

one **large garlic clove, put through a press or minced**

¼ **teaspoon salt**

Generous seasoning freshly ground black pepper

¼ **cup olive oil**

The Salad:
two **(15-ounce) cans chickpeas, rinsed & well drained**

two **ripe tomatoes, diced**

½ cup slivered red onion

four cups flat-leaf spinach, stems discarded & leaves torn into small pieces

1. Mix all of the dressing ingredients in a jar with a decent-fitting lid & shake well, or whisk them together in a bowl.
2. In a big serving bowl mix the chickpeas, tomatoes, & onion. Pour on the dressing & toss to coat everything completely. Let marinate not less than half-hour or up to several hours. If serving time is greater than half-hour away, chill, then bring to room temperature. Add the spinach, toss well, & let the salad sit 10 minutes to slightly wilt the spinach. Serve on large plates or in pasta bowls, accompanied by some chewy European-style bread, if desired.

TIP: Flat-leaf spinach is usually known as baby spinach, but as many gardeners know, it's really a distinct variety from its crinkled-leaf cousin. Its smaller, thinner leaves are perfect for salads.

BLACK BEAN, MANGO, & JICAMA SALAD WITH CITRUS VINAIGRETTE

Tropical flavors come together right here to make a splendidly flavorful salad that requires no cooking & might be assembled with ease. A terrific choice for a hot summer time day or as a prelude to a Mexican feast. In case you are unacquainted with jicama, it's a humble vegetable that resembles a raw potato & provides an intriguing crunch to salads.

SERVES four AS A MAIN COURSE
¾ pound *(½ of a medium-size)* jicama

two **(15-ounce) cans black beans, rinsed well in a strainer & drained**

one **ripe mango, cut into ½-inch cubes (learn "Mango Mania,")**

½ cup finely diced red onion

two **jalapeño peppers, minced & seeds removed (put on rubber gloves) (see Tip)**

⅓ cup Citrus Vinaigrette

two **tablespoons minced cilantro**

1. Peel the jicama with a vegetable peeler. Slice into ¼-inch-thick slices, stack, & cut into ¼-inch-thick strips. Cut the jicama into ¼-inch cubes. It's best to have 1½ cups.
2. **2**. In a big bowl mix the jicama, black beans, mango, red onion, jalapeño peppers, & vinaigrette & toss gently. Let marinate half-hour or up to four hours to mix the flavors. Stir in the cilantro just before serving.

TIPS: You can substitute ¼ teaspoon crushed red pepper flakes for the jalapeños in case you need.

Jicama (pronounced HEE-ca-ma) will be present in most supermarkets.

SICILIAN POTATO & VEGETABLE SALAD

Red-skin potatoes are chosen for this salad as a result of they're waxy and, consequently, maintain together thoroughly when cooked. In the summertime this can be a essential course in our home, & it's particularly pleasing when preceded by corn on the cob; nevertheless, it will also make an excellent side dish at a barbecue or transport thoroughly to a picnic.

SERVES four-6 AS A MAIN COURSE

The Dressing:

two **tablespoons red wine vinegar**

two **garlic cloves, pressed or minced**

½ teaspoon salt

Generous seasoning freshly ground pepper

⅓ cup olive oil

The Salad:

½ pound green beans, tips removed & every bean cut in half

five **medium-large (2 pounds) red-skin potatoes (skins left on), cut into 1½-inch pieces**

one **ripe tomato, cut into ½-inch dice**

one **(15-ounce) can white beans, such as Nice Northern or navy beans, rinsed well & drained, or 1½ cups freshly cooked white beans**

⅓ cup slivered red onion

sixteen-20 black olives, preferably Niçoise

two **teaspoons drained capers**

1. To make the dressing mix all of the ingredients in a jar with a decent-fitting lid & shake vigorously.
2. Fill a stockpot midway with water & bring to a boil. Drop in the green beans & cook four-5 minutes, or till tender when tasted. Utilizing a sieve, remove the green beans right into a bowl. Keep the water boiling. Cover the green beans with cold running water, drain, & cover once more. Let sit till cold all through, at the least five minutes. Drain well & place on a cotton kitchen towel to dry.
3. Drop the potatoes into the boiling water & cook till tender, 10-quarter-hour. Don't overcook or they are going to get mushy. Drain completely in a colander. Place the potatoes in a medium-size bowl & pour on half the dressing. Utilizing a rubber spatula, toss the potatoes gently with the dressing. Let cool to room temperature.
4. Place the green beans in a big bowl. Add the tomato, white beans, onion, olives, & capers. Pour on the remaining dressing & toss. When the potatoes are cool, gently fold them into the salad. Serve the salad at room temperature.

COMPOSED SALAD PLATTER

This salad is comprised of a mattress of dressed greens topped with an assortment of separate bundles of marinated greens such as beets, green beans, & cherry tomatoes, plus roasted tofu, baked goat cheese, & olives. You can let the market dictate what's freshest, but the thought is to create a major-course salad platter that shows individual mounds of fantastically dressed greens. Other decisions may very well be marinated mushrooms, potato salad, & marinated peppers. That is an excellent summer time meal that's finest when made in levels so it may be easily assembled just before serving.

MAKES four MAIN-COURSE PLATTERS
The Dressing:
2½ tablespoons red wine vinegar

one **teaspoon Dijon-style mustard**

one **large garlic clove, pressed or minced**

¼ teaspoon salt

Generous seasoning freshly ground pepper

⅔ cup olive oil

The Salad:
one **recipe (1 pound) Roasted Tofu**

eight small or four medium-size beets, (red, striped, or golden variety)

½ pound green beans, tips removed

one **tablespoon minced fresh basil, dill, or parsley**

12 cherry tomatoes, each cut in half

12 black olives, your favourite form

one **slice white bread**

four-ounce log goat cheese, cut into four slices

one **tablespoon olive oil**

12 cups combined greens (such as romaine, green leaf, & Boston lettuces, & arugula)

½ cup slivered red onion

1. Mix all of the ingredients for the dressing in a jar with a decent-fitting lid & shake vigorously.
2. Make the Roasted Tofu & chill till very cold.
3. Trim the greens off the beets, leaving a ½-inch stem. Boil the beets till tender. The time will fluctuate depending on the size of the beets. Drain well. Slip their skins off & discard. Cut the beets into bite-size chunks & toss with about one tablespoon of the dressing. Chill. Bring a medium-size saucepan of water to a boil. Drop in the green beans & cook till tender, about five minutes.

4. Place the beans in a big bowl & instantly fill with very cold water. Drain & fill once more. When the beans are cold all through, remove them & dry on a cotton kitchen towel. Place in a bowl & toss with about one tablespoon of the dressing & the fresh herb of your choice. Cover & chill.
5. Toss the cherry tomatoes with a little dressing, & set the olives apart.
6. Preheat the oven to 425 degrees just before serving the salad.
7. Place the slice of bread in a blender to make bread crumbs. Pour them onto a small plate.
8. Lightly brush each slice of goat cheese with the tablespoon of olive oil & press the cheese into the crumbs to coat either side. Place the cheese on a baking sheet. Bake 10 minutes, or till hot & scorching but not in order that the cheese is runny.
9. Place the combined greens & onion in a big salad bowl. Pour on the remaining salad dressing & toss. You can current the salad on four individual dinner plates, or let company serve themselves from one large platter. Arrange the greens accordingly. On middle of the mattress of greens place the beets, then encompass with mounds of Roasted Tofu (you may not need all of it), green beans, tomatoes, olives, & baked goat cheese. Serve without delay.

TIP: The dressing, roasted tofu, & the beets might be prepared up to three days prematurely.

LEMON BREAD

MAKES one LOAF, 10-12 SERVINGS
eight tablespoons (1 stick) unsalted butter, very soft

½ cup sugar

two **large eggs**

Zest of one lemon

⅓ cup frozen lemonade focus, thawed

one **teaspoon vanilla extract**

two **cups unbleached flour**

two **teaspoons baking powder**

½ teaspoon salt

¾ cup half-and-half

Lemon-Almond Glaze:
one **tablespoon melted butter**

one **tablespoon fresh lemon juice**

one **teaspoon milk**

⅛ **teaspoon almond extract**

¼ **teaspoon vanilla extract**

¾ **cup confectioners' sugar**

1. Preheat the oven to 350 degrees. Generously butter & flour a nine X 5-inch loaf pan. In a big bowl, utilizing an electrical mixer, cream the butter & sugar till very smooth. Add the eggs & beat till very fluffy, not less than three minutes. Add the zest, lemonade focus, & vanilla, & beat till combined.
2. In a medium-size bowl mix the flour, baking powder, & salt. Sprinkle it into the butter combination & beat a few seconds. Pour in the half-and-half & beat just till the batter is evenly moistened. Scrape the batter into the prepared loaf pan.
3. Bake 50-60 minutes, or till a tester or knife inserted in the middle of the bread comes out clean. Cool the bread completely on a wire rack.
4. To make the glaze: mix the butter, lemon juice, milk, & almond & vanilla extracts in a medium-size bowl. Add the confectioners' sugar & beat vigorously with a fork Let the combination sit a minute so the sugar can take in the liquid, then stir once more till smooth. Check the consistency Add 1-2 drops of milk if the glaze is just too thick to spread. Spread or drizzle the glaze over the top of the bread. Let harden, about quarter-hour, before slicing the bread.

DRIED CRANBERRY & ORANGE BREAD

MAKES one LOAF, 10-12 SERVINGS
two **cups unbleached flour**

two **teaspoons baking powder**

½ **teaspoon salt**

½ **cup dried cranberries**

six **tablespoons butter, very soft**

¾ **cup sugar**

Zest of two oranges

two **large eggs**

½ **cup orange juice**

½ **cup low-fat milk**

1. Preheat the oven to 350 degrees. Butter & flour a nine X 5-inch loaf pan.
2. **2**. Place the flour, baking powder, & salt in a medium-size bowl & mix well. Put the cranberries in a small bowl & toss with one tablespoon of the flour combination.
3. In a big bowl, utilizing an electrical mixer, beat the butter, sugar, & orange zest together till creamy, not less than two minutes. Add the eggs & beat till very fluffy, at the very least three minutes more. Alternately add half the flour & half the orange juice & milk. Beat just till combined, then repeat, mixing only till mixed. Fold in the cranberries by hand. Scrape the batter into the loaf pan. Bake 50-fifty five minutes, or till a tester inserted in the middle of the bread comes out dry. Cool on a wire rack for five minutes before unmolding. Let the bread cool completely before slicing, at the very least two hours.

SPICED APPLE RUM BREAD

MAKES one LOAF, 10–12 SERVINGS
two **cups unbleached flour**

one **cup sugar**

one **teaspoon baking powder**

one **teaspoon baking soda**

one **teaspoon cinnamon**

one **teaspoon powdered ginger**

¼ **teaspoon ground cloves**

¼ **teaspoon nutmeg**

½ **cup finely chopped pecans or walnuts**

½ **teaspoon salt**

two **large eggs**

½ **cup canola oil**

one **cup unsweetened applesauce**

¼ **cup rum or apple cider**

1. Preheat the oven to 350 degrees. Butter & flour a nine X 5-inch (1½-quart) loaf pan.
2. In a big bowl totally mix the flour, sugar, baking powder, baking soda, cinnamon, ginger, cloves, nutmeg, nuts, & salt.
3. In a medium-size bowl beat together the eggs, oil, applesauce, & rum. Add to the flour combination & stir till evenly moistened. Scrape into the prepared pan.
4. Bake one hour, or till a knife inserted in the middle of the bread comes out clean. Let stand on a wire rack for 10 minutes before eradicating from the pan. Cool completely before slicing, about two hours.

BANANA BRAN BREAD

MAKES one LOAF
one **cup unbleached flour**

½ **cup bran**

⅔ **cup sugar**

one **teaspoon baking powder**

one **teaspoon baking soda**

½ **teaspoon salt**

½ **cup finely chopped walnuts**

two **large eggs**

one **cup completely mashed ripe bananas (2-three bananas)**

six **tablespoons unsalted butter, melted**

1. Preheat the oven to 350 degrees. Butter a nine X 5-inch (1½-quart) loaf pan.
2. In a big bowl mix the flour, bran, sugar, baking powder, baking soda, salt, & walnuts.
3. Whisk the eggs in a medium-size bowl. Totally whisk in the mashed banana & butter. Scrape this into the flour combination & stir just till evenly moistened. Pour the batter into the prepared pan.
4. Bake 50 minutes, or till a knife inserted in the middle of the loaf comes out clean. Cool on a wire rack for 10 minutes before eradicating from the pan. Cool completely, not less than two hours, before slicing.

SWEET POTATO BREAD

MAKES one large loaf, 12-14 servings
two **cups unbleached flour**

1¼ **cups sugar**

1¼ **teaspoons baking powder**

½ **teaspoon baking soda**

¾ **teaspoon salt**

one **teaspoon cinnamon**

½ **teaspoon ground cloves**

½ **cup finely chopped pecans**

two **large eggs**

½ teaspoon vanilla extract

one **cup cooked, well-mashed sweet potato (from one large potato)**

½ cup canola oil

½ cup low-fat milk

1. Preheat the oven to 350 degrees. Butter & flour a nine × five × three-inch loaf pan (see Tip).
2. In a medium-size bowl completely mix the flour, sugar, baking powder, baking soda, salt, cinnamon, cloves, & pecans.
3. Whisk the eggs in a big bowl till blended. Whisk in the vanilla & sweet potato till thoroughly blended. Whisk in the oil & milk. Add the flour combination & whisk just till the batter is smooth & blended. Scrape the batter into the prepared pan.
4. Bake one hour & 20 minutes, or till a knife inserted in the middle of the bread comes out clean. Remove the loaf from the pan & cool completely on a wire rack before slicing, no less than two hours.

OATMEAL RAISIN BREAD

MAKES one LOAF, 10-12 SERVINGS
1¼ cups quick oats

½ cup whole wheat flour

¼ cup unbleached flour

¼ cup wheat bran

½ teaspoon cinnamon

two **teaspoons baking powder**

½ teaspoon salt

⅔ cup raisins

two **large eggs**

½ **cup firmly packed light brown sugar**

¼ **cup canola oil**

1¼ **cups buttermilk**

1. Preheat the oven to 350 degrees. Butter a nine X 5-inch (1½-quart) loaf pan.
2. In a big bowl completely mix the oats, the two flours, bran, cinnamon, baking powder, & salt. Add the raisins & toss to coat well.
3. Beat the eggs in a medium-size bowl with a fork or whisk Beat in the sugar & oil till well combined. Beat in the buttermilk till blended. Pour this combination into the flour combination & stir just till the batter is evenly moistened. Scrape the batter into the prepared pan.
4. Bake 50 minutes, or till a knife inserted in the middle of the bread comes out clean. Remove the loaf from the pan & cool on a wire rack. Cool to room temperature, no less than two hours, before slicing.

CLASSIC CORN BREAD

SERVES 6
one **cup cornmeal**

one **cup unbleached flour**

one **tablespoon baking powder**

¼ **cup sugar**

½ **teaspoon salt**

one **large egg**

four tablespoons unsalted butter, melted

1¼ **cups low-fat milk**

1. Preheat the oven to four hundred degrees. Butter an eight X eight-inch baking pan.

2. In a big bowl completely whisk together the cornmeal, flour, baking powder, sugar, & salt.

3. Whisk the egg in a medium-size bowl. Whisk in the butter & milk till well blended. Pour into the cornmeal combination & whisk just till the batter is evenly moistened. Don't overbeat. With a rubber spatula scrape the batter into the prepared pan.

4. Bake 25 minutes, or till very lightly golden on top & a knife inserted in the middle of the bread comes out dry. Let cool on a wire rack a minimum of 10 minutes before cutting. Serve warm or at room temperature.

CORN BREAD WITH CHILIES

SERVES 6
1¼ cups cornmeal

¼ cup unbleached flour

one **tablespoon baking powder**

½ teaspoon salt

¼ cup sugar

one **cup frozen corn, thawed**

one **(four-ounce) can chopped (mild) green chilies, well drained**

one **cup grated Monterey Jack cheese with jalapeño peppers**

two **large eggs**

one **cup milk**

¼ cup canola oil

1. Preheat the oven to four hundred degrees. Butter an eight X eight-inch baking pan.

2. In a big bowl totally mix the cornmeal, flour, baking powder, salt, & sugar. Stir in the corn, chilies, & cheese till well coated.
3. Beat the eggs in a medium-size bowl. Beat in the milk & oil. Pour into the cornmeal combination & stir just till evenly moistened. Scrape the batter into the prepared pan. Bake half-hour. Let cool on a wire rack at the least quarter-hour before cutting into squares. Serve barely warm or at room temperature.

CORN BREAD LOAF

MAKES one LOAF, 10-12 SERVINGS
Butter for greasing pan

1¼ **cups unbleached flour, plus extra for dusting the pan**

1¼ cups cornmeal

½ cup sugar

one **teaspoon baking powder**

½ teaspoon salt

two **large eggs**

½ cup canola oil

one **cup low-fat milk**

one **cup frozen corn kernels, thawed**

1. Preheat the oven to 350 degrees. Butter & flour a nine X 5-inch loaf pan.
2. In a big bowl completely mix the flour, cornmeal, sugar, baking powder, & salt.
3. Beat the eggs in a medium-size bowl. Beat in the oil & milk. Pour into the flour combination & stir just till evenly moistened. Stir in the corn. Scrape the batter into the prepared loaf pan.
4. Bake quarter-hour. Lower the heat to 325 degrees & bake one hour more, or till a knife inserted in the middle of the bread comes out clean. Let the loaf cool in the pan for quarter-hour before eradicating it. Cool on a wire rack till warm or at room temperature before slicing, at the least one hour.

SODA BREAD

MAKES one LOAF, 12-14 SERVINGS
2½ cups unbleached flour, plus extra for dusting

½ cup whole wheat flour

½ cup sugar

¾ teaspoon salt

two **teaspoons baking soda**

four tablespoons (½ stick) butter, cut into bits, plus extra for greasing

one **cup raisins**

1½ **tablespoons caraway seeds**

1½ cups buttermilk, or plain yogurt thinned with milk

Milk for brushing on top

1. Preheat the oven to 350 degrees. Butter & flour a spherical eight x 2-inch cake pan.
2. In a big bowl place the two flours, sugar, salt, & baking soda, & totally mix together. Drop in the butter bits & toss to coat with the flour. Rub the butter into the flour with your fingertips till little pea-size pieces form. Stir in the raisins & caraway seeds.

three. Pour in the buttermilk & stir to moisten the dough evenly. Sprinkle a little flour on the work surface, then place the dough on it. Knead the dough a few times simply to make it pliable. Form it right into a ball, then put it in the baking pan & flatten it. With a pointy knife cut an "x" in it. Use your fingers to coat the surface of the dough with a little milk to provide it a slight sheen. Bake fifty five-60 minutes, or till a wealthy golden brown. Remove the bread from the pan & let cool completely on a wire rack, a minimum of two hours, before slicing it.

ANGEL BISCUITS

MAKES one DOZEN BISCUITS

¼ **cup warm water**

½ **packet (about 1⅛ teaspoons) dry active yeast**

2½ **cups unbleached flour**

two **tablespoons sugar**

½ **teaspoon baking powder**

½ **teaspoon baking soda**

¾ **teaspoon salt**

four tablespoons unsalted butter, chilled

one **cup buttermilk**

one **tablespoon butter, melted**

1. Place the water in a small bowl & sprinkle on the yeast. Let sit two minutes, then stir it into the water till blended.
2. Completely mix the flour, sugar, baking powder, baking soda, & salt in a big bowl. Cut the butter into bits & toss it in the flour combination. Rub the butter into the flour with your fingertips or a pastry cutter till small pellets form. Pour in the yeast combination & buttermilk, & stir just till evenly moistened. Cover the bowl with plastic wrap & refrigerate a minimum of one hour or up to four days.
3. Preheat the oven to 450 degrees. Place the oven rack in the top third of the oven.
4. Place the dough on a lightly floured surface & knead a few times. Roll it right into a ½-inch thickness. Use a three-inch biscuit cutter to chop out the biscuits & place them on a greased baking sheet. Brush the tops lightly with melted butter. Bake eleven–thirteen minutes, or till deeply golden.

GIANT CORN MUFFINS

MAKES six LARGE MUFFINS
Butter for greasing

1¼ cups unbleached flour

¾ cup cornmeal

one **tablespoon baking powder**

½ teaspoon salt

⅓ cup sugar

one **large egg**

¼ cup canola oil

one **cup milk**

1. Preheat the oven to four hundred degrees. Butter a jumbo-size (¾-cup) muffin pan.
2. In a big bowl totally mix the flour, cornmeal, baking powder, salt, & sugar.
3. Beat the egg in a medium-size bowl. Beat in the oil & milk. Pour into the dry ingredients & stir just till evenly moistened. Spoon into the prepared muffin cups.
4. Bake 22 minutes, or till a knife inserted in the middle of a muffin comes out clean. Serve warm, not piping hot, for optimum flavor & texture.

POPPY SEED MUFFINS

MAKES one DOZEN MUFFINS
1½ cups unbleached flour

⅓ cup sugar

one **½ tablespoons poppy seeds**

½ teaspoon salt

two **teaspoons baking powder**

½ teaspoon baking soda

two **tablespoons grated orange zest (about two oranges)**

one **egg**

one **cup buttermilk**

six **tablespoons butter, melted**

two **tablespoons orange juice**

1. Preheat the oven to four hundred degrees. Generously butter the insides & top of an everyday-size (⅓-cup) muffin pan.
2. In a big bowl totally mix the flour, sugar, poppy seeds, salt, baking powder, baking soda, & zest.
3. Beat the egg in a medium-size bowl. Beat in the buttermilk, butter, & orange juice. Pour into the flour combination & stir just till evenly moistened. Don't overmix the batter. Spoon into the muffin pan. Bake 18-20 minutes, or till a tester inserted in a muffin comes out clean. Instantly remove the muffins from the pan & cool on a wire rack Serve warm or at room temperature.

MIXED BERRY MUFFINS

MAKES one DOZEN MUFFINS
1¼ **cups frozen combined berries**

two **cups unbleached flour**

½ **cup sugar**

one **tablespoon baking powder**

¾ **teaspoon salt**

two **large eggs**

one **teaspoon vanilla extract**

1¼ **cups low-fat milk**

six **tablespoons butter, melted**

1. Preheat the oven to four hundred degrees. Generously butter the insides & top of a daily-size (⅓-cup) muffin pan or line the pan with paper muffin cups. With a big, sharp knife cut any large frozen berries, such as strawberries & blackberries, into small pieces, then place the berries in a small bowl.
2. In a big bowl totally mix the flour, sugar, baking powder, & salt. Sprinkle one tablespoon of the flour combination on the berries & toss to coat.
3. Beat the eggs in a medium-size bowl. Beat in the vanilla, milk, & melted butter. Pour into the flour combination & stir a few strokes to evenly moisten the batter, then gently fold in the berries. Don't overmix.
4. Fill the muffin cups with the batter; it would reach the top of the pan. Bake 20-22 minutes, or till a knife inserted in the middle of a muffin comes out dry. These muffins are most flavorful when served at room temperature.

BANANA GINGER MUFFINS

MAKES one DOZEN MUFFINS
two **cups unbleached flour**

½ **cup sugar**

one **tablespoon baking powder**

one **teaspoon cinnamon**

½ **teaspoon salt**

½ **cup finely chopped crystallized ginger**

two **large eggs**

one **cup totally mashed ripe bananas (2-three bananas)**

six **tablespoons butter, melted**

¾ **cup low-fat milk**

1. Preheat the oven to four hundred degrees. Butter the insides & top of a daily-size (⅓-cup) muffin pan.
2. In a big bowl totally whisk together the flour, sugar, baking powder, cinnamon, salt, & ginger.
3. Whisk the eggs in a small bowl. Whisk in the mashed banana, butter, & milk till completely mixed. Scrape this combination into the flour combination & whisk just till evenly moistened. Don't over-beat. Spoon the combination into the prepared muffin pan. It would reach the top of every cup.
4. Bake 18 minutes, or till a knife inserted in the middle of a muffin comes out dry. Remove the muffins from the pan & let cool on a wire rack. Serve warm or at room temperature.

MORNING MUFFINS

MAKES one DOZEN MUFFINS
two **cups unbleached flour**

½ **cup sugar**

two **teaspoons baking powder**

two **teaspoons cinnamon**

½ **teaspoon salt**

one **cup grated carrots (about two carrots)**

one **tart apple (such as Granny Smith), peeled, cored, & grated**

½ **cup raisins**

⅓ **cup sweetened shredded coconut**

½ **cup finely chopped pecans**

two **large eggs**

½ **cup canola oil**

one **teaspoon vanilla extract**

⅔ cup low-fat milk

1. Preheat the oven to 375 degrees. Butter the insides & top of a daily-size (⅓-cup) muffin pan.
2. In a big bowl completely mix the flour, sugar, baking powder, cinnamon, & salt. Stir in the grated carrots, apple, raisins, coconut, & pecans, & toss to coat well.
3. Beat the eggs in a medium-size bowl. Beat in the oil, vanilla, & milk. Add to the flour combination & stir to mix. Don't overheat the batter.
4. Spoon the batter into the muffin cups. Bake 20-22 minutes, or till a knife inserted in the middle of a muffin comes out clean. Cool the muffins on a wire rack for five minutes, then remove from the pan & let cool some more. These muffins are finest served barely warm or at room temperature—not hot.

CRANBERRY OAT MUFFINS

MAKES one DOZEN MUFFINS
1¼ cups unbleached flour

¼ cup whole wheat flour

one **cup oats**

½ cup sugar

one **tablespoon baking powder**

½ teaspoon cinnamon

½ teaspoon salt

one **cup fresh or frozen thawed cranberries**

one **large egg**

one **cup milk**

six **tablespoons butter, melted & cooled**

1. Preheat the oven to four hundred degrees. Generously butter the insides & top of a daily-size (⅓-cup) muffin pan.
2. In a big bowl completely mix the two flours, oats, sugar, baking powder, cinnamon, & salt.
3. Place the cranberries in a processor & roughly chop them, or place on a cutting board & chop by hand with a big knife. Mix the cranberries into the flour combination.
4. Beat the egg in a medium-size bowl. Beat in the milk & butter. Pour into the flour combination & stir just till the batter is evenly moistened. Don't overmix it. Spoon the batter into the prepared muffin pan.
5. Bake 18 minutes, or till a knife inserted in the middle of a muffin comes out clean. Remove the muffins from the pan & cool on a wire rack. Serve slightly warm or at room temperature.

APPLE CIDER MUFFINS

MAKES one DOZEN MUFFINS
Streusel Topping:
¼ cup unbleached flour

¼ cup sugar

three tablespoons chilled unsalted butter, cut into bits

The Muffins:
two **cups unbleached flour**

½ cup whole wheat flour

one **tablespoon baking powder**

½ teaspoon cinnamon

½ teaspoon ground cloves or allspice

½ teaspoon salt

one **apple, grated (skin left on)**

one **large egg**

½ cup firmly packed light brown sugar

153

½ cup canola oil

one **cup apple cider**

1. To make the streusel: mix the flour & sugar in a small bowl. Toss the butter bits with the combination, then use your fingers to rub the butter into the flour till moist pellets form. Put aside.
2. Preheat the oven to four hundred degrees. Generously butter the insides & top of a daily-size (⅓-cup) muffin pan.
3. In a big bowl totally mix the two flours, baking powder, cinnamon, cloves, & salt. Add the apple & toss with the combination till it no longer stays in clumps.
4. Beat the egg in a medium-size bowl. Beat in the brown sugar, oil, & apple cider. Add to the flour combination & stir just till blended. Spoon the batter into the muffin cups. With your fingers sprinkle some streusel on each muffin, then pat it down lightly.
5. Bake 17–18 minutes, or till a knife inserted in one of many muffins comes out clean. Cool on a rack for five minutes before eradicating the muffins from the pan. Serve slightly warm or at room temperature.

JAMMIES

MAKES one DOZEN MUFFINS
two **cups unbleached flour**

½ cup sugar

one **tablespoon baking powder**

½ teaspoon salt

Pinch nutmeg

one **large egg**

six **tablespoons butter, melted & cooled**

1¼ cups milk

one **teaspoon vanilla extract**

¼ cup jam (roughly)

1. Preheat the oven to 425 degrees. Generously butter the insides & top of a daily-size (⅓-cup) muffin pan.
2. In a big bowl completely mix the flour, sugar, baking powder, salt, & nutmeg.
3. Beat the egg in a medium-size bowl. Beat in the butter, milk, & vanilla. Pour into the dry ingredients & stir just till the batter is evenly moistened. Don't overheat.
4. Spoon about ⅓ of the batter into all of the muffin cups. (They are going to be lower than half stuffed.) Place a teaspoon of jam in the middle of every muffin, then cover with the remaining batter.
5. Bake 15-20 minutes, or till evenly golden on top. Cool on a wire rack for a couple of minutes before eradicating from the pan.

POPOVERS

MAKES six POPOVERS
two **large eggs**

two **tablespoons butter, melted, plus extra for greasing**

one **cup milk**

one **cup unbleached flour**

two **teaspoons sugar**

½ teaspoon salt

1. Butter six custard cups (¾ cup capability) & place on a baking sheet.
2. Whisk the eggs in a big bowl. Pour in the melted butter & milk, & mix. Add the flour, sugar, & salt, & whisk till the batter is smooth. Don't overmix.

   three. Fill the custard cups with the batter. Place the baking sheet with the custard cups on it in the cold oven, then set the heat at 425 degrees. Bake forty minutes. Don't peek in the oven before the popovers are done, or they might deflate. Tip the popovers on their sides in the cups & cut a slit in the sides to let steam escape. Serve inside quarter-hour.

CLASSIC CURRANT SCONES

MAKES one DOZEN SCONES
two **cups unbleached flour**

⅓ **cup sugar**

two **teaspoons baking powder**

½ **teaspoon baking soda**

½ **teaspoon salt**

six **tablespoons unsalted butter, chilled**

½ **cup currants**

one **large egg**

¾ **cup buttermilk, or yogurt thinned with a little milk**

Milk for glazing

1. Place the oven rack in the top third of the oven. Preheat the oven to four hundred degrees. Lightly butter a baking sheet.
2. In a big bowl mix the flour, sugar, baking powder, baking soda, & salt, & mix together completely. Cut the butter into bits & toss them into the flour combination. Rub the butter into the combination with your fingertips till small pellets form. Stir in the currants.
3. Beat the egg in a small bowl. Beat in the buttermilk. Pour into the flour combination & stir with a fork till the dough is evenly moistened. Sprinkle a little flour on a piece surface & drop the dough on it. Collect the dough right into a ball & knead a few times. Pat the dough right into a three/four-inch disk. Cut the disk into 12 triangles with a big knife. Brush the top of the scones with a little milk & place on the baking sheet.
4. Bake quarter-hour, or till lightly golden. Cool on a wire rack before serving.

GINGER CREAM SCONES

MAKES one dozen scones
two **cups unbleached flour**

⅓ **cup sugar**

two ½ **teaspoons baking powder**

½ **teaspoon salt**

⅓ **cup finely diced crystallized ginger**

1⅓ **cups heavy cream**

one **teaspoon vanilla extract**

Milk for glazing

1. Place the oven rack in the top third of the oven. Preheat the oven to four hundred degrees. Lightly butter a baking sheet.

    2.In a big bowl completely mix the flour, sugar, baking powder, salt, & crystallized ginger.

3. Mix the cream & vanilla together, then pour into the flour combination. Stir with a big spoon just till the dough is evenly moistened. Lightly flour a piece surface & place the dough on it. Knead one or two times, then pat right into a three/four-inch-thick disk. Cut the disk into 12 triangles. Place the scones on the baking sheet & brush the tops lightly with some milk.
4. Bake quarter-hour, or till the scones are lightly golden. Cool till slightly warm or at room temperature before serving.

IRISH WHOLEMEAL SCONES

At Area's market in Skibbereen, County Cork, Eire, we had one of the best scones of our journey across the Emerald Isle. These scones resemble Irish brown bread as a result of they're made with the same Irish "wholemeal" flour that's extensively utilized in that nation. The closest flour we've got right here is whole wheat flour, but that lacks the graininess that's so pleasing of their variety. I used to be thrilled to find that I might duplicate wholemeal flour by adding some oats & wheat germ or bran to our whole wheat flour. Though crammed with whole grain goodness, these memorable scones are light & tender.

MAKES one DOZEN SCONES

one **cup unbleached flour**

½ **cup whole wheat flour (preferably stone-ground)**

¼ **cup oats**

¼ **cup toasted wheat germ or bran**

two **tablespoons sugar**

two **teaspoons baking powder**

½ **teaspoon baking soda**

½ **teaspoon salt**

six **tablespoons unsalted butter, chilled**

one **large egg**

¾ **cup buttermilk, or plain yogurt thinned with a little milk**

Milk for glazing

1. Place the oven rack in the top third of the oven. Preheat the oven to four hundred degrees. Lightly butter a baking sheet.
2. In a big bowl totally mix the two flours, oats, wheat germ, sugar, baking powder, baking soda, & salt. Cut the butter into bits & toss into the combination to coat the pieces of butter. Rub the butter into the combination with your fingertips till small pellets form.
3. Beat the egg in a small bowl. Beat in the buttermilk. Pour into the flour combination & stir with a fork till the flour is evenly moistened. Let the combination sit for one minute so it will possibly take in the liquid.

4. Lightly flour a piece surface & place the dough on it. Knead one or two times, adding flour if it's too sticky. Form right into a disk & pat to a ¾ inch thickness. Cut the dough in half, then cut each half into six triangles to make 12 scones. Place the scones on the baking sheet. Brush the top of every scone with some milk.
5. Bake quarter-hour, or till lightly golden. Cool on a wire rack before serving.

DOUBLE ALMOND SCONES

MAKES L DOZEN SCONES
7-eight ounces almond paste

1¾ cups unbleached flour

two **tablespoons sugar**

Grated zest of one orange

2½ teaspoons baking powder

½ teaspoon salt

five **tablespoons chilled unsalted butter, cut into bits**

½ cup sliced almonds

one **large egg**

⅔ cup buttermilk, or plain yogurt thinned with a little milk

Milk for brushing

1. Place the oven rack in the top third of the oven. Preheat the oven to four hundred degrees. Lightly butter a baking sheet.
2. Place the almond paste in a food processor & process till it's the texture of coarse sand. Scrape it into a big bowl & completely mix in the flour, sugar, orange zest, baking powder, & salt. Add the butter bits & toss to coat with the flour combination. Rub the butter into the flour with your fingertips till coarse crumbs form. Stir in the sliced almonds.

3. Beat the egg in a small bowl. Beat in the buttermilk. Pour into the flour combination & stir just till evenly moistened. Lightly flour a piece surface & drop the dough on it. Knead two or three times, then pat right into a ¾-inch-thick disk. Cut the disk in half with a big, sharp knife & cut each half into six triangles to make 12 scones. Place the scones on the baking sheet. Brush the top of every scone with some milk. **5,** Bake about 17 minutes, or till golden. Cool completely on a wire rack before serving.

CHEESE SCONES

MAKES 24 SMALL SCONES
2½ cups unbleached flour

one **tablespoon baking powder**

½ teaspoon dry mustard

¾ teaspoon salt

⅛ teaspoon cayenne pepper

six **tablespoons chilled unsalted butter, cut into bits**

1½ cups grated extra-sharp cheddar cheese

two **large eggs**

¾ cup plus two tablespoons low-fat milk

1. Place the oven rack in the top third of the oven. Preheat the oven to four hundred degrees. Lightly butter a big baking sheet.
2. In a big bowl totally mix the flour, baking powder, mustard, salt, & cayenne.
3. Drop in the butter bits & toss to coat them with the butter. With your fingertips rub the butter into the flour combination till it's the texture of very coarse crumbs.
4. Add one cup of the cheese & use your fingertips to coat the cheese pieces with the combination. In a medium-size bowl, beat the eggs. Beat in the milk. Pour this into the flour combination & stir till the dough is evenly moistened.
5. Lightly flour your work surface & drop the dough onto it. Knead two or three times, then form right into a ball & divide it into two pieces. Pat every bit right into a disk ½–¾ inch thick (no thicker). With a big, sharp knife cut each disk in half, & cut each half into six

triangles to make 24 scones. Place the scones on the baking sheet (in case your baking sheet is small, bake the scones in two batches) & place among the remaining grated cheese on top of every scone.

6. Bake on the top rack for 10-12 minutes, or till golden. Remove the scones from the baking sheet & cool slightly on a wire rack. Serve warm.

YOGURT FRUIT PARFAIT

SERVES four
one **cup plain yogurt**

1½–2 tablespoons honey

Dash cinnamon

four cups (roughly) assorted fruit (such as melon, berries, kiwi, banana, mango, & pear), cut into bite-size pieces

Mint sprigs or sliced almonds for garnish

1. Mix the yogurt, 1½ tablespoons honey, & cinnamon in a bowl & mix well. Taste for sweetness & add more honey if necessary.
2. Fill four ornamental goblets or large wine glasses about midway with the fruit. Spoon on a layer of yogurt. Top with more fruit & once more cover with yogurt. Garnish with a mint sprig or a few sliced almonds. Serve inside one hour.

PANCAKES

SERVES four
2¼ cups unbleached flour

¼ cup sugar

2¼ teaspoons baking powder

¾ teaspoon salt

three large eggs

2¼ **cups milk**

four tablespoons (½ stick) butter, melted

Oil for greasing the pan

Maple syrup (optional; see Tip)

1. In a big bowl whisk together the flour, sugar, baking powder, & salt.
2. Whisk the eggs in a medium-size bowl. Whisk in the milk & melted butter. Pour into the flour combination & whisk just till mixed. The batter ought to be a little lumpy, not completely smooth.
3. Cover the griddle or frying pan with a thin movie of oil. Heat the pan over medium heat till a drop of water dances when flicked on the pan.

PUMPKIN PANCAKES

SERVES four GENEROUSLY
two **large eggs**

¼ cup canned pumpkin (puree)

¼ cup canola oil

2¼ cups low-fat milk

2¼ cups unbleached flour

¼ cup sugar

2½ **teaspoons baking powder**

¾ teaspoon salt

one **teaspoon cinnamon**

¾ teaspoon allspice

¼ teaspoon nutmeg

Canola oil for frying

Maple syrup for topping

1. Whisk the egg in a medium-size bowl. Add the pumpkin, oil, & milk, whisking till smooth.
2. In a big bowl completely whisk together the flour, sugar, baking powder, salt, cinnamon, allspice, & nutmeg. Pour the egg combination into these dry ingredients & whisk till just blended & with a few lumps remaining. Don't overbeat.
3. Pour a thin movie of oil in a big skillet & heat over medium heat till a drop of water dances when dropped on the surface. Lower the heat to rather less than medium, & it ought to be good. Spoon on some batter to make a few pancakes; they shouldn't be too thick. When some bubbles have appeared & burst & the bottom of the pancake is a wealthy golden color, flip them over & cook till golden brown. Repeat with the remaining batter. Serve with maple syrup.

BUTTERMILK CORN PANCAKES

SERVES three
1¼ **cups unbleached flour**

¼ cup cornmeal

two **tablespoons sugar**

1¼ teaspoons baking powder

¼ teaspoon baking soda

one **teaspoon salt**

two **large eggs**

1¾ cups buttermilk

three tablespoons butter, melted

one **cup frozen corn, thawed**

Oil for greasing

Maple syrup

1. In a medium-size bowl whisk together the flour, cornmeal, sugar, baking powder, baking soda, & salt.
2. Whisk the eggs in a big bowl after which whisk in the buttermilk & melted butter. Gently whisk in the flour combination & the corn just till the batter is evenly moistened. Don't overbeat.
3. Pour a thin movie of oil on a griddle or large skillet & heat over medium heat. Test to see if the pan is hot enough by flicking a drop of water on it; it ought to sizzle. When the pan is prepared, put a few tablespoons of batter on the pan to make three-inch pancakes. Flip the pancakes over when they're golden brown beneath; this could take a couple of minutes on all sides. Not like traditional pancakes, this batter doesn't bubble up as it cooks. Repeat with the remaining batter, lightly oiling the pan in between batches. Serve the pancakes with maple syrup.

WHOLE-GRAIN WAFFLES

MAKES one DOZEN 6-INCH WAFFLES
½ cup oats

½ cup whole wheat flour

one **cup unbleached flour**

one **tablespoon sugar**

½ teaspoon salt

one **½ teaspoons baking powder**

one **teaspoon baking soda**

four large eggs

two **cups buttermilk**

eight tablespoons (1 stick) butter, melted

Maple syrup (see Tip)

1. Preheat the waffle iron.
2. Place the oats in a blender or food processor & grind right into a powder. Pour into a big bowl & completely mix in the two flours, sugar, salt, baking powder, baking soda, & salt.
3. Beat the eggs in a medium-size bowl. Beat in the buttermilk & melted butter. Pour this combination into the dry ingredients & stir just till blended but still a little lumpy. Don't overheat.
4. Cook the waffles in accordance to the producer's instructions. Serve instantly

FRENCH TOAST

SERVES
four large eggs

⅔ cup low-fat milk

¼ cup Grand Marnier or Triple Sec (or other orange liqueur)

¼ cup sugar

Oil for frying (preferably canola)

eight slices good-quality white bread

Maple syrup

1. In a medium-size bowl completely beat the eggs till completely blended. Beat in the milk, Grand Marnier, & sugar. Pour right into a shallow dish such as a glass pie plate.
2. Pour a thin movie of oil in a fiying pan & heat over medium heat till a drop of water dances when dropped on it.
3. Place the slices of bread one after the other in the egg combination & let sit a few seconds. Carefully turn each over & moisten the opposite side. Place a slice of soaked

bread in the frying pan & repeat with one other slice. Cook on either side till golden brown & cooked through. Regulate the heat so the bread doesn't brown too quick. Serve with a little bit of maple syrup.

BAKED APPLE FRENCH TOAST

SERVES four GOOD EATERS
four tablespoons (½ stick) unsalted butter

three medium-large apples (such as Cortland, Macoun, or Empire), peeled & thinly sliced (four–4½ cups) (see Tips)

¾ cup firmly packed light or dark brown sugar

two **tablespoons water**

one **teaspoon cinnamon**

6–eight slices Italian or extensive French bread (four–5 inches in diameter), cut one inch thick (see Tips)

four large eggs

1¼ cups milk

two **teaspoons vanilla extract**

1. Melt the butter in a big skillet & add the apple slices. Sauté five minutes, tossing often. Mix in the brown sugar, water, & cinnamon. Cook, stirring, eight–10 minutes, or till the apples are very tender. Scrape the combination right into a thirteen X nine X 2-inch Pyrex baking dish or other shallow three-quart casserole.
2. Cover the apples with the bread slices, trimming the bread if necessary, to completely cover the surface.
3. Beat the eggs totally, then beat in the milk & vanilla. Pour throughout the bread. Cover the dish with plastic wrap & refrigerate overnight.
4. Remove the dish from the fridge in the morning & let sit at room temperature whilst you preheat the oven to 375 degrees. Bake the casserole, uncovered, for 30–35 minutes, or till the bread is golden & firm. Let sit 10 minutes before unmolding.
5. Run a knife across the edges of the dish. If in case you have a platter or tray large enough to suit over the casserole, place it on top & thoroughly flip over the baking dish

to unmold it. In any other case, cut the French toast into individual parts and, utilizing a spatula, lift one portion from the dish. Invert a serving plate & place on the French toast portion, then flip over so the apple layer is on top.

PANETTONE FRENCH TOAST

SERVES four
six **large eggs**

½ cup low-fat milk

Canola oil for frying

four–6 **slices (cut ¾ inch thick) panettone**

Maple syrup

1. Beat the eggs completely in a medium-size bowl. Beat in the milk till blended. Pour the combination right into a shallow dish large enough to maintain a slice of panettone.
2. Pour a thin layer of oil in one or two large frying pans & heat over medium heat till a drop of water flicked on the pan sizzles.
3. Dip one slice of panettone into the egg combination, then shortly turn it over to soak the opposite side. As a result of the panettone is so soft & porous, you'll must moisten it shortly so it doesn't get too saturated & break. Place the slice instantly in the hot oil. Repeat with one other slice in case you are utilizing two pans. Cook till a wealthy golden brown, flip over, & cook once more till browned. Serve with maple syrup.

ZUCCHINI, TOMATO, & BASIL FRITTATA

SERVES four
three tablespoons olive oil one large onion, finely diced

one **(14-ounce) can prepared-cut diced tomatoes, drained well & juice reserved**

two **small zucchini, halved lengthwise & thinly sliced**

eight large eggs

⅓ cup grated Parmesan cheese

two **tablespoons minced fresh basil, or ½ teaspoon dried**

½ teaspoon salt

Liberal seasoning freshly ground pepper

1. Heat two tablespoons oil in a 10-inch skillet, preferably nonstick, over medium heat. Add the onion & sauté till softened, about 10 minutes. Add the drained tomatoes & cook slowly with the onions till the onions are very tender, about 10 minutes. Stir in the zucchini & cover the pan. Cook stirring often, till the zucchini is tender, about 10 minutes. Add a little of the reserved cooking liquid if the greens start to stay Scrape the combination right into a bowl & let cool.
2. Clean the skillet during which the greens have been cooked. Pour in the remaining tablespoon of oil & swirl it across the pan to coat the sides as well because the bottom. In case your pan isn't nonstick you'll in all probability need a bit more oil. Heat the pan over medium heat.
3. In the meantime, beat the eggs totally. Beat in the cheese, basil, salt, & pepper. Stir in the zucchini combination. Pour into the prepared pan. After about five minutes, when the edges start to set, loosen the edges of the frittata with a rubber spatula & tilt the pan to permit the uncooked egg to reach the bottom. It ought to take about quarter-hour for the frittata to become almost completely set.
4. In the meantime, preheat the broiler. When the frittata is about eighty % cooked, slide it under the broiler for a minute or so, till the top is about. (If the handle of your pan isn't ovenproof, wrap a few layers of foil round it before putting it under the broiler.) Let the frittata cool 10 minutes before cutting it into wedges.

SWISS CHARD & POTATO FRITTATA

SERVES three
six **large Swiss chard leaves**

one **tablespoon olive oil**

one **medium onion, diced**

one **garlic clove, minced**

one **medium boiling (waxy) potato, peeled & diced into ½-inch cubes (no greater)**

six **large eggs**

¼ cup grated Parmesan cheese

¼ teaspoon salt

Generous seasoning freshly ground pepper

one **tablespoon unsalted butter**

1. Wash the Swiss chard & pat very dry. Cut off & discard the stems, then collect the leaves into a decent bundle & finely chop them.
2. Heat the oil in a 9-or 10-inch nonstick skillet over medium heat. Add the onion & garlic, & sauté till the onion turns golden, about 10 minutes. Mix in the potato & cover the pan. Cook, shaking the pan often, till the potato is tender & the onions are brown, about 10–quarter-hour. Remove the cover & pile on the Swiss chard. Cover once more & cook, tossing often, till the leaves are wilted, about five minutes. Scrape this combination onto a plate & let cool. Wipe the pan clean.
3. Beat the eggs totally in a big bowl. Beat in the cheese, salt, & pepper. Stir in the cooled vegetable combination.
4. Melt the butter in the skillet over low heat & swirl it round to coat the sides of the pan. Pour in the egg combination. After about five minutes, when the edges start to set, help the liquid egg pour over the sides of the frittata by often loosening the edges with a rubber spatula & tilting the pan. It ought to take about quarter-hour for the frittata to become almost completely set.
5. Preheat the broiler. When the frittata is about eighty p.c cooked, slide it under the broiler for a minute or so, till the top is ready. (If the handle of your pan isn't ovenproof, wrap a few layers of foil round it before putting it under the broiler.) Let the frittata cool 10 minutes before cutting it into wedges.

ONION FRITTATA

two **tablespoons olive or canola oil, divided**

three strips tempeh "bacon"

one **medium-large onion, finely diced**

eight large eggs

⅓ cup grated Asiago or Parmesan cheese

¼ teaspoon salt

Freshly ground pepper to taste

one **tablespoon unsalted butter**

1. Heat one tablespoon oil in a 10-inch (preferably nonstick) skillet over medium-high heat. Lay the tempeh strips in the hot oil & fry on either side till brown & crisp. Remove the strips with tongs, place on a big plate, & chop into ½-inch pieces.
2. Pour the remaining oil into the skillet. Add the onion & lower the heat to medium. Sauté till the onion is very soft & golden brown, about 10 minutes. Scrape the onion onto the plate containing the bacon.
3. Beat the eggs in a big bowl till well blended. Beat in the cheese, salt, & pepper. Stir in the bacon & onion. Melt the butter in the skillet over low heat, swirling the pan round so the butter also coats the sides. Pour in the egg combination.
4. After about five minutes, when the edges start to set, help the liquid egg pour over the sides of the frittata by often loosening the edges with a rubber spatula & tilting the pan. It ought to take about quarter-hour for the frittata to become almost completely set.
5. In the meantime, preheat the broiler. When the frittata is about eighty p.c cooked, slide it under the broiler for a minute or so, till the top is about. (If the handle of your pan isn't ovenproof, wrap a few layers of foil round it before inserting it under the broiler.) Let the frittata cool 10 minutes before cutting it into wedges.

SPANISH TORTILLA

SERVES three
four tablespoons olive oil, divided

two **medium boiling potatoes, peeled & cut into ¼-inch dice (2 cups diced)**

Salt to taste

Freshly ground pepper to taste

two **medium onions, diced**

six **large eggs**

1. Heat three tablespoons oil in a 9-or 10-inch nonstick skillet over medium-high heat. When the oil is hot but not smoking, add the potatoes & cook till golden brown throughout & tender, a minimum of 10 minutes. If the potatoes become brown before they're tender, turn the heat to medium-low & cook a couple of minutes more. Season generously with salt & pepper. Remove the potatoes with a slotted spoon & place on a plate, leaving any oil behind.
2. Add the onions to the skillet & cook till very tender & golden brown, no less than 10 minutes. Spoon onto the plate containing the potatoes. Wipe the skillet clean, pour in the remaining tablespoon of oil, & place the pan over medium heat.
3. Beat the eggs in a big bowl. Mix in the potatoes & onions. When the skillet is hot but not smoking, pour in the egg combination. Let set a couple of minutes, then loosen the edges with a spatula. Cook the tortilla till it's about ninety % set. Shake the pan often to be sure that the tortilla doesn't stick with the bottom. Lower the heat a little if it's getting too brown. Place a plate over the skillet & invert the skillet so the tortilla is bottom side up on the plate. Shortly slide the tortilla back onto the skillet. Cook one or two minutes. Slide the tortilla back onto the plate & cut into wedges.

MUSHROOM, ONION, & CHEESE OMELET

SERVES 2
one **tablespoon olive oil**

one **medium onion, halved & really thinly sliced**

two **cups (6 ounces) thinly sliced mushrooms**

four large eggs

¼ teaspoon salt

two **tablespoons water**

two **teaspoons unsalted butter**

½ **cup grated smoked Gouda cheese**

1. To make the filling: heat the oil in a medium-size skillet over medium heat. Add the onion & cover the pan. Sauté, stirring often, till the onion is very tender & golden, about **10** minutes. Mix in the mushrooms & sauté, uncovered, till brown & juicy, about **10** minutes. Keep warm over low heat.
2. Beat the eggs completely with the salt & water in a medium-size bowl.
3. Make one omelet at a time. Heat one teaspoon butter in an eight-inch skillet, preferably nonstick, over medium-high heat. When the pan is highly regarded but not but smoking, pour in half of the egg combination. It should instantly start to set on the edges. Use an inverted spatula to push the edges towards the middle of the omelet whereas tipping the pan to permit the liquid egg to run onto the hot pan. When little or no of the uncooked egg stays, spoon half of the hot mushroom filling onto one side of the omelet. Cover with half of the grated cheese. Instantly fold the omelet in half, then slide onto a plate. Repeat to make an extra omelet.

EGG & PEPPER BREAKFAST BURRITOS

SERVES 2
one **tablespoon olive oil**

one **small onion, finely diced**

one **small to medium green bell pepper, finely diced**

two **(eight-inch) flour tortillas**

four eggs, well beaten

Salt to taste

⅔ **cup grated Monterey Jack cheese with jalapeño peppers**

1. Heat the oil in a small skillet over medium heat. Add the onion & green pepper, & cook two minutes. Cover the pan & cook till the green pepper is very soft & an olive color, not less than 10 minutes.
2. In the meantime, heat the tortillas utilizing a technique outlined.
3. When the peppers are cooked, pour in the eggs & stir with a spoon till scrambled. Season with salt & take away the pan from the heat.
4. Place each warm tortilla on a big plate & sprinkle half the cheese down the middle of every one. Cover with the eggs, then tightly roll up, burrito-style. Serve without delay.

SPINACH, ARTICHOKE, & RED

SERVES eight

one **tablespoon olive oil**

one **large red bell pepper, cut into thin strips two inches long**

one **(10-ounce) package frozen chopped spinach, thawed**

nine **large eggs**

3½ cups low-fat milk

½ cup grated Parmesan cheese

¼ teaspoon nutmeg

one **teaspoon salt**

Generous seasoning freshly ground pepper

2½ tablespoons butter, softened

nine **slices (roughly) firm white bread (see Tips)**

two **(6-ounce) jars marinated artichoke hearts, well drained**

two **scallions, very thinly sliced**

three cups grated extra-sharp cheddar cheese

1. Heat the oil in a medium-size skillet over medium heat & sauté the red pepper till tender, about seven minutes. Put aside.
2. Place the thawed spinach in a strainer & press out all of its liquid with the back of a giant spoon. Put aside.
3. Totally beat the eggs in a big bowl. Beat in the spinach, milk, Parmesan cheese, nutmeg, salt, & pepper.
4. Utilizing ½ tablespoon butter, grease a thirteen X nine X 2-inch baking dish. With the remaining two tablespoons butter, coat one side of every slice of bread. Cut the bread into 1-inch cubes. You have to nine cups of cubed bread.
5. Place half of the bread cubes in the baking dish. Sprinkle on half of the red pepper strips, one jar of artichokes, & half of the scallions. Ladle on half of the spinach combination, then sprinkle on half of the cheddar cheese. Repeat this layering & finish with the cheddar cheese. Cover the dish with plastic wrap or foil & refrigerate overnight.
6. Remove the dish from the fridge at the least half-hour before baking. Preheat the oven to 350 degrees. Bake the strata, uncovered, for one hour, or till golden brown on top & firm in the middle. Let the strata sit quarter-hour before cutting it into squares.

MIXED PEPPER STRATA

SERVES 6

two **teaspoons olive oil**

one **red bell pepper, cut into ½-inch dice**

one **green bell pepper, cut into ½-inch dice**

one **onion, finely diced**

two **tablespoons butter, softened**

six **slices (roughly) firm white bread, such as sourdough**

two **cups grated Monterey Jack cheese with jalapeño peppers**

five **large eggs**

one **cup light cream**

one **cup milk**

¼ **teaspoon salt**

½ teaspoon dried oregano

1. Heat the oil in a big skillet over medium heat. Add the peppers & onion, & sauté till very tender, about **10** minutes. Put aside to chill.
2. Utilizing 1½ tablespoons butter, coat one side of every slice of bread. Cut the bread into 1-inch cubes. You need six cups of cubed bread.
3. Utilizing ½ tablespoon butter, grease a 12 X seven x 2-inch shallow 2½-quart baking dish (such as a Pyrex glass dish). Scatter the bread cubes in the dish, spread on the peppers, after which sprinkle on the cheese. Beat the eggs in a bowl. Beat in the cream, milk salt, & oregano. Pour the combination throughout the bread combination.
4. Cover the casserole with foil or plastic wrap & refrigerate overnight.
5. Remove the dish from the fridge not less than half-hour before baking. Preheat the oven to 350 degrees. Bake the strata, uncovered, for 35 minutes, or till golden brown on top & firm in the middle. Let the strata sit quarter-hour before cutting it into squares.

BUNS

MAKES one DOZEN ROLLS
one **cup firmly packed light brown sugar, divided**

¼ cup water

four tablespoons (½ stick) unsalted butter, at room temperature, divided

one **pound frozen bread dough, thawed**

Flour for dusting

two **teaspoons cinnamon**

½ cup chopped pecans

1. Set out a shallow 10-inch baking dish.
2. In a small saucepan mix ⅔ cup brown sugar, the water, & a couple of tablespoons butter. Heat, stirring often, just till the sugar has melted & the combination blends. Pour all but three tablespoons of the caramel into the baking dish & spread it round.

3. On a lightly floured surface form the dough right into a rectangle. With a rolling pin roll it right into a sixteen x 10-inch rectangle. (If the dough resists being stretched, let it rest a couple of minutes & roll once more.) Spread the remaining two tablespoons butter throughout the dough. Sprinkle on the remaining ⅓ cup brown sugar, the cinnamon, & pecans. Drizzle with the remaining three tablespoons of caramel. Beginning on the long finish, roll the dough right into a log. Tightly pinch the seam together. With a serrated knife & utilizing a sawing movement, cut the log crosswise into 12 pieces. Place the buns, cut side up, on the caramel in the baking dish. Let rise half-hour.
4. Preheat the oven to 350 degrees. Bake the buns half-hour, or till golden. Cool on a wire rack for five minutes, then cover the baking dish with a platter & invert the buns so the caramel is on top. Serve warm, not piping hot.

GRANOLA

MAKES 12 CUPS
½ cup canola oil

½ cup honey

six **cups old school oats**

⅓ cup bran

⅓ cup toasted wheat germ

½ teaspoon salt

one **tablespoon cinnamon**

one ½ **cups unsweetened coconut (bought at a natural meals store)**

¼ cup sunflower seeds

¼ cup sesame seeds

two **cups chopped walnuts**

1⅓ cups raisins

1. Preheat the oven to 350 degrees.
2. Mix the oil & honey in a big stockpot & heat, stirring often, just till blended. You don't need the combination to boil. Stir in all of the remaining ingredients besides the raisins. Mix well to coat everything evenly.
3. Bake the granola in three batches. Spread ⅓ of the combination evenly on a big baking sheet (with sides). Bake 15–20 minutes. For the last 5–10 minutes toss the granola often with a spatula to permit it to cook evenly. The granola tends to burn alongside the sides of the pan, so be watchful. When done, the granola might be lightly browned but still soft.
4. Place this batch in a bowl & stir in ⅓ of the raisins. Let cool completely before storing in jars. Repeat with the remaining two batches of granola.

SOFT PRETZELS

MAKES 18 FAT PRETZELS
½ cup warm water

one **packet active dry yeast**

two **cups milk (preferably whole milk)**

¼ cup sugar

Salt

¼ cup canola oil

six **cups unbleached flour**

Butter for greasing

one **egg white**

Kosher (coarse) salt

1. Place the warm water in a small bowl & sprinkle on the yeast. Let sit a couple of minutes to melt, then stir it into the water. Let sit five minutes more.
2. Warm the milk to a lukewarm temperature. Pour into a big bowl (or the bowl of a mixer if in case you have a dough hook) & stir in the sugar, 1½ teaspoons salt, oil, & the yeast

177

liquid. Sprinkle in the flour & stir to form an evenly moistened dough, or use the dough hook in your mixer & mix till moistened. Knead the dough for eight–10 minutes, or till pliable, or use the mixer to knead it for eight minutes.

3. Lightly grease a big bowl. Press the dough into the bowl, then flip it over so it's greased-side up. Cover the bowl with plastic wrap & let rise till double in size, about one hour.

4. Punch down the dough. On a lightly floured surface roll it right into a 12 x 18-inch rectangle. Cut the dough into 18 strips. With your hands roll the strips into spherical ropes. Form into pretzel shapes. (I make an inverted "U," crisscross the ends, after which decide them up & firmly press them into the top of the "U.") Place the pretzels on baking sheets & let rise half-hour.

5. Fill a big pot midway with water plus two tablespoons salt & bring to a boil. Place the oven racks so one is in the middle & one is above it. Preheat the oven to four hundred degrees.

6. At this level a little group will go an extended way. Place a big cooling rack on a big tray or a smaller rack on a plate. (That is for the pretzels when they're faraway from the water.) Place a baking sheet containing the pretzels close by. With a big spatula lift up a pretzel & lower it into the boiling water. Let sit five seconds, then lift it out of the water with the spatula & drain on the cooling rack. Repeat till the cooling rack is stuffed. Place the boiled pretzels on plates or a piece surface so you can also make room on the cooling rack for the next batch. Repeat with all of the pretzels.

7. Butter two baking sheets. Place the pretzels on the sheets, leaving a 1-inch space between them. Lightly brush with the egg white, then sprinkle generously with kosher salt. Place one sheet on the middle rack & one on the rack above it, & bake 17 minutes, or till lightly golden. Swap the place of the baking sheets midway in the course of the cooking time. Cool the pretzels on a cooling rack. Serve warm.

DOUGHNUTS

MAKES one DOZEN
three cups unbleached flour

one **tablespoon baking powder**

½ **teaspoon cinnamon**

⅛ **teaspoon nutmeg**

½ **teaspoon salt**

two **large eggs**

¼ cup sugar

three tablespoons butter, melted

½ cup milk

one **teaspoon vanilla extract**

Oil for frying

For Dipping:
½ cup sugar

1¼ teaspoons cinnamon

1. In a medium-size bowl totally mix the flour, baking powder, cinnamon, nutmeg, & salt.
2. Whisk the eggs & sugar together in a big bowl till light & smooth. Whisk in the butter, milk, & vanilla. Add the dry ingredients, whisking just till blended. Don't overmix.
3. Turn the dough onto a lightly floured surface (it will likely be soft) & knead two or three times. Use a rolling pin to roll the dough a hair lower than $^{three}/_{four}$ inch thick (no thinner). Cut out the doughnuts with a floured 2½-inch doughnut cutter. Roll the little middle pieces into balls to form doughnut "holes." You need to get about 12 doughnuts & holes. Fill a three-quart saucepan or deep flying pan with about three inches oil.
4. Heat over medium heat till a tiny pellet of dough dropped in the oil sizzles & instantly rises to the surface, about 370 degrees. In the meantime, mix the sugar & cinnamon in a bowl & put aside.
5. When the oil is prepared, fly a few doughnuts at a time till golden brown, turning once. It can take about one minute on either side. Remove with tongs & drain on paper towels or brown paper bags. Whereas still hot, dip in the cinnamon-sugar combination till well coated. Fry the doughnut holes in the same method. Serve warm, preferably, or at room temperature.

MAPLE OATCAKES

MAKES sixteen OATCAKES
three cups old style oats

½ teaspoon salt

one **stick (eight tablespoons) unsalted butter, at room temperature, plus extra for greasing**

⅓ **cup heavy cream**

⅓ **cup pure maple syrup**

1. Place the oats & salt in the container of a food processor & process till as fine as flour. Pour the combination into a big bowl.
2. Put the butter, cream, & maple syrup in the processor & process till blended. Pour the oats back into the processor & process till mixed with the butter combination, about 30 seconds.
3. Preheat the oven to 325 degrees. Lightly butter the bottom & a little bit up the sides of two 9-inch spherical cake pans. Divide the oat combination into two parts. Utilizing your fingers, press a portion into each pan, making them as evenly thick as possible.
4. Use a rubber spatula to smooth over the tops. With a pointy knife cut almost right through to make eight triangles in each pan.
5. Bake half-hour. Remove from the oven & cut all over to separate the triangles. Remove the triangles with a spatula & place on a baking sheet. (The best strategy to remove the triangles is by sliding the spatula under their sides.) Lower the oven heat to 275 degrees.
6. Return the oatcakes to the oven & bake half-hour more, or till dark beige throughout.

ORANGE-ALMOND BISCOTTI

MAKES ABOUT forty
¾ **cup almonds**

two **cups unbleached flour**

one **teaspoon baking powder**

¼ **teaspoon salt**

two **large eggs**

one **cup sugar**

½ **teaspoon vanilla extract**

¼ teaspoon almond extract

Grated zest of one orange

1. Preheat the oven to 350 degrees.
2. Place the almonds in a shallow baking dish & toast till aromatic & golden, about eight minutes. Let cool completely, then use a big knife to cut them coarsely. In the meantime, line a baking sheet with parchment paper or butter & flour it.
3. In a small bowl mix the flour, baking powder, & salt.
4. In a big bowl mix the eggs, sugar, vanilla & almond extracts, & orange zest. Beat with an electrical mixer till pale & creamy.
5. Add the almonds & dry ingredients, & beat just till mixed. Collect the dough into two balls. Place the balls on the baking sheet & form every one right into a smooth 12 X 2-inch log.
6. Bake 35 minutes, or till lightly golden. Remove the pan from the oven & lower the heat to 325 degrees. Let the loaves cool a full 10 minutes; they may crumble if they're sliced when too hot.
7. Place the loaves on a cutting board & use a serrated knife to chop the loaves on a pointy diagonal into ½-inch-thick slices. Place the slices, cut side down, on the baking sheet.
8. Return the biscotti to the oven & bake 15–20 minutes more, turning each slice over after 10 minutes. The biscotti can be lightly golden when done, but still considerably soft. They are going to harden upon cooling. Transfer the biscotti to a cooling rack & cool totally before storing in a covered tin for up to two weeks.

SUGAR & SPICE NUTS

MAKES four CUPS
½ cup sugar

one **tablespoon cinnamon**

one **teaspoon ground cloves**

one **teaspoon ground ginger**

Dash salt

six **tablespoons unsalted butter**

one **teaspoon vanilla extract**

one **pound (four cups) pecans**

1. Preheat the oven to 300 degrees.
2. Mix the sugar, cinnamon, cloves, ginger, & salt in a small bowl.
3. Melt the butter & vanilla in a big skillet over medium heat. Stir in ⅓ of the sugar combination till blended. Add the pecans & toss well to coat them totally. With a rubber spatula scrape the nuts onto a baking sheet & spread them out in order that they don't touch one another. Bake quarter-hour, or till completely toasted but not dark.
4. Drop the nuts into a big bowl. Sprinkle on the remaining sugar combination & toss. Let cool completely before storing in a tightly covered container.

PARMESAN GARLIC BREAD

MAKES one loaf, serves four–6
one **loaf French bread (about sixteen inches long)**

two **tablespoons olive oil**

four garlic cloves, put through a press

two **tablespoons butter, softened**

two **tablespoons grated Parmesan cheese**

Salt to taste

1. Cut the bread in half horizontally.
2. Pour the oil right into a small saucepan or skillet & heat over medium heat. Add the garlic & cook only about 30 seconds, or till hot all through & by no means coloured. Instantly pour the garlic oil right into a small bowl. Let cool to room temperature.

3. Stir the soft butter & cheese into the oil. Spread the flavored butter throughout the cut sides of the bread. Sprinkle with salt. Preheat the broiler. Broil the bread till golden brown on top. Serve instantly.

BERRY SMOOTHIE

MAKES two GLASSES
½ (12-ounce) package frozen combined berries (about *1⅔* cups) (see Tip)

one **½ cups lemonade or orange juice**

two **tablespoons sugar**

four ice cubes

1. Mix the berries, lemonade or orange juice, & sugar in the container of a blender & let sit five minutes to partially soften the berries.

2.Add the ice cubes & mix till completely smooth. You'll most likely must turn off the blender every now & then to stir the contents which have adhered to the sides. Taste the drink to see if it wants additional sugar. In that case, mix once more. Serve in glasses with straws.

CANTALOUPE MILK SHAKE

MAKES one TALL MILK SHAKE
½ very ripe medium-large cantaloupe

¼ cup milk

two **teaspoons sugar (provided that fruit isn't sweet)**

1. Use a spoon to scoop the flesh out of the cantaloupe; it is best to get about two cups. Place in a bowl & chill till very cold.
2. Mix the cantaloupe & milk in a blender & mix till smooth. Taste the drink. You may need so as to add the sugar & mix once more for a few seconds. Let the milk shake rest a

couple of minutes before pouring it in a tall glass so the foam can deflate. Serve with a straw.

MANGO LASSI

MAKES two GLASSES LASSI
one **cup whole-milk yogurt**

one **cup mango nectar or juice (such because the Goya model)**

two **tablespoons sugar**

Ice cubes

Mix the yogurt, mango nectar, & sugar in the container of a blender & mix one minute, or till the sugar is dissolved. Fill two glasses with ice cubes & pour in the lassi. Serve instantly.

MASALA CHAI

MAKES four CUPS TEA
2⅔ cups water

1½ cups milk, preferably low-fat

2–three teaspoons loose black tea (depending on power of tea), or three tea bags

one **teaspoon garam masala, *or* one cinnamon stick, four cloves, & four cardamom pods, *or* ¼ teaspoon *each* ground cinnamon, cloves, & cardamom (see Tip)**

two **tablespoons sugar**

Mix the water & milk in a medium-size saucepan & bring to a boil over medium heat. As quickly because the combination begins to froth up, add the tea, spices, & sugar. Cover the pot, & take away the pan from the heat. Let steep three minutes. Strain the tea through a fine strainer & serve instantly.

ICED GINGER TEA

MAKES two TALL GLASSES TEA
2¼ cups water

three tablespoons finely chopped fresh ginger, skin left on

three tablespoons sugar

one **cup cold water**

Mix the water & ginger in a small saucepan & bring to a boil. Reduce the heat & simmer 10 minutes. Strain right into a glass jar or pitcher & stir in the sugar till dissolved. Mix in the cup of cold water. Chill till ice cold. Serve in tall glasses over ice.

CLASSIC VEGETABLE MELT

MAKES four SANDWICHES
one **tablespoon olive oil**

three cups (eight ounces) thinly sliced mushrooms

one **onion, thinly sliced**

one **red bell pepper, cut into thin strips**

one **(10-ounce) bag triple-washed spinach, stems discarded**

two **teaspoons tamari soy sauce**

Salt to taste

four slices home made-style bread, such as sourdough or multigrain

three tablespoons mayonnaise

one **cup grated Monterey Jack cheese with jalapeño peppers**

185

1. Heat the oil in a big skillet over medium heat. Add the mushrooms, onion, & red pepper, & sauté till tender, about 10 minutes.
2. Pile on the spinach & cover the pan. Cook just till the spinach wilts, about three minutes. Sprinkle on the tamari & salt, & take away from the heat.

   three. Preheat the broiler.

4. Toast the bread in a toaster. Spread the mayonnaise on one side of every piece, then lay them on a baking sheet & top with the vegetable combination. Sprinkle on the cheese.
5. Broil the sandwiches just till the cheese is melted. Serve instantly. This can be a sandwich to eat with a knife & fork

PORTOBELLO MUSHROOM SANDWICHES

MAKES two SANDWICHES
½ tablespoon unsalted butter
two **large (5-inch diameter) Portobello mushrooms, stems discarded, caps cleaned, & thinly sliced**
Salt to taste
3½ tablespoons mayonnaise
one **very small garlic clove, put through a press or minced**
one **tablespoon lemon juice**
Generous seasoning freshly ground pepper
four slices Tuscan-style bread or two sandwich rolls
one **small-to medium-size ripe tomato, thinly slice**d
10 leaves arugula, each torn in half

1. Melt the butter in a medium-size skillet over medium heat. Add the mushrooms & sauté till brown throughout & juicy, about 10 minutes. Season with salt & let cool.
2. Mix the mayonnaise, garlic, lemon juice, & pepper in a small bowl.
3. To make the sandwiches, spread a few of the mayonnaise combination on each bread slice. Place the mushrooms, tomato slices, & arugula on two of the slices & top with the remaining bread. Serve directly.

two **SANDWICHES**
¼ cup mayonnaise
two **(6-inch) chunks French bread, each sliced horizontally**
one **ripe Haas (dark, pebbly-skinned) avocado, peeled & thinly sliced**
one **ripe tomato, thinly sliced**
eight thin slices cucumber
two **paper-thin slices red onion**
Salt to taste
Liberal seasoning freshly ground pepper

Spread the mayonnaise on the cut sides of the French bread. Layer the avocado, tomato, cucumber, & red onion on the bottom halves of the bread, & season with salt & pepper. Near make a sandwich, then cut in half. Serve without delay.

TIP: This sandwich can also be fabulous served open-confronted. Finish the layering with the avocado on top after which season with salt & pepper.

EGGPLANT & TOMATO SANDWICHES WITH PESTO MAYONNAISE

For a few years eggplant in sandwiches was restricted to its use in hot eggplant Parmesan grinders (also called submarines & heroes). Having found that breaded eggplant slices are scrumptious cold, with little effort we are able to now create wonderful sandwiches which have a suitable Provençal theme. This one's a winner.

MAKES four SANDWICHES
one **small-to medium-size eggplant, peeled & sliced ½ inch thick**
⅓ cup olive oil
⅓ cup dry bread crumbs
Salt to taste
Freshly ground pepper to taste
⅓ cup mayonnaise
⅓ cup Traditional Pesto
four (6-inch) pieces French bread, each halved horizontally
one **ripe tomato, thinly sliced**

1. Preheat the broiler.
2. Place the eggplant slices in entrance of you, the oil in a small bowl, & the bread crumbs on a small plate. Utilizing a pastry brush, coat each side of the eggplant slices with some oil, then press the slices into the bread crumbs to coat on each side. Place the slices on a baking sheet.
3. Broil the eggplant on each side till golden brown & really tender. Season with salt & pepper, & let cool to room temperature.
4. Mix the mayonnaise & pesto in a small bowl & stir till well blended. Spread a few of this combination on each slice of French bread. Stack eggplant & tomato slices on the

bottom pieces of the French bread & cover with the top sections. Cut each sandwich in half & serve inside two hours.

MEDITERRANEAN STUFFED SANDWICH

MAKES four SANDWICHES
one **extensive loaf Italian or French bread (about 24 inches long)**
eight tablespoons olive oil (roughly)
two **large garlic cloves, put through a press or minced**
two **tablespoons minced fresh basil**
one **teaspoon dried oregano**
Freshly ground pepper to taste
eight ounces very thinly sliced cheese, preferably provolone or a smoked cheese
two **large ripe tomatoes, sliced**
one **(7-ounce) jar roasted red peppers, drained thoroughly & patted dry**
one **green bell pepper, thinly sliced into rings**
four thin slices red onion
20 black olives (your favourite sort), pitted

1. Slice the bread lengthwise & take away among the interior bread to make two considerably hollow shells. Drizzle the oil over the cavity of each pieces of bread & spread it round with a knife. Sprinkle on the garlic, basil, oregano, & pepper.

2.Layer all of the remaining ingredients on one half of the bread. Top with the opposite piece of bread. Cut it into four sandwiches. Tightly wrap each sandwich in plastic wrap & let marinate at the very least one hour or up to four hours. If the sandwiches are going to sit greater than one hour, refrigerate them & bring to room temperature before serving.

GRILLED JALAPEÑO CHEESE SANDWICH

MAKES two SANDWICHES
four slices good-quality white bread, such as Tuscan-style, sourdough, or Vienna

12 thin slices (about five ounces) Monterey Jack cheese with jalapeño peppers

½ (7-ounce) jar roasted red peppers, patted very dry & thinly sliced
four thin slices ripe tomato
1½ tablespoons very soft unsalted butter

1. Heat a big skillet over medium-low heat.
2. Place two slices of bread in entrance of you. Lay three cheese slices on each slice of bread. Top with the red pepper strips, tomato slices, & remaining six slices of cheese. Cover with the opposite two slices of bread to make two sandwiches. Utilizing half the butter, spread a thin layer on the top two pieces of bread.
3. Place each sandwich buttered side down in the hot skillet. Butter the tops of the sandwich with the remaining butter. Cook till golden brown, at the very least five minutes, then flip & cook the opposite side. Make sure the sandwich cooks slowly so the cheese melts correctly. Cut in half & serve.

ROASTED SWEET POTATO QUESADILLAS

SERVES four
two **medium (1 pound total) sweet potatoes (preferably dark orange), peeled, quartered lengthwise, & thinly sliced**
one **tablespoon olive oil**
Salt to taste
eight (6-inch) flour tortillas
one **cup canned black beans, rinsed in a strainer**
two **large scallions, very thinly sliced**
four tablespoons finely chopped cilantro
two **cups grated Monterey Jack cheese with jalapeño peppers**
Butter for greasing the pan

1. Preheat the oven to 425 degrees.
2. Mix the sweet potatoes & oil in a big bowl & toss to coat evenly. Spread the sweet potatoes out on a baking sheet in one layer. Bake about quarter-hour, or till tender. Season lightly with salt, then let cool. Turn off the oven.

three. Place four of the tortillas on a piece surface in entrance of you. Sprinkle ¼ of the sweet potatoes, beans, scallions, cilantro, & cheese on each tortilla. Cover with the remaining tortillas & press down gently to assist them adhere.

4. In case your tortillas are flaky & tender, you'll in all probability not need so as to add butter to the skillet. In any other case, melt a little butter in a big skillet over medium heat. Place one quesadilla in the skillet & cook till golden beneath, pressing down with a spatula now & again to assist the quesadilla stick together. Spread some butter very lightly on top of the quesadilla, then carefully flip & cook the opposite side till golden. Remove & cut into wedges. Repeat with the remaining quesadillas. Wait a couple of minutes before serving as a result of the quesadillas lure a whole lot of heat & will burn your mouth.

MUSHROOM & SWISS CHEESE QUESADILLAS

SERVES 2
one **tablespoon olive oil**
one **large onion, halved & thinly sliced**
eight ounces (three cups) thinly sliced mushrooms
Salt to taste
Freshly ground black pepper to taste
four (eight-inch) flour tortillas
1¼ cups grated Swiss cheese
Butter for greasing the pan

1. Heat the oil in a big skillet over medium heat. Add the onion & sauté till golden, about 10 minutes. Mix in the mushrooms & sauté till they're brown & juicy & the onion has browned. Season with salt & pepper. Remove from the heat & let cool.
2. Place two tortillas on a piece surface. Divide the mushroom combination between them & spread it round evenly. Sprinkle each with half the Swiss cheese. Top with the remaining tortillas.
3. Melt some butter in a medium-large skillet over medium heat. Place one quesadilla in the pan & cook till golden beneath. Press the quesadilla down with a spatula to assist the melted cheese adhere. Lightly butter the top of the quesadilla, then carefully flip it over to cook on this side. When golden brown, slide onto a plate & cut into wedges. Repeat with the remaining quesadilla.

CUCUMBER & WATERCRESS SANDWICHES WITH WASABI MAYONNAISE

MAKES four SANDWICHES
two **teaspoons wasabi powder**
two **teaspoons water**
½ cup mayonnaise
eight slices chewy Tuscan-style sourdough or other good-quality bread
one **small cucumber, peeled & thinly sliced**
one **bunch watercress, stems discarded**

1. Mix the wasabi & water in a small bowl & stir to make a paste. Let sit 10 minutes for the flavour to develop. Stir in the mayonnaise.
2. Spread the wasabi mayonnaise on all of the bread slices. Lay the cucumber slices on half of the bread slices. (You might need some cucumber left over.) Place some watercress

on top of the cucumber, then cover with the remaining bread to make sandwiches. Slice the sandwiches & serve inside one hour.

VEGETABLE SUBS

MAKES two SANDWICHES
two **submarine (grinder) rolls, sliced horizontally almost all through**
two **tablespoons mayonnaise (see Tips)**
Freshly ground black pepper to taste
four lettuce leaves
four thin slices tomato
two **thin slices red onion**
four thin rings green or red bell pepper
eight thin slices cucumber
six **thin slices smoked Gouda (see Tips)**

1. Spread the bread halves with the mayonnaise, then season generously with pepper.
2. Divide the ingredients in half. Layer them in each sandwich & shut tightly, pressing down on the bread gently to assist it adhere. Slice each sandwich in half.

HOT EGG & PEPPER GRINDERS

MAKES two SANDWICHES
four teaspoons olive oil
one **green bell pepper, cut into thin strips**
two **grinder, hero, or submarine rolls, sliced open**
one **tablespoon mayonnaise**
two **large eggs, beaten**
Salt to taste
½ cup grated smoked Gouda cheese

1. Preheat the oven to 350 degrees.
2. Heat two teaspoons oil in a big nonstick skillet over medium heat. Add the green pepper & cover the pan. Cook till very soft & tender, about 10 minutes. Place on a plate & let cool a little.
3. Heat the rolls in the oven for a couple of minutes till hot. Remove & let cool a bit.
4. Spread a thin layer of mayonnaise on each half.
5. Heat the remaining two teaspoons oil in the skillet over medium-high heat. Mix the pepper into the egg. Pour the combination into the skillet. Let cook undisturbed for a

couple of minutes, then flip the omelet over. Cook just till set. Season with salt. Cut the omelet in half & place every bit in a grinder roll. Sprinkle on the cheese & shut the sandwich. Cut in half & serve.

FALAFEL

MAKES four SANDWICHES
one **(10-ounce) box falafel mix**
The Sauce:
½ cup tahini (sesame butter)
½–¾ cup water
¼ cup lemon juice
one **large garlic clove, put through a press or minced**
Salt to taste
Oil for frying
four pita breads, each cut in half to make pockets
two **ripe tomatoes, finely diced**
eight lettuce leaves, shredded

1. Prepare the falafel in accordance to the package instructions & let sit quarter-hour to soak up the liquid. Form the combination into 24 balls, then flatten into patties.
2. To make the sauce: place the tahini in a medium-size bowl. With a fork slowly beat in the ½ cup water, lemon juice, garlic, & salt. Check the consistency; it needs to be pourable like honey. Beat in additional water if needed.
3. Pour about ¼ inch of oil in a big skillet & heat over medium heat till hot but not smoking. Fry the patties on each side till golden brown. Drain on paper towels.
4. To make the sandwiches heat the pita halves in the oven or a toaster for only a few minutes, or till warm & soft.
5. Fill each pita half with three patties, some tomato, & lettuce. Drizzle the sauce over the filling. Serve instantly.

VEGETABLE WRAPS

MAKES three SANDWICHES
one **(eight-ounce) package Neufchâtel (light cream cheese), at room temperature**
two **scallions, very thinly sliced**

one **small garlic clove, pressed or minced**
½ **teaspoon minced fresh dill, or one teaspoon dried**
three single rounds large (10-inch) pita bread
½ **cucumber, quartered & really thinly sliced**
½ **red bell pepper, cut into paper-thin strips**
one **small tomato, thinly sliced**
½ **cup very thinly sliced red onion**
three romaine lettuce leaves, torn into small pieces
Salt to taste
Freshly ground pepper to taste

1. In a medium-size bowl mix the cream cheese, scallions, garlic, & dill, & beat along with a fork till nice & creamy.
2. Divide the combination into three parts & spread a portion on the inside (tough) side of every pita disk leaving a 1-inch border throughout. Sprinkle ⅓ of the cucumbers, peppers, tomatoes, onion, & lettuce throughout each pita. Season with salt & pepper. Beginning on the finish in entrance of you, tightly roll each pita right into a log. Cut in half on the diagonal before serving.

VEGETABLE BURGER ROLL-UPS

MAKES two ROLL-UPS
two **(eight-inch) flour tortillas**
one **tablespoon canola oil**
two **vegetable-style burgers (your favourite type; mine is frozen Gardenburgers)**
three tablespoons mayonnaise
one **tomato, thinly sliced**
two **thin slices red onion, separated into rings**

1. Preheat the oven to 350 degrees.
2. Wrap the tortillas in foil. Heat in the oven till hot all through, about five minutes.
3. Warm the oil in a medium skillet. Cook the burger in accordance to package instructions.
4. Place the tortillas on large plates. Spread each with half the mayonnaise. Crumble up the burger & sprinkle it on the bottom half of the tortilla. Top with the tomato & onion. Roll up the sandwich tightly, then cut it in half on the diagonal. Serve instantly.

ROASTED RED PEPPER & CREAM CHEESE SPREAD

ENOUGH FOR four SLICED BAGELS
(eight HALVES)
¼ **cup roasted red peppers (half of a 7-ounce jar)**
one **(eight-ounce) package Neufchâtel (light**
cream cheese), at room temperature
two **tablespoons minced red onion**
½ **teaspoon sweet paprika**
one **teaspoon minced fresh dill, or ½ teaspoon dried**
Dash cayenne pepper
Dash salt

1. Place the peppers in a cotton kitchen towel & collect the towel right into a ball. Squeeze out all of the moisture. Drop the peppers onto a cutting board & mince; the pepper pieces should be very tiny.
2. Place the peppers in a bowl with all of the remaining ingredients & beat with a fork till whipped & really smooth. Cover the bowl with plastic wrap & chill at the least one hour so the flavors can meld. Serve with bagels.

ORZO PILAF

SERVES four AS A SIDE DISH
three cups vegetable broth/stock, store-purchased or selfmade

eight ounces (1 cup) orzo (rice-formed pasta)

½ **tablespoon unsalted butter**

three tablespoons grated Parmesan cheese

two **tablespoons minced fresh parsley or one tablespoon minced fresh basil or dill**

¼ **teaspoon salt**

Freshly ground black pepper to taste

1. Bring the broth/stock to a boil in a medium-size, heavy-bottomed saucepan. Stir in the orzo & lower the heat. Cook the orzo at a energetic simmer for 20 minutes, stirring often. Throughout the last five minutes of cooking you'll need to lower the heat once more & stir more frequently to prevent the orzo from sticking. When done, the orzo may have absorbed just about all the broth/stock & must be al dente, that's, slightly firm in the middle, not mushy.
2. Stir in the remaining ingredients. If the orzo has become dry rather than creamy, mix in a few tablespoons of broth/stock. Serve instantly.

EGG NOODLES WITH GARLIC & HERBS

SERVES four
eight ounces huge egg noodles

1½ tablespoons unsalted butter

one **tablespoon olive oil**

one **large garlic clove, put through a press or minced**

Salt to taste

¼ cup minced fresh parsley or two tablespoons minced chives or fresh basil

1. Bring a stockpot of water to a boil. Drop in the noodles & cook, stirring frequently, till al dente, about 5–7 minutes.
2. Melt the butter with the oil in a small skillet or saucepan. Add the garlic & cook about one minute, or till hot all through but in no way coloured. Instantly remove the pan from the heat.
3. Drain the noodles in a colander & return to the pot. Pour on the garlic butter & toss well. Add the salt & parsley, & toss once more. Serve instantly.

COUSCOUS PILAF WITH TOASTED PINE NUTS

SERVES four
one **tablespoon unsalted butter**

one **medium onion, minced**

¼ **cup pine nuts**

one ½ **cups vegetable broth/stock, either store-purchased or home made**

¼ **teaspoon salt**

one **cup couscous**

1. Melt the butter in a medium-size saucepan over medium heat. Add the onion & sauté till soft, about five minutes. Add the pine nuts and, stirring often, toast them till golden, about five minutes.
2. Pour in the vegetable broth/stock & salt, & bring to a boil. Stir in the couscous, cover the pot, & take away from the heat. Let the couscous sit not less than five minutes & up to fifteen minutes. Fluff with a fork before serving.

ISRAELI COUSCOUS WITH BUTTER & CHEESE

SERVES four
one **teaspoon olive or canola oil**

one **cup Israeli couscous (generally called**

"pearl pasta")

two **tablespoons unsalted butter**

¼ **teaspoon salt**

Freshly ground pepper to taste

⅓ cup grated Parmesan cheese

1. Fill a medium-size saucepan ⅔ full with water & bring to a boil. Add the oil & couscous, & return to a boil. Lower the heat slightly & cook the couscous till al dente, about eight minutes. Drain completely in a strainer or colander
2. Instantly return the couscous to the pot. Stir in the butter, salt, pepper, & cheese. Serve directly.

ISRAELI COUSCOUS WITH TOMATO & SCALLIONS

SERVES four
one **teaspoon olive or canola oil**

one **cup Israeli couscous (typically called**

"pearl pasta")

two **tablespoons unsalted butter**

one **plum tomato, very finely diced**

two **scallions, very thinly sliced**

¼ teaspoon salt

Freshly ground black pepper to taste

¼ cup grated Parmesan cheese

1. Fill a medium-size saucepan ⅔ full with water & bring to a boil. Add the oil & couscous, & return to a boil. Lower the heat slightly & cook the couscous till al dente, about eight minutes. Drain in a strainer or colander.
2. Instantly melt the butter in the saucepan. Stir in the tomato & scallion, & cook two minutes. Mix in the couscous, salt, pepper, & cheese. Toss well & serve.

PESTO MASHED POTATOES

SERVES four–6
five **large (three pounds) boiling potatoes (preferably Yukon Gold), peeled & cut into even-size pieces**

½ cup milk

one **tablespoon unsalted butter**

½ cup Traditional Pesto

1. Bring a stockpot of water to a boil & add the potatoes. Cook, partially covered, till tender. The time depends upon the size of the potato pieces. Drain the potatoes in a colander.
2. Instantly pour the milk in the stockpot & heat it. Return the potatoes to the pot. Use an electrical mixer (my favourite technique) or a potato masher to mash the potatoes till smooth. Heat gently over low heat till piping hot.
3. Stir in the butter till it melts. Spoon on the pesto & stir it in gently just till streaks are fashioned; you don't need it completely blended. Serve instantly.

WASABI MASHED POTATOES

**SERVES four VERY GENEROUSLY
(AS YOU'LL WANT THEM SERVED)**
five **large (three pounds) boiling potatoes (preferably Yukon Gold), peeled & quartered**

one **tablespoon wasabi powder**

one **tablespoon water**

⅔ cup milk (roughly)

three tablespoons unsalted butter

½ teaspoon salt

1. Bring a stockpot of water to a boil & add the potatoes. Cook, partially covered, till tender, about 20 minutes. The time will rely on the size of the potato pieces.
2. Mix the wasabi & water in a small bowl & let sit no less than quarter-hour to develop its flavor.
3. Drain the potatoes in a colander. A. Heat the milk in the pot by which the potatoes cooked. Add the potatoes & switch the heat to low. Use an electrical hand mixer to whip the potatoes till smooth. Add a little more milk if the potatoes are too thick. Stir in the butter & salt. Keep warm till prepared to serve. Just before serving, stir in the wasabi.

SPICY OVEN FRIES

SERVES four
four baking (Idaho or russet) potatoes

three tablespoons olive oil

two **teaspoons chili powder**

Salt to taste

1. Preheat the oven to 425 degrees.
2. Peel the potatoes & slice them in half lengthwise. Cut each part into ¼-inch-thick slices. Place on a baking sheet & drizzle with oil. Use your hands to toss the potatoes so that they become well coated.
3. Bake 20–25 minutes, tossing after quarter-hour. When done, the potatoes can be golden & really tender. Sprinkle the chili powder throughout the fries & toss well with a spatula to coat them evenly. Season generously with salt & serve.

MIXED POTATO HOME FRIES

SERVES four–6
two **large sweet potatoes (preferably dark orange), peeled, quartered lengthwise, & sliced ¼ inch thick**

two **large baking (Idaho or russet) potatoes, peeled, quartered lengthwise, & sliced ¼ inch thick**

one **large onion, cut into 1-inch dice**

three tablespoons olive oil

Salt to taste

1. Preheat the oven to 425 degrees.
2. Mix the potatoes, onion, & oil in a big bowl & toss to coat evenly with the oil. Spread on a big baking sheet or in a roasting pan in one layer.
3. Bake 25–half-hour, tossing with a spatula after quarter-hour. When done, the potatoes might be tender & brown. Season with salt before serving.

TIPS: As quickly as you chop the potatoes, toss them in oil to prevent darkening.

Make certain to cook these in one layer to allow them to brown evenly. In case your baking pan is small, use two to prevent overcrowding.

Kale

one of many hardiest: of greens, kale really advantages from being harvested after a frost, which improves its flavor. You can continue to grow kale in the Northeast till after Christmas & enjoy strolling through your snow-covered backyard through the holidays to reap it. Surprisingly, kale also grows well in the heat of the American South. The adaptability of this member of the cabbage household most likely explains its reputation in two contrasting climates in Europe—the cool nations of Scandinavia, Germany, Holland, & Scotland, & warm Portugal.

SAUTÉED KALE

SERVES four
1½ pounds kale (together with four-inch stems)

three tablespoons olive oil

three garlic cloves, minced

⅓ cup water

one ½ tablespoons balsamic vinegar

Salt to taste

1. Wash the kale by running individual leaves under cold water. Tear the leaves off the stems & discard the stems. Chop the kale into bite-size pieces. It is best to get about sixteen cups of leaves.
2. Heat the oil in a big skillet over medium heat. Add the garlic & sauté about one minute, or simply till it begins to sizzle. Use tongs to combine in the kale, coating it with the garlic & oil as much as possible. Add the water & cover the pan.
3. Steam the kale till it wilts & will get tender, about 5–7 minutes. Remove the cover & toss it round often. When it's tender & just about all the water has evaporated, drizzle with the vinegar & season with salt. Cook a few seconds after which serve.

ZUCCHINI & RED PEPPER GRATIN

SERVES 6
three medium zucchini, halved lengthwise & sliced ¼ inch thick on the diagonal

two **red bell peppers, cored, halved, & really thinly sliced**

two **medium onions, halved vertically, very thinly sliced, & sections separated**

¼ cup olive oil

three tablespoons tomato sauce, store-purchased or Easy Marinara Sauce

Salt to taste

Freshly ground black pepper to taste

The Topping:
two **slices bread, whole wheat or white**

one **tablespoon olive oil**

1. Preheat the oven to four hundred degrees.
2. In a big bowl mix the zucchini, red peppers, onions, oil, & tomato sauce. Sprinkle with salt & pepper. Place the combination in a shallow 2½ quart casserole (such as a 12 X seven X two Pyrex dish) & flatten the top.
3. Bake forty five minutes, tossing the combination after the first half-hour. Flatten once more.
4. In the meantime, place the bread in a food processor & process to make crumbs. Drizzle on the oil & rub it into the crumbs with your fingers. Sprinkle the crumbs throughout the greens & bake quarter-hour more, or till golden brown on top. Let the gratin sit quarter-hour before serving so the juices can settle & thicken.

BANANA MINT RAITA

SERVES 6
one **cup plain yogurt, preferably low-fat (not fat-free)**

one **small-to medium-size ripe banana, finely diced**

one **tablespoon finely chopped fresh mint, or one teaspoon dried**

¼ teaspoon sugar

Dash salt

Mint sprig for garnish

Mix all of the ingredients besides the mint sprig in a bowl. Cover & chill a minimum of half-hour but no more than two hours before serving. Garnish with a mint sprig, if out there.

CUCUMBER & TOMATO RAITA

SERVES four–6
½ cucumber, peeled

½ cup very finely diced tomato

one **cup plain yogurt**

¼ teaspoon salt

Pinch ground cumin

Cut the cucumber piece in half lengthwise. With a small spoon scoop out all of the seeds & discard them. Grate the cucumber utilizing a hand grater & place in a serving bowl. Stir in the remaining ingredients. Cover & chill not less than half-hour or up to two hours before serving.

FRESH MANGO CHUTNEY

SERVES four
one **ripe mango**

one **tablespoon minced cilantro**

A few dashes cayenne pepper

A few dashes salt

1. To chop the mango, learn Mango Mania, reverse.
2. Place all of the ingredients in the container of a food processor & pulse a few times just till the combination is coarsely chopped. Place in a bowl, cover, & chill no less than half-hour but no quite a lot of hours before serving.

SHIITAKE MUSHROOM & GOAT CHEESE QUICHE

SERVES 6
Flaky Pie Crust, savory model

½ tablespoon unsalted butter

six ounces shiitake mushrooms, stems discarded & caps thinly sliced (three cups sliced)

four large eggs

one cup light cream, or ½ cup heavy cream & ½ cup milk

½ teaspoon salt

Generous seasoning freshly ground black pepper

⅛ teaspoon grated nutmeg

½ cup crumbled goat cheese (such as Montrachet)

½ cup grated Swiss cheese

1. Prepare the pie crust in accordance to instructions. Line a 9-inch tart pan with a detachable rim or a glass pie plate with the pastry & prick it throughout with a fork. Chill not less than half-hour.
2. Preheat the oven to 375 degrees.
3. Line the pastry with aluminum foil & fill it with pie weights, dried beans, or raw rice to maintain it in place. Bake quarter-hour. Remove the foil & weights & return the crust to the oven. Bake five minutes more. Let cool. Keep the oven on.
4. Melt the butter in a medium-size skillet over medium heat. Add the mushrooms & sauté till brown & juicy. Let cool.
5. To make the filling beat the eggs in a big bowl. Beat in the cream, salt, pepper, nutmeg, & mushrooms. Carefully stir in the goat cheese so the pieces keep intact quite than mix with the custard.
6. Place the tart pan on a baking sheet to move it to the oven easily. Sprinkle the Swiss cheese on the bottom of the crust. Carefully ladle in the filling. Bake half-hour, or till golden on top. Cool on a wire rack. Serve warm, not hot.

SPINACH, RED PEPPER, & FETA CHEESE QUICHE

SERVES 6

Flaky Pie Crust, savory model

two **teaspoons olive oil**

one **red bell pepper, cut into very thin 2-inch-long strips**

one **(10-ounce) package triple-washed spinach, stems discarded & leaves** torn, or one 10-ounce box frozen chopped spinach, defrosted & squeezed dry

three large eggs

¼ cup grated Parmesan cheese

½ cup heavy cream

½ cup milk

¼ teaspoon salt

Generous seasoning freshly ground black pepper

⅔ cup (three ounces) crumbled feta cheese

1. Prepare the pie crust in accordance to instructions. Line a 9-inch tart pan with a detachable rim or a glass pie plate with the pastry & prick it throughout with a fork. Chill at the least half-hour.
2. Preheat the oven to 375 degrees.

    three. Line the pastry with aluminum foil & fill it with pie weights, dried beans, or raw rice to maintain it in place. Bake quarter-hour. Remove the foil & weights & return the crust to the oven. Bake five minutes more. Let cool. Keep the oven on.

4. To make the filling: heat the oil in a big skillet over medium heat. Add the red pepper & sauté till tender, about seven minutes. In case you are utilizing fresh spinach, pile it on & tightly cover the pan. Cook just till the spinach wilts, about three minutes. (If there may be any liquid in the pan at this level, boil it away on high heat.) In case you are utilizing cooked spinach, add it & cook uncovered, till all liquid has evaporated, about two minutes. Remove the pan from the heat.

5. Beat the eggs in a big bowl. Beat in the Parmesan cheese, cream, milk, salt, & pepper. Stir in the cooled spinach combination & the feta cheese. Place the tart pan on a baking sheet to hold it to the oven. Pour the filling into the crust.
6. Bake 30–35 minutes, or till a knife inserted in the middle of the filling comes out clean. Remove the outer rim of the tart pan. Cool the quiche on a wire rack for quarter-hour before serving.

CARAMELIZED ONION TART

SERVES 6
one **sheet (half of a 17-ounce package) frozen puff pastry**

one **tablespoon olive oil**

two **pounds onions, thinly sliced (9 cups sliced)**

two **large eggs**

½ **cup heavy cream**

Dash cayenne pepper

½ **teaspoon salt**

½ **cup grated Swiss cheese**

1. Remove the puff pastry from the package & let thaw at room temperature for about half-hour, or till no longer frozen but still cool.
2. To make the filling: heat the oil in a big stockpot over medium heat. Add the onions & partially cover the pot. Cook stirring often, for forty minutes, or till the onions are a deep caramel color & really soft. Turn down the heat a little once the onions start to melt to allow them to cook slowly, & scrape the bottom of the pot as necessary. When done, the onions might be evenly brown & almost jamlike. Let cool. (The onions may be prepared & refrigerated up to forty eight hours prematurely. Bring to room temperature before inserting in the filling.)
3. Lightly butter a dark-coloured 9-inch tart pan with a detachable rim or a glass pie plate. On a lightly floured surface roll the puff pastry into an eleven-inch sq.. Healthy it into the tart pan or pie plate. Use scissors to trim off the overhanging pieces of pastry. Refrigerate the crust quarter-hour or cover & refrigerate up to eight hours.

4. Preheat the oven to 425 degrees.
5. Beat the eggs in a big bowl. Beat in the cream, cayenne, & salt. Stir in the cheese & onions.
6. Spoon the combination into the tart pan or pie plate. Bake 30–35 minutes, or till the custard is about & the crust is deeply golden. In case your pie plate is glass, you can peek on the bottom of the crust to make sure that it's cooked in the middle. When the tart is finished, remove the outer ring in case you used a tart pan with a detachable rim. Cool the tart on a wire rack for 15–20 minutes before serving as a result of it needs to be served warm, not hot.

SPINACH & PESTO TART

SERVES four–6
one **sheet frozen puff pastry (half of a 17-ounce package)**

two **(10-ounce) bags triple-washed fresh spinach, stems discarded**

two **medium-size boiling potatoes, peeled & sliced ¼ inch thick**

two **large eggs**

two **scallions, very thinly sliced one cup grated Gruyère or other Swiss cheese**

¼ teaspoon salt

Generous seasoning freshly ground black pepper

Butter for greasing

½ cup Basic Pesto

1. Let the puff pastry thaw at room temperature for about half-hour, or till defrosted but still slightly cold.
2. Place the spinach in a big stockpot with a few tablespoons of water & cook over medium heat just till wilted, about four minutes. Drain the spinach in a colander. Let cool till room temperature. Squeeze all of the moisture from the spinach with your hands.
3. Fill a medium-size saucepan with water & bring to a boil. Drop in the potatoes & cook till tender, about eight minutes. Drain completely.

4. Beat the eggs in a medium-size bowl. Remove about two tablespoons of egg & place in a small bowl to make use of later as an egg wash. Mix the spinach, scallions, cheese, salt, & pepper into the beaten eggs.
5. Preheat the oven to 375 degrees. Butter a big baking sheet.
6. Lightly flour a piece surface. Use a rolling pin to roll the sheet of puff pastry till it's about 12 x 14 inches. Place on the baking sheet; a little will overhang. Spread the pesto on the puff pastry, leaving a 1½-inch border. Cover the pesto with the sliced potatoes. Spoon the spinach combination throughout the potatoes, once more leaving a border. Fold the border over the filling. Utilizing a pastry brush coat the border with the reserved egg. (You can chill the tart up to four hours before baking.)
7. Bake 25 minutes, or till the pastry is a wealthy golden brown. Let sit 10 minutes before cutting into squares & serving.

EASY ZUCCHINI, TOMATO, & CHEESE TART

SERVES four–6 AS A MAIN COURSE
one **sheet (half of a 17-ounce package) frozen puff pastry**

two **tablespoons olive oil**

one **onion, finely diced**

two **garlic cloves, minced**

two **medium zucchini, quartered lengthwise & thinly sliced**

one **(14-ounce) can prepared-cut diced tomatoes, well drained**

three **large eggs**

one **cup grated smoked Gouda cheese**

½ **teaspoon salt**

Generous seasoning freshly ground black pepper

1. Remove the puff pastry from the package & let thaw at room temperature for about half-hour, or till no longer frozen but still cool.

2. In the meantime, heat the oil in a big skillet over medium heat. Add the onion & garlic, & cook five minutes, or till the onion is slightly tender. Stir in the zucchini & sauté just till it begins to melt, about five minutes. Mix in the drained tomatoes & lift the heat to medium-high. Cook stirring often, till the zucchini is tender but not mushy & the juices have evaporated. Let cool.
3. Lightly butter a dark-coloured 9-inch tart pan with a detachable rim or a glass pie plate.
4. On a lightly floured surface roll the puff pastry into an eleven-inch sq.. Healthy it into the tart pan or pie plate. Trim off the overhanging pieces of pastry with scissors. Refrigerate the crust, uncovered, for quarter-hour, or up to eight hours, covered.
5. Preheat the oven to 425 degrees.
6. Beat the eggs in a big bowl. Stir in the cheese, salt, pepper, & cooled greens.
7. Spoon the combination into the tart pan. Bake 25–half-hour, or till the pastry is brown & a knife inserted in the middle of the tart comes out clean. Remove the outer rim of the tart pan. Let the tart cool on a wire rack for 20 minutes before slicing. It's greatest to serve this tart very warm moderately than piping hot.

LEEK TART

SERVES four–6 AS A MAIN COURSE
one **sheet (half of a 17-ounce package) frozen puff pastry**

three large leeks (about two pounds)

1½ tablespoons unsalted butter, plus extra for greasing

½ cup heavy cream

½ teaspoon salt

Freshly ground black pepper to taste

three large eggs

one **large egg yolk**

½ cup whole milk

1. Remove the puff pastry from the package & let thaw at room temperature for about half-hour, or till no longer frozen but still cool.

2. In the meantime, cut the roots off the leeks & all but two inches of their green tops. Slice the leeks in half vertically & rinse thoroughly under cold runing water to do away with the sand. Use your fingers to flip through the leaves to disclose any hidden grime. Drain well. Slice the leeks thinly crosswise, utilizing all of the white part & a little of the sunshine green interior leaves. You need five cups sliced leeks.
3. Melt the butter in a big skillet over medium heat. Add the leeks & sauté five minutes, or till they start to melt. Pour in the cream & cook five minutes more. Stir in the salt & pepper, & take away the pan from the heat. Let cool.
4. Lightly butter a dark-coloured 9-inch tart pan with a detachable rim or a glass pie plate. On a lightly floured surface roll the puff pastry into an eleven-inch sq.. Healthy it into the tart pan or pie plate. Trim off the overhanging pieces of pastry with scissors. Refrigerate the crust, uncovered, for quarter-hour, or up to eight hours, covered.
5. Preheat the oven to 425 degrees.
6. Beat the eggs & yolk together in a big bowl. Stir in the milk & the leek combination. Pour this into the cold pie shell. Bake 25–half-hour, or till richly golden. Remove the outer rim of the tart pan. Let the tart cool on a wire rack for quarter-hour before slicing. Serve warm, not hot.

BROCCOLI & MUSHROOM TART

SERVES four–6
one **sheet (half of a 17-ounce package) frozen puff pastry**

one **tablespoon olive oil**

three cups thinly sliced mushrooms (eight ounces)

3½–four cups tiny broccoli florets (no stalks)

¼ cup water

three large eggs

¼ cup milk

½ teaspoon salt

one **cup grated Monterey Jack cheese with jalapeño peppers**

1. Remove the puff pastry from the package & let it thaw at room temperature for about half-hour, or till no longer frozen but still cool.

2.In the meantime, heat the oil in a big skillet over medium heat. Add the mushrooms & sauté till brown. Mix in the broccoli & water, & cover the pan. Cook the broccoli till tender but still shiny green, about five minutes. Remove the cover & cook till all of the liquid evaporates. Remove the pan from the heat & let the greens cool to room temperature.

3. Lightly butter a dark-coloured 9-inch tart pan with a detachable bottom or a glass pie plate. On a lightly floured surface roll the puff pastry into an eleven-inch sq.. Healthy it into the tart pan. Trim off the overhanging pieces of pastry with scissors. Refrigerate the crust quarter-hour, or cover & chill up to eight hours.
4. Preheat the oven to 425 degrees.
5. Beat the eggs in a big bowl. Stir in the milk, greens, salt, & cheese.
6. Spoon the combination into the tart pan. Bake 25—half-hour, or till the pastry is brown & a knife inserted in the middle of the tart comes out clean. Remove the outer rim of the tart pan in case you are utilizing such a pan. Let the tart cool on a wire rack for quarter-hour before slicing. Serve the tart hot but not piping hot.

VEGETABLE TARTS

SERVES four
one **sheet (half of a 17-ounce package) frozen puff pastry**

Sun-Dried Tomato Pesto

one **medium-large boiling potato (preferably Yukon Gold), peeled, halved, & sliced ¼ inch thick**

two **tablespoons olive oil**

one **medium zucchini, sliced ¼ inch thick**

1. Defrost the puff pastry for forty five minutes, or till thawed but still cold.
2. In the meantime, make the Sun-Dried Tomato Pesto & put aside.

3. Fill a saucepan midway with water & bring to a boil. Drop in the potato slices & cook till tender but not mushy, about five minutes. Drain & unfolded on a plate to let cool.
4. Heat the oil in a big skillet till hot but not smoking. Fry the zucchini slices till golden on all sides. Remove to a plate & let cool.
5. On a lightly floured surface roll the puff pastry into an eleven X eleven-inch sq.. Utilizing a 5-inch cutter or inverted bowl, cut four disks from the pastry. Place the disks on a baking sheet & pierce throughout with a fork. Keep refrigerated till you're prepared to assemble the tarts.
6. Preheat the oven to four hundred degrees.
7. Spread two tablespoons pesto on each pastry disk leaving a ½-inch border. You should have some pesto left over; refrigerate for an additional use (see Tip). Cover the pesto with some potato slices, then cover the potatoes with zucchini slices organized in a circle. You might have some potato & zucchini left over.
8. Bake 15–20 minutes, or till the pastry is golden brown. Serve without delay.

SHIITAKE MUSHROOM TARTS IN PUFF PASTRY

SERVES four
two **garlic cloves, minced**

five **tablespoons olive oil**

one **sheet (half of a 17-ounce package) frozen puff pastry**

two **medium onions, thinly sliced**

½ cup chopped walnuts

Salt to taste

Freshly ground black pepper to taste

six **ounces shiitake mushrooms, stems discarded & caps thinly sliced (three cups sliced)**

four ounces usual white mushrooms, thinly sliced (1½ cups sliced)

1. Defrost the puff pastry for forty five minutes, or till thawed but still cold.

2. Mix three tablespoons oil with the garlic in a small bowl & let sit no less than forty five minutes.
3. Heat one tablespoon oil in a skillet. Add the onions & sauté till golden brown & really soft, about quarter-hour. Stir in the walnuts & cook two minutes. Season with salt & pepper. Puree the combination in a food processor & let cool.
4. Heat the remaining tablespoon of oil in the skillet & sauté the mushrooms till brown, about 10 minutes. Let cool.
5. On a lightly floured surface roll the puff pastry into an eleven X eleven-inch sq.. Utilizing a 5-inch cutter or inverted bowl, cut four disks from the pastry. Place them on a baking sheet & chill till you might be prepared to assemble the tarts.
6. Strain the garlic oil through a strainer. Discard the garlic & put aside the oil.
7. Preheat the oven to four hundred degrees.
8. Spread ¼ of the onion combination on each pastry disk, leaving a ½-inch border. Cover each tart with ¼ of the mushrooms. Brush a little garlic oil on each tart. Bake 15–20 minutes, or till the pastry is golden brown. Brush the tarts once more with some oil before serving. Serve instantly.

GREENS, POTATO, & FETA CHEESE PIE

SERVES four
½ tablespoon unsalted butter, at room temperature

¼ cup dry bread crumbs

two **medium boiling potatoes (such as red-skinned), peeled & cut into ½-inch dice (about 1½ cups)**

6–7 large leaves Swiss chard, faraway from stems, or one 10-ounce package fresh spinach, stems discarded, or a mixture of each

1½ tablespoons salt

one **cup crumbled feta cheese**

two **scallions, thinly sliced**

two **tablespoons chopped fresh parsley**

Generous seasoning freshly ground black pepper

two **large eggs, well beaten**

¼ **cup milk**

two **tablespoons olive oil**

1. Coat the bottom & sides of a 9-inch pie plate with the ½ tablespoon butter. Sprinkle the crumbs on the plate, then rotate the plate till they cover all the bottom & sides. This may form the crust.
2. Place the potatoes in a medium-size saucepan & cover with water. Bring to a boil, then lower the heat to a simmer. Cook the potatoes till tender, about 10 minutes. Drain well & place in a big bowl.
3. Wash the Swiss chard or spinach & place in a colander. Sprinkle the salt throughout the leaves & let sit for half-hour; it will trigger the juices to "sweat." With your hands collect the leaves right into a ball & squeeze out all of the juices. Chop the leaves roughly & add them to the potatoes. Mix in all of the remaining ingredients.
4. Preheat the oven to 375 degrees.
5. Place the greens combination in the prepared pie plate. Bake forty minutes, or till a knife inserted in the middle of the pie comes out clean. Let sit 10 minutes before serving.

RED PEPPER, & SPINACH PIE

SERVES four
½ **tablespoon butter, at room temperature**

¼ **cup dry bread crumbs**

one **tablespoon olive oil**

one **red bell pepper, cut into ½-inch dice**

four large garlic cloves, minced

three medium yellow squash, quartered vertically & thinly sliced

one **(10-ounce) package triple-washed spinach, stems discarded & leaves torn, or one 10-ounce box frozen chopped spinach, defrosted & squeezed dry**

three large eggs

¼ cup milk

¼ teaspoon salt

Generous seasoning freshly ground black pepper

one ½ cups grated Swiss cheese

1. Slather the butter throughout the inside a 9-inch pie plate. Sprinkle the bread crumbs on the plate, then rotate the plate so the crumbs adhere to the sides & bottom. A thicker layer of crumbs on the bottom is okay.
2. Heat the oil in a big skillet over medium heat. Add the red pepper & cover the pan. Cook five minutes, tossing often. Add the garlic & cook, uncovered, for two minutes.
3. Mix in the squash & sauté, tossing often, till the squash is tender, about 10 minutes.
4. In case you are utilizing fresh spinach, pile it on & cover the pan. Cook two minutes, or till the spinach wilts. If any juices are on the bottom of the pan, elevate the heat & allow them to evaporate. In case you are utilizing frozen spinach, add it & cook till all its liquid evaporates, about three minutes. Let the combination cool.
5. Preheat the oven to 375 degrees.
6. Beat the eggs in a big bowl. Stir in the milk, salt, pepper, & cooled greens. Spoon half the combination into the prepared pie plate. Sprinkle on one cup cheese. Spoon on the remaining combination & top with the remaining cheese.
7. Bake half-hour, or till a knife inserted in the middle comes out clean. Cool quarter-hour before cutting the pie into wedges.

SHEPHERD'S PIE

SERVES four–6
three tablespoons olive oil

three garlic cloves, minced

one cup canned crushed tomatoes or tomato puree

½ cup water

one **cup fresh or frozen green beans, cut into 1-inch lengths**

one **cup cooked chickpeas or white beans, rinsed well if canned**

two **tablespoons minced fresh basil, or one teaspoon dried**

½ **teaspoon salt**

Generous seasoning freshly ground black pepper

two **medium zucchini, quartered lengthwise & thinly sliced**

one **cup fresh or frozen corn**

The Topping:
four large (2½ pounds) boiling potatoes, peeled & quartered

½ **cup milk (roughly)**

two **tablespoons unsalted butter**

¼ **teaspoon salt**

three tablespoons grated Parmesan cheese

1. Heat the oil in a three-quart saucepan over medium heat. Add the garlic & cook 1–2 minutes, or till softened but by no means coloured. Stir in the crushed tomatoes, water, green beans, chickpeas, basil, salt, & pepper, & cook, stirring often, for 10 minutes. Add the zucchini & corn, & simmer 10 minutes more, or till the greens are tender but not mushy.
2. In the meantime, cook the potatoes in boiling water till tender. Drain thoroughly in a colander & return to the pot. Add the milk (see Tip), butter, & salt, & mash with an electrical mixer or potato masher till smooth, adding a little more milk if necessary.
3. Preheat the oven to 375 degrees.
4. Pour the stew right into a shallow 2½-quart baking dish, such as a l2X7X2 Pyrex dish. Spread the mashed potatoes throughout the top of the stew, being cautious to go to the fringe of the casserole. Sprinkle the top with the Parmesan cheese.
5. Bake half-hour, or till bubbly & brown on top. Let sit 10 minutes before serving.

TIPS: Watch out with the quantity of milk you add to the potatoes whenever you mash them. You need them to be creamy but considerably thick as a result of the steam from the casserole will moisten them additional & thin them a little.

You can easily prepare this pie in phases. The stew might be cooked up to 24 hours prematurely. The potatoes might be placed on top up to eight hours prematurely. If refrigerated, bring to room temperature before baking.

CLASSIC VEGETABLE POT PIE

SERVES four
two **cups water**

two **carrots, thinly sliced**

one **celery rib, thinly sliced**

one **cup diced green beans, fresh or frozen**

two **tablespoons olive oil**

one **medium onion, finely diced**

three cups (eight ounces) sliced mushrooms

one **red bell pepper, cut into ½-inch dice**

⅓ cup unbleached flour one cup milk

one **tablespoon tamari soy sauce**

¼ teaspoon dried basil Pinch dried oregano

½ teaspoon salt

Generous seasoning freshly ground pepper one sheet (half of 17-ounce box) puff pastry Flour for dusting

one **egg beaten with one tablespoon water**

1. Place the water in a medium-size saucepan & bring to a boil. Add the carrots & celery, & cook two minutes. Add the green beans & simmer till the greens are tender, about five minutes. Put aside. (Don't drain the greens.)
2. Heat the oil in a big skillet over medium heat. Add the onion, mushrooms, & red pepper, & sauté till the mushrooms are juicy & the peppers are tender, not less than 10 minutes.
3. Sprinkle the flour over the greens. Toss & cook, stirring continually, for two minutes. The greens will likely be dry & the flour will brown slightly.
4. Pour in the carrot & liquid combination, milk, & soy sauce, & stir constantly till the gravy involves a boil. Scrape the bottom of the skillet to remove & incorporate any crusty tidbits. Boil one minute, or simply till the combination thickens. Stir in the basil, oregano, salt, & pepper. Scrape the combination right into a shallow 2½-quart baking dish (such as a 12 X seven X 2-inch Pyrex dish). Let cool to room temperature.
5. In the meantime, thaw the puff pastry at room temperature for half-hour, or till completely defrosted but still cool.
6. Preheat the oven to four hundred degrees.
7. Lightly flour a piece surface & the top of the pastry sheet. Roll the pastry till it's a little bigger than the top of the baking dish. Place the pastry on the cooled filling & let it prolong one inch or so up the sides of the dish. Trim it with scissors to suit evenly. With a pointy knife cut a few slits in the pastry to create steam vents. Brush the pastry with the beaten egg combination. (You can prepare the pie so far & refrigerate up to two hours. Bring to room temperature before cooking.)
8. Bake the pie half-hour, or till the pastry is a wealthy golden brown. Serve directly.

CLASSIC PIZZA DOUGH

FOR two (12-INCH) PIZZAS
one **cup warm water, divided**

one **teaspoon sugar**

one **packet (2¼ teaspoons) active dry yeast**

three tablespoons olive oil, plus extra for greasing

2½ cups unbleached flour, plus extra for dusting

½ teaspoon salt

1. Place ¼ cup warm water in a small bowl. Add the sugar & stir till dissolved. Sprinkle the yeast onto the surface of the water. Let the yeast sit undisturbed for one minute, then stir it into the water till blended. Let the yeast "proof" for 10 minutes; it ought to become considerably bubbly due to the presence of the sugar. If it doesn't bubble in any respect, it's outdated & inactive.
2. Pour the yeast into a big bowl & stir in the remaining water, oil, flour, & salt. Mix the dough with a wooden spoon till it forms a ball. Lightly flour a piece surface & place the dough on it. Knead the dough for 10 minutes, or till it's smooth & elastic. Flour the work surface as essential to prevent the dough from sticking.
3. Coat the inside of a big glass or ceramic bowl with oil. Press the ball of dough into the bottom of the bowl, then flip the dough over so the oiled side is on top. Cover the bowl with plastic wrap & let the dough rise in a warm place till it doubles in bulk, about 1½ hours.
4. Punch down the dough & knead it a few times. Divide it in 2, then proceed with your recipe.

SEMOLINA PIZZA DOUGH

FOR three (eleven-INCH) PIZZAS
1¼ cups warm water, divided one teaspoon sugar

one **packet (2¼ teaspoons) active dry yeast**

two **tablespoons olive oil, plus extra for greasing**

½ teaspoon salt

two **cups unbleached flour, plus extra for dusting**

one **cup semolina**

1. Place ¼ cup warm water in a small bowl. Stir in the sugar till dissolved. Sprinkle the yeast onto the surface of the water. Let the yeast sit undisturbed for one minute, then stir it into the water till blended. Let the yeast "proof" for 10 minutes; it ought to become considerably bubbly due to the presence of the sugar. If it doesn't bubble in any respect, it's outdated & inactive.
2. Pour the yeast into a big bowl. Mix in the remaining water, oil, & salt. Add the flour & semolina, & stir with a wooden spoon till a ball of dough forms.

3. Turn the dough onto a lightly floured surface & knead about 10 minutes. Flour the work surface as essential to prevent the dough from sticking. When prepared, the dough needs to be smooth & elastic.
4. Lightly oil a big ceramic or glass bowl. Place the dough inside, then flip it over so the oiled side is on top. Cover with plastic wrap & place in a warm place to rise till it doubles in bulk, about 1½ hours. Proceed with your pizza recipe.

QUICK BAKING POWDER PIZZA DOUGH

FOR four (eight-INCH) PIZZAS
2½ cups unbleached flour, plus extra for dusting

1½ teaspoons baking powder

½ teaspoon salt

four tablespoons unsalted butter, chilled & cut into pieces

one **cup low-fat milk**

Olive oil for greasing or cornmeal for sprinkling

1. Place the flour, baking powder, & salt in a big bowl. Add the butter & toss to coat. Rub the butter into the flour with your fingertips till the combination resembles coarse meal. You are able to do this in a food processor, if desired. Add the milk slowly & mix just till the dough is evenly moistened.
2. Turn the dough onto a lightly floured surface & knead two or three times, or simply till it's pliable. Divide the dough into four balls.
3. Lightly oil a big baking sheet, or if you'll be utilizing a pizza stone, sprinkle some cornmeal on a pizza peel. Utilizing a lightly floured rolling pin, roll out each ball into an eight-inch circle. Place two on the baking sheet or one on the pizza peel. Proceed with your recipe.

.

BEER PIZZA DOUGH

FOR two (12-INCH) PIZZAS
three cups unbleached flour, plus extra for dusting

one **tablespoon baking powder**

½ teaspoon salt

one **(12-ounce) can or bottle beer (an affordable beer is ok)**

Oil for greasing or cornmeal for sprinkling

1. Mix the flour, baking powder, & salt in a big bowl & mix completely. Pour in the beer & mix well; the dough will probably be sticky. Spread a small handful of flour on a piece surface & place the dough on it. Roll the dough round to coat it with the flour & stop it from sticking. Knead it two or three times to make it pliable. Form the dough right into a ball, then divide it in 2.
2. Grease two baking sheets, or if you'll use a baking stone, sprinkle some cornmeal on a pizza peel. Use a rolling pin to roll each ball right into a 12-inch circle. Place a spherical of dough on each baking sheet or put one spherical on the pizza peel. Proceed with your recipe.

TORTILLA PIZZA SHELLS

MAKES four (eight-INCH) PIZZA SHELLS
four (eight-inch) flour tortillas

1½ tablespoons olive oil

1. Preheat the oven to 375 degrees.
2. Use two baking sheets & place two tortillas side by side on each sheet. With a pastry brush lightly coat each tortilla with some oil. Flip the tortillas & coat once more.
3. Bake eight–10 minutes, flipping the tortillas & alternating the position of the baking sheets midway through the cooking time. Through the first jiffy use a knife level to pop any air bubbles which may develop. The tortillas must be golden & crisp when done. Proceed with your recipe.

CLASSIC PIZZA

MAKES two (12-INCH) PIZZAS
SERVES four
Traditional Pizza Dough or other pizza dough from this chapter

Cornmeal for sprinkling or olive oil for greasing

one **cup Easy Marinara Sauce**

1½ cups grated mozzarella cheese

1½ cups grated Muenster cheese

1. Prepare the pizza dough in accordance to the recipe.
2. Preheat the oven to 450 degrees. If you're utilizing a pizza stone, heat it at the very least forty five minutes before cooking the pizza on it.
3. Lightly flour the work surface. Punch down the dough & place it on the work surface. Divide it in half. Use a rolling pin to roll one portion right into a 12-inch circle. If the dough resists stretching, let it rest a couple of minutes, then roll once more. In case you are utilizing a pizza stone, sprinkle some cornmeal on a pizza peel & place one circle of dough on the peel. In any other case, lightly grease a baking sheet & place the dough on it.
4. Spread half the sauce on one crust, then top with half of the mozzarella & Muenster cheeses. Bake 10–12 minutes if cooking instantly on a baking stone; add a couple of minutes if cooking the pizza on a baking sheet. When done, the pizza might be golden on top & beneath. Repeat with the remaining ingredients to make one other pizza.

MIXED MUSHROOM & FONTINA PIZZA

MAKES three (eleven-INCH) PIZZAS
SERVES four–6
Semolina Pizza Dough or other pizza dough from this chapter

The Topping:
two **tablespoons olive oil**

three medium onions, halved & thinly sliced

1½ pounds combined mushrooms (such as white button, shiitake, cremini, & oyster), very thinly sliced

two **sprigs fresh thyme, leaves removed & stems discarded, or ¼ teaspoon dried**

½ teaspoon salt

Generous seasoning freshly ground black pepper

Oil or cornmeal for baking the pizzas

½ cup sour cream

4½ cups grated fontina cheese

1. Make the pizza dough as directed.
2. Whereas the dough is rising, make the topping. Heat the oil in a big skillet over medium heat & add the onions. Cook stirring frequently, till the onions are golden brown throughout, about 20 minutes. Mix in the mushrooms & cook till brown & juicy, about five minutes. Remove the pan from the heat & season with thyme, salt, & pepper.
3. Preheat the oven to 450 degrees. In case you are utilizing a pizza stone, heat it a minimum of forty five minutes before cooking the pizza on it.
4. Punch down the dough & place it on a piece surface. Divide it into **three.** Lightly flour the work surface, then use a rolling pin to roll one portion of the dough into an eleven-inch circle. If the dough resists stretching, let it rest a couple of minutes, then roll once more. In case you are utilizing a pizza stone, sprinkle some cornmeal on a pizza peel & place the dough on the peel; in any other case, lightly grease a baking sheet & place the dough on it.
5. Spread ⅓ of the sour cream throughout the dough. Sprinkle on ⅓ of the fontina cheese, then scatter ⅓ of the mushroom combination over all. If you're cooking the pizza on a baking stone, bake eight–10 minutes, or till the crust is golden brown beneath. If cooked on a baking sheet, the pizza will take a couple of minutes longer. Repeat with the remaining ingredients.

FRESH MOZZARELLA, TOMATO, & BASIL PIZZA

MAKES two (12-INCH) PIZZAS
SERVES four
Basic Pizza Dough or other pizza dough from this chapter

Cornmeal for sprinkling or olive oil for greasing

four tablespoons olive oil, divided

six **plum tomatoes, seeded & minced**

four garlic cloves, minced

Salt to taste

Freshly ground black pepper to taste

⅔ cup (four ounces) sliced fresh mozzarella (quarter-size pieces)

½ cup grated or shaved Parmesan cheese

12 large basil leaves, stacked, tightly rolled, & thinly sliced into shreds (chiffonade)

1. Prepare the pizza dough in accordance to the recipe.
2. Preheat the oven to 450 degrees. If you're utilizing a pizza stone, heat it a minimum of forty five minutes before cooking the pizza on it.
3. Lightly flour the work surface. Punch down the dough & divide it in half. Use a rolling pin to roll one portion of the dough right into a 12-inch circle. If the dough resists stretching, let it rest a couple of minutes, then roll once more.
4. If you're utilizing a pizza stone, sprinkle some cornmeal on a pizza peel & place one circle of dough on the peel; in any other case, lightly grease a baking sheet & place the dough on it.
5. Heat two tablespoons oil in a medium-size skillet over medium heat. Add the tomatoes & garlic, & sauté five minutes, or till the tomatoes have softened. Season generously with salt & pepper & let cool.
6. Utilizing half of the combination, spoon little mounds throughout one crust. Scatter half of the mozzarella & Parmesan cheeses alongside the tomato.
7. Bake 12 minutes, or till the crust is golden beneath. Remove the pizza from the oven, instantly drizzle one tablespoon oil throughout the top, & sprinkle with half the shredded basil. Serve instantly. Repeat with the remaining ingredients to make one other pizza.

PIZZA WITH POTATOES, GARLIC, & TOMATOES

MAKES two (12-INCH) PIZZAS
SERVES four
Basic Pizza Dough

four cups peeled & diced (½inch) boiling potatoes (about four medium potatoes) (see Tip)

1½ cups finely diced tomatoes, fresh or canned

three tablespoons olive oil, plus extra for greasing

four garlic cloves, pressed or minced

1½ teaspoons fresh rosemary, minced, or ½ teaspoon dried, finely crumbled

½ teaspoon salt

Generous seasoning freshly ground black pepper

1. Preheat the oven to 450 degrees. In case you are utilizing a pizza stone, heat it a minimum of forty five minutes before cooking the pizza on it.
2. Lightly flour the work surface. Punch down the dough & place it on the work surface. Divide it in half. Use a rolling pin to roll one portion of the dough right into a 12-inch circle. If the dough resists stretching, let it rest a couple of minutes, then roll once more. In case you are utilizing a pizza stone, sprinkle some cornmeal on a pizza peel & place the circle of dough on the peel; in any other case, lightly grease a baking sheet & place the dough on it. In either case, to prevent the dough from rising once more, place it in the fridge till the topping is prepared.
3. Fill a medium-size saucepan midway with water & bring to a boil. Add the potatoes & cook till tender, about 10 minutes. Drain completely & place in a bowl. Let cool to room temperature, then stir in the tomatoes.
4. Heat the oil in a small skillet over medium heat. Add the garlic & cook only about 15 seconds, or simply enough to eliminate its raw taste. Don't let it get in any respect brown. Pour it over the potatoes & toss. Mix in the rosemary, salt, & pepper.
5. Spread half of the combination on the pizza. Bake about 12 minutes if you're baking instantly on a pizza stone; add a couple of minutes in case you are utilizing a baking

sheet. Check the bottom of the crust to ensure it's golden brown. Cut the pizza into wedges. Make one other pizza with the remaining ingredients.

PIZZA BIANCO

MAKES two (12-INCH) PIZZAS
SERVES four

Traditional Pizza Dough or other pizza dough from this chapter

Cornmeal for sprinkling or olive oil for greasing

one **cup ricotta cheese**

two **garlic cloves, put through a press or minced**

¼ cup grated Parmesan cheese

three cups grated mozzarella cheese

1. Prepare the pizza dough in accordance to the recipe.
2. Preheat the oven to 450 degrees. If you're utilizing a pizza stone, heat it a minimum of forty five minutes before cooking the pizza on it.
3. Lightly flour the work surface. Punch down the dough & divide it in half. Use a rolling pin to roll one portion of the dough right into a 12-inch circle. If the dough resists stretching, let it rest a couple of minutes, then roll once more. In case you are utilizing a pizza stone, sprinkle some cornmeal on a pizza peel & place one circle of dough on the peel; in any other case, lightly grease a baking sheet & place the dough on it.
4. Mix the ricotta cheese, garlic, & Parmesan cheese in a medium-size bowl. Spread half of the combination on the pizza crust, leaving a 1-inch border. Sprinkle half of the mozzarella cheese on top.
5. Bake 10–12 minutes if cooking immediately on a baking stone. Add a few extra minutes if utilizing a baking sheet. When done, the pizza shall be golden on top & beneath. Repeat with the remaining ingredients to make one other pizza.

CARAMELIZED ONION, WALNUT, & GOAT CHEESE PIZZA WITH A BEER CRUST

MAKES two (12-inch) pizzas
SERVES four

two **tablespoons olive oil**

three pounds (6 large) onions, very thinly sliced

Salt

Freshly ground black pepper

½ cup finely chopped (not ground) walnuts

Beer Pizza Dough or other pizza dough from this chapter

1½ cups (eight ounces) crumbled soft, mild goat cheese

1. Heat the oil in a big stockpot over medium heat. Add the onions & a generous quantity of salt & pepper. Toss to coat well, then cover the pot. Cook tossing often, till the onions are very soft & are caramel brown throughout. After 10 minutes or so, lower the heat to prevent sticking. The onions have to be cooked slowly over low heat to caramelize correctly; this can take about forty five minutes. You should use much less oil in case you cook them *covered.* Remove the cover from the pan & stir in the walnuts. Cook five minutes, tossing frequently. Remove from the heat & let cool. (You can prepare the onions thus far & refrigerate them up to two days inadvance.)
2. Preheat the oven to 450 degrees. If you will cook your pizzas on a pizza stone, heat it at the least forty five minutes.
3. To assemble the pizzas, spread half the onion combination on each prepared crust, then sprinkle with the crumbled goat cheese. If you're cooking the pizza on a baking sheet, you should use two pans & cook each pizzas directly. Place the pans on two totally different oven racks & alternate the pans midway through the cooking. Bake 12– quarter-hour, or till golden brown on top & beneath. Use a spatula to peek beneath the crust to ensure it's golden & well cooked.

PESTO PIZZA

MAKES four (eight-inch) pizzas
SERVES four
Quick Baking Powder Pizza Dough or other pizza dough from this chapter

1⅓ cups Basic Pesto or Winter Pesto

four cups grated mozzarella cheese

1⅓ cups diced roasted red peppers, store-purchased or freshly roasted, patted very dry

24 black olives, pitted & halved

1. Preheat the oven to 450 degrees. If you'll cook your pizzas on a pizza stone, heat it at the very least forty five minutes. Have the rolled crusts in entrance of you either on a pizza peel (1 crust) or on a baking sheet (2 crusts each).
2. Divide the topping ingredients into four parts. Spread one portion of every ingredient on each pizza. Sprinkle on ¼ of the mozzarella cheese, then top with ¼ of the roasted peppers & olives. Bake 12–quarter-hour, or till richly golden on top & beneath. Use a spatula that can assist you peek on the underside of the crust.

TORTILLA PIZZAS WITH FETA CHEESE

MAKES four (eight-INCH) PIZZAS
SERVES four
Tortilla Pizza Shells

The Topping:
four plum tomatoes, finely diced

12 black olives (such as Kalamata), pitted & halved

one **medium zucchini, halved lengthwise & sliced paper-thin**

½ cup thin slivers red onion

228

four teaspoons finely chopped fresh oregano, or two teaspoons dried

Generous seasoning freshly ground black pepper

three tablespoons fruity olive oil

eight ounces (1½ cups) finely crumbled feta cheese

1. Preheat the oven to 375 degrees.
2. Place two cooked tortillas on each of two baking sheets.
3. In a big bowl mix the tomatoes, olives, zucchini, onion slivers, oregano, pepper, & oil, & toss well. Gently fold in the feta cheese. Scatter throughout the four tortillas.
4. Bake 12 minutes, or till the feta is scorching & the zucchini is softened. Alternate the position of the baking sheets midway throughout the cooking time. Cut & serve instantly.

SPINACH CALZONES

MAKES four CALZONES
five **cups (5 ounces) spinach, stems discarded & leaves torn into small**
pieces

two **medium boiling potatoes, peeled & cut into ½-inch dice (2 cups diced)**

one **scallion, very thinly sliced**

two **tablespoons olive oil, plus extra for greasing**

one **cup grated smoked mozzarella or Gouda cheese**

Salt to taste

Freshly ground black pepper to taste

one **pound frozen bread dough, thawed Flour for dusting**

1. Fill a medium-size saucepan midway with water & bring to a boil. Drop in the spinach & cook 30 seconds, or simply till it wilts. Use tongs to scoop out the spinach & place in a

strainer in the sink. Press out all of the liquid from the spinach with the back of a giant spoon. Put in a medium-size bowl.

2. Let the water return to a boil. Add the potatoes & cook till tender, about quarter-hour. Drain totally & mix with the spinach. Let cool, then mix in the scallion, oil, cheese, salt, & pepper.

3. Preheat the oven to 375 degrees. Lightly oil a baking sheet.

4. Divide the dough into four equal pieces & roll each bit right into a ball. Place a small bowl of water in entrance of you. Lightly mud the work surface with some flour. Use a rolling pin to roll a ball of dough right into a 7-inch circle, dusting the dough with a little flour as necessary. Dip your finger in the water & moisten the fringe of the circle of dough. Spoon ¼ of the potato combination on half of the circle, then fold over the dough to form a half-moon. Pinch the edges of the dough together, stretching the bottom layer slightly over the top as you pinch. Repeat with the remaining three parts.

5. Place the calzones on the baking sheet. Use your fingers or a pastry brush to lightly coat the tops of the calzones with some oil. Bake 25 minutes, or till a deep golden brown. Let cool quarter-hour before consuming to avoid being burned by the internal steam.

CALZONE PIE

SERVES four
two **medium boiling potatoes, peeled & cut into ½-inch dice (2 cups diced)**

two **tablespoons olive oil, plus extra for greasing**

two **medium zucchini, cut lengthwise into quarters & thinly sliced**

six **garlic cloves, minced**

one **(14-ounce) can prepared-diced tomatoes, well drained**

½ teaspoon oregano

½ teaspoon salt

Generous seasoning freshly ground pepper

¼ cup grated Parmesan cheese

one **pound frozen pizza dough, thawed & at room temperature**

Flour for dusting

one **cup grated mozzarella cheese**

1. Fill a saucepan midway with water & bring to a boil. Add the potatoes & boil till tender, about 10 minutes. Drain well & let cool.
2. Heat the oil in a big skillet over medium heat till hot. Add the zucchini & sauté till crisp but tender, about five minutes. Sprinkle on the garlic & sauté two minutes. Stir in the tomatoes, oregano, salt, & pepper, & cook two minutes more. Remove from the heat, stir in the Parmesan cheese, & let cool.
3. Preheat the oven to four hundred degrees. Lightly oil a big baking sheet.
4. Divide the pizza dough into two equal pieces. Lightly flour a piece surface & form every bit into an ideal ball. Roll one ball into an eleven-or 12-inch circle, dusting the top of the dough as necessary. Place the circle on the baking sheet. (If the dough resists being rolled easily, let sit a couple of minutes to loosen up the gluten, then attempt once more.)
5. Spoon the vegetable filling throughout the dough, leaving a 1-inch border. With a little water moisten the border with your fingers. Top with the mozzarella cheese. Pull the bottom fringe of the dough over the top edge, pinch together, & seal the edges. Prepare the opposite ball of dough in the same way.
6. Brush each pie with some oil. Cut a steam vent in the middle of the pie. Bake 20–25 minutes, or till golden throughout. Remove from the oven & brush once more with oil. Remove the pie from the baking sheet & cool on a wire rack for 10 minutes. Cut into wedges & serve.

ROASTED TOFU

SERVES 2–four
one **pound extra-firm tofu**

one **½ tablespoons tamari soy sauce**

one **tablespoon Asian sesame oil**

one **tablespoon dry sherry**

1. Slice the tofu into ½-inch-thick slices. Place them on a clean cotton towel or on paper towels. Use one other towel or more paper towels to pat the tofu very dry. Cut each slice in half vertically, then cut the pieces into triangles, or cut the slices into three/four-inch cubes.
2. Mix the soy sauce, sesame oil, & sherry in a big bowl. Add the tofu & use a rubber spatula to softly toss it with the marinade. Let marinate a minimum of half-hour, or cover & chill up to 24 hours.
3. Preheat the oven to 450 degrees.
4. Place the tofu & its marinade in a single layer in a big shallow baking dish. Bake 25–half-hour, or till golden throughout. Shake the dish after quarter-hour to prevent the tofu from sticking. You can serve the tofu warm, but it's much more scrumptious when cooled to room temperature after which chilled till very cold, about two hours.

MARINATED TOFU

one **pound extra-firm tofu**

two **tablespoons tamari soy sauce**

one **tablespoon Asian sesame oil**

one **tablespoon canola oil**

1. Slice the tofu into ½-inch-thick slices & lay them on one finish of a cotton kitchen towel or on paper towels. Use the remaining half of the towel or more paper towels to pat the tofu very dry. Cut into ½-inch cubes & pat dry once more.
2. mix the soy sauce & sesame oil in a big bowl. Drop in the tofu & use a rubber spatula to softly toss it round in the marinade. Let marinate 20–half-hour, or cover & refrigerate up to eight hours.
3. Heat the canola oil in a big nonstick skillet over medium-high heat. When the oil is highly regarded but not but smoking, add the tofu. Cook till it's golden beneath, about five minutes. Shake the pan often to prevent it from sticking. Use a spatula to toss the tofu round till it's golden throughout, one other 5–7 minutes. Place the tofu on a big plate & let cool. Serve barely warm or at room temperature, or chill till very cold. This tofu could be eaten alone, combined into stir-fries, or tossed into salads.

CLASSIC STIR-FRIED TOFU & VEGETABLES HOISIN

SERVES four
¼ cup hoisin sauce

two **tablespoons tamari soy sauce**

one **tablespoon Chinese rice wine or sherry**

one **tablespoon Asian sesame oil**

four tablespoons canola oil, divided

one **pound extra-firm tofu, cut into ½-inch slices & patted very dry, then cut into ½-inch cubes & patted very dry once more**

5–6 cups tiny broccoli florets

one **red bell pepper, cut into 1-inch dice**

three tablespoons water

one **teaspoon minced fresh ginger**

four garlic cloves, minced

four cups hot cooked rice (created from one cup raw rice)

1. To make the sauce mix the hoisin sauce, tamari, wine, & sesame oil, & put aside.
2. Over medium-high heat, heat two tablespoons canola oil in a big nonstick skillet or wok till highly regarded but not smoking. Add the tofu & let sit one minute or so to brown. Shake the skillet a few times to prevent sticking. Toss the tofu & cook till evenly golden throughout. Remove to a platter.
3. Place the broccoli & red pepper in the skillet, toss, then add the water. Cover the pan & cook till all of the water has evaporated & the broccoli is starting to get tender but continues to be fairly crisp, about three minutes.
4. Make a well in the middle of the pan & pour in the remaining two tablespoons canola oil. Add the ginger & garlic, stir a few seconds, then toss with the greens. Add the tofu & stir-fry till hot, about one minute. Pour the sauce over the combination & stir-fiy 30 seconds. Serve over hot rice.

TIP: As with all stir-fried dishes, be sure you have all of the ingredients laid out before you start cooking. Have your rice completely cooked, covered, & stored warm over low heat before the stir-hying begins. Keep the skillet or wok extremely popular when stir-frying.

STIR-FRIED SZECHUAN TOFU

SERVES four
The Sauce:
two **teaspoons cornstarch**

¼ cup water

one **tablespoon chili paste with garlic**

¼ cup tamari soy sauce

¼ cup sherry

one **teaspoon sugar**

The Greens:
three tablespoons canola oil

one **pound extra-firm tofu, cut into ½-inch slices & patted very dry, then cut into ½-inch cubes & patted very dry once more**

three cups (eight ounces) sliced mushrooms

5–6 cups tiny broccoli florets (from one bunch broccoli)

two **carrots, very thinly sliced on the diagonal**

½ cup water

four cups hot cooked rice (produced from one cup raw rice)

1. Place the cornstarch in a small bowl & stir in the water till smooth. Stir in all of the remaining sauce ingredients. Put aside.
2. Heat the oil in a big, preferably nonstick, skillet over medium-high heat till very popular but not smoking. Add the tofu & stir-fry till deeply golden throughout. Remove the tofu to a plate & put aside.

3. Add the mushrooms to the pan & stir-fry till they start to release their juices. Stir in the broccoli & carrots, then pour in the water. Cover the pan & cook about five minutes, or till the broccoli begins to get tender but remains to be a shiny green.
4. Return the tofu to the pan & toss. Stir the sauce once once more & rapidly add to the pan. Toss a few seconds till it thickens. Serve instantly over hot rice.

TIP: As with all stir-fried dishes, be sure to have all of the ingredients laid out before you start cooking. Have your rice completely cooked, covered, & saved warm over low heat before the stir-frying begins. Keep the skillet or wok highly regarded when stir-frying.

PENNE WITH ROASTED TOFU, SPINACH, & RED PEPPERS IN GARLIC SAUCE

SERVES four–6
Roasted Tofu:
one **tablespoon tamari soy sauce**

one **tablespoon Asian sesame oil**

one **pound extra-firm tofu, sliced ½ inch thick, patted very dry, then cut into ½-inch cubes**

The Sauce:
½ cup olive oil

one **red bell pepper, cut into strips ½ x two inches**

six **large garlic cloves, minced**

¼ teaspoon crushed red pepper flakes

one **12-ounce package triple-washed spinach, stems discarded & leaves torn**

½ cup vegetable broth/stock, store-purchased or selfmade

½ teaspoon salt

one **pound penne**

Freshly grated Parmesan cheese

1. Preheat the oven to 450 degrees.
2. Mix the soy sauce & oil in a medium-size bowl. Stir the dry tofu into the combination & toss to coat. Let sit at the least 20 minutes or up to two hours.
3. Spread the tofu in a baking dish in one layer. Bake about 25 minutes, or till golden throughout. Toss with a spatula midway through the cooking time. Let the tofu cool when you prepare the pasta; it can get firmer. You can roast the tofu up to 24 hours prematurely, if desired.
4. Bring a big stockpot of water to a boil for the penne.
5. To make the sauce, heat the oil in a big skillet over medium heat. Add the red pepper & sauté till tender but crisp, about five minutes. Stir in the garlic & red pepper flakes, & toss well. Cook two minutes, stirring often. Mix in the spinach, broth/stock, & salt, & cover the pan. Cook just till the spinach wilts, about two minutes. Remove the cover & stir in the tofu. Keep the heat low whilst you cook the penne.
6. Put the penne in the boiling water & cook till al dente, about 12–quarter-hour. Drain completely & return to the pot. Stir in the greens & sauce together with a handful of Parmesan cheese. Toss well. Serve instantly with extra Parmesan cheese on the table.

CLASSIC POLENTA WITH WILD MUSHROOM RAGU

SERVES four
The Ragù:
three tablespoons olive oil

four large garlic cloves, minced

12 ounces white button mushrooms, thinly sliced

eight ounces combined unique mushrooms (such as shiitake, oyster, & cremini), thinly sliced

1½ cups canned crushed tomatoes or tomato puree

¼ teaspoon sugar

½ teaspoon salt

Generous seasoning freshly ground black pepper

The Polenta:
four cups vegetable broth/stock, store-purchased or home made

¼ teaspoon salt

1¼ cups cornmeal

one **tablespoon unsalted butter**

⅓ cup grated Parmesan cheese

1. To make the ragu, heat the oil in a three-quart saucepan over medium heat. Add the garlic & cook gently about one minute, or till very aromatic but under no circumstances coloured. Stir in the mushrooms & sauté, stirring often, till brown & juicy, about seven minutes. Mix in all of the remaining ingredients & partially cover the pan. Simmer 10 minutes, or till the sauce is thick & fragrant.
2. To make the polenta, bring the broth/stock & salt to a boil in a medium-size heavy-bottomed saucepan. Very slowly drizzle in the cornmeal, whisking all of the whereas with a wire whisk. Lower the heat to a simmer & continue to whisk the polenta till it's the consistency of soppy mashed potatoes, about five minutes.
3. Remove the polenta from the heat. Whisk in the butter & cheese. (You can cover the polenta & keep it warm for up to 10 minutes.) On large plates or in pasta bowls serve a mound of polenta topped with the mushroom ragu.

SMOKED CHEESE POLENTA WITH MIXED PEPPER TOPPING

SERVES four
The Topping:
two **tablespoons olive oil**

four garlic cloves, minced

¼ teaspoon crushed red pepper flakes

one **large red bell pepper**

two **large green bell peppers**

⅔ **cup canned crushed tomatoes or tomato puree**

¼ **teaspoon dried oregano**

¼ **teaspoon salt**

The Polenta:
four cups water

½ **teaspoon salt**

1¼ **cups cornmeal**

¼ **cup sour cream**

⅔ **cup grated smoked Gouda cheese**

1. To make the topping, heat the oil in a big skillet over medium heat. Add the garlic & crushed pepper flakes, & cook 30 seconds, or simply till they sizzle a bit. Mix in the peppers & sauté five minutes, tossing often. Cover the pan & cook till the peppers are very soft, about 10–quarter-hour. Remove the cover & mix in the crushed tomatoes, oregano, & salt. Cook about five minutes more, or simply till the sauce thickens. Keep warm over low heat. (You can prepare the sauce up to 24 hours prematurely. Reheat till hot, adding a few tablespoons of water if it has gotten too thick.)

2. To make the polenta, mix the water & salt in a heavy-bottomed saucepan & bring to a boil over high heat. Turn the heat to medium-low, then very slowly drizzle in the cornmeal, whisking all of the whereas with a wire whisk. Cook the polenta, whisking repeatedly, till it begins to tear away from the sides of the pan, about seven minutes. Whisk in the sour cream & smoked cheese. (You can cover the pan & keep the polenta warm for up to 10 minutes.) Spoon the polenta onto each serving plate & top with a few spoonfuls of the peppers & their sauce.

GORGONZOLA POLENTA

SERVES four
The Green Beans:
one **tablespoon olive oil one onion, finely diced**

one **(14-ounce) can prepared-cut diced tomatoes with their juice**

one **pound green beans, cut into 1-inch lengths**

¼ **teaspoon salt**

The Polenta:
3½ **cups water**

½ **teaspoon salt**

1¼ **cups cornmeal**

one **tablespoon butter**

two **tablespoons grated Parmesan cheese**

four **ounces (¾ cup) diced Gorgonzola or other blue cheese**

1. To make the beans, heat the oil in a medium-size saucepan over medium heat & add the onion. Sauté till it softens, about five minutes. Add the tomatoes, green beans, & salt, & partially cover the pan. Simmer till the green beans are very tender, about 20 minutes.
2. To make the polenta, bring the water & salt to a boil in a medium-size heavy-bottomed saucepan. Drizzle in the cornmeal very slowly, whisking all of the whereas with a wire whisk. When all of the cornmeal has been added, turn the heat to medium-low & continue to whisk the polenta till it has thickened & is the consistency of mashed potatoes, about seven minutes. Whisk in the butter & Parmesan & Gorgonzola cheeses. Serve instantly or remove from the heat, cover the pan, & let sit 10 minutes. Spoon onto serving plates & mound the braised green beans on top.

YELLOW SQUASH & RED PEPPER SAUTÉ ON POLENTA

SERVES four
two **tablespoons olive oil**

two **red bell peppers, cut into strips two inches by one inch**

two **yellow squash, halved lengthwise & sliced ¼ inch thick**

one **tomato, cored, seeded, & finely diced, or ½ cup canned diced tomatoes**

four garlic cloves, minced

Salt to taste

Generous seasoning freshly ground black pepper

two **tablespoons minced fresh basil, or one teaspoon dried**

two **tablespoons minced fresh parsley**

The Polenta:
four cups vegetable broth/stock, store-purchased or selfmade

¼ teaspoon salt

1¼ cups cornmeal

two **tablespoons unsalted butter**

⅓ cup grated Parmesan cheese

1. Heat the oil in a big skillet over medium heat till hot but not smoking. Add the red peppers & sauté two minutes. Cover the pan & cook till the peppers are soft & browned throughout but not mushy, about seven minutes. They need to sizzle fairly a bit whereas cooking.
2. Remove the cover of the pan & stir in the squash, tomato, garlic, salt, & pepper. Elevate the heat to medium-high & cook uncovered, till the squash is tender, about seven

minutes more. Toss the greens frequently. The combination will become juicy after which start to dry. Stir in the the basil & parsley. Keep warm over low heat.

3. To cook the polenta, bring the broth/stock & salt to a boil in a medium-size saucepan. Drizzle in the cornmeal very slowly, whisking all of the whereas with a wire whisk. Turn the heat to low & cook the polenta, whisking repeatedly, till it turns into like soft mashed potatoes, about five minutes. Whisk in the butter & cheese. Spoon a mound of polenta on each serving & top with among the greens.

VEGETABLE TAGINE

SERVES four generously
The Stew:
three tablespoons olive oil

one **medium onion, minced**

three garlic cloves, minced

two **teaspoons ground cumin**

one **teaspoon ground ginger**

1½ teaspoons paprika

½ teaspoon turmeric

¼ teaspoon cinnamon

⅛ teaspoon cayenne pepper

1½ cups canned crushed tomatoes or tomato puree

two **cups water**

⅛ teaspoon crushed saffron

one **carrot, thinly sliced**

one **sweet potato, peeled & cut into ½-inch dice**

two **cups diced green beans**

¼ cup raisins

½ teaspoon salt

l (15-ounce) can chickpeas, rinsed in a strainer

one zucchini, cut lengthwise into sixths & diced

The Couscous:
2¼ cups water

two tablespoons unsalted butter

½ teaspoon salt

1½ cups couscous

1. Heat the oil in a big stockpot over medium heat. Add the onion & garlic, & sauté till the onion begins to melt, about five minutes. Sprinkle in all of the spices & sauté two minutes, stirring often.
2. Mix in the tomatoes, water, saffron, carrot, sweet potato, beans, raisins, & salt. Bring the combination to a boil. Cover the pot, lower the heat to a simmer, & cook 20 minutes, or till the sweet potatoes are tender. Stir often.
3. Mix in the chickpeas & zucchini, cover the pot, & cook 10 minutes, or till the zucchini is tender. At this level check the consistency of the sauce. If it appears too watery, cook uncovered a couple of minutes to thicken it.
4. To make the couscous, mix the water, butter, & salt in a medium-size saucepan & bring to a boil. Stir in the couscous, cover the pot, & take away from the heat. Let sit 10 minutes to soak up all of the liquid. Fluff with a fork before serving. Place a portion of couscous in the middle of every serving plate & top with a mound of greens.

COUSCOUS TOPPED WITH ZUCCHINI

SERVES four
two tablespoons olive oil

one medium onion, very finely diced

four garlic cloves, minced

one **green bell pepper, cut into ½-inch dice**

two **small to medium zucchini, quartered lengthwise & thinly sliced**

one **(14-ounce) can prepared-cut diced tomatoes**

½ teaspoon dried oregano

Generous grating fresh pepper

one **cup frozen corn**

1½ cups vegetable broth/stock (store-purchased or selfmade), or water

one **tablespoon unsalted butter**

½ teaspoon salt (or much less if the broth/stock is salty)

one **cup couscous**

½ cup finely crumbled feta cheese (optional)

1. Heat the oil in a big skillet over medium heat. Add the onion & garlic, & sauté, stirring often, for five minutes. Add the green pepper & cook five minutes. Add the zucchini, toss well, & sauté five minutes. Stir the combination often.
2. Stir in the tomatoes with their juice, oregano, & pepper. Simmer the greens, uncovered, till the zucchini is tender & the juices have thickened slightly. Stir in the corn & keep warm over low heat. (You can prepare the combination thus far up to eight hours upfront. To reheat, add a few tablespoons of water to create a little bit of sauce.)
3. To cook the couscous, bring the broth/stock or water to a boil in a medium-size saucepan. Add the butter & salt, stir, then mix in the couscous. Cover the pan & take away it from the heat. Let the couscous sit five minutes. Fluff with a fork cover once more, & let sit a couple of minutes more.
4. Serve a mound of couscous on each serving plate & top with the vegetable combination. Sprinkle some feta cheese on each serving, if desired.

BULGUR & GREENS

SERVES three–four AS A MAIN COURSE
⅓ cup olive oil

two **large onions, finely diced**

six **garlic cloves, minced**

three scallions, very thinly sliced, divided

¼ teaspoon crushed red pepper flakes

1¼ cups coarse bulgur

one **cup water**

¼ teaspoon salt

one **pound (about 1½ bags) prewashed fresh spinach, stems removed & leaves torn into small pieces, or one pound Swiss chard, stems diced & leaves finely chopped (keep stems & leaves separate)**

1. Heat the oil in a big (three-quart) saucepan over medium heat. Add the onions, garlic, all but two tablespoons scallions, & the crushed red pepper flakes (and Swiss chard stems if utilizing) & sauté 10 minutes, or till the onions start to melt.
2. Add the remaining ingredients (besides the reserved two tablespoons scallions), stuffing the spinach or Swiss chard leaves on top. Cover the pot tightly, lower the heat to a simmer, & cook half-hour. Remove the cover often & stir to distribute the greens. Remove the pot from the heat & let sit undisturbed for 10 minutes so all of the liquid will get absorbed. Serve with a sprinkling of the reserved scallions on top of every serving.

BRAISED WHITE BEANS WITH TOMATOES, ZUCCHINI, & GARLIC

SERVES four

¼ **cup olive oil**

six **garlic cloves, minced**

¼ **teaspoon crushed red pepper flakes**

one **(14-ounce) can prepared-cut diced tomatoes**

¼ **cup water**

two **medium boiling (all-purpose) potatoes, peeled & cut into ½-inch dice**

two **small to medium zucchini, quartered lengthwise & thinly sliced**

two **(14-ounce) cans small white beans, such as Nice Northern or navy,** rinsed well in a strainer

¼ **teaspoon dried rosemary, crumbled**

Salt

1. Heat the oil in a big skillet over medium heat. Stir in the garlic & red pepper flakes, & cook 1–2 minutes, or till the garlic is very tender but under no circumstances coloured. Stir in the tomatoes, water, & potatoes, & cover the pan. Cook at a vigorous simmer for quarter-hour, or till the potatoes are almost cooked through.
2. Mix in the zucchini, beans, rosemary, & salt. Cover the pan once more & cook, stirring often, 10 minutes more, or till the zucchini & potatoes are tender. At this level check the consistency of the sauce; it must be thick & soupy, not dry or watery. Add a little bit of water if the combination doesn't have much sauce; cook it uncovered if the juices appear watery. Serve in large pasta bowls, preferably, or on plates.

BRAISED WHITE BEANS

SERVES three–four
¼ **cup olive oil**

six **garlic cloves, minced**

one **pound (1 head) escarole, well washed & torn into small pieces (see Tip)** two **tablespoons water**

two **(14-ounce) cans small white beans, such as Nice Northern or navy, rinsed well in a strainer**

two **teaspoons balsamic vinegar**

Salt to taste

Generous seasoning freshly ground black pepper

1. Heat the oil in a big skillet over medium heat. Mix in the garlic & cook about 30 seconds, or till scorching & aromatic but under no circumstances coloured. Add handfuls of the escarole, tossing it with the garlic after each addition. (Utilizing tongs may be useful right here.) Pour in the water & cover the pan. Cook the escarole, tossing often, till wilted & tender, about five minutes.
2. Remove the cover & stir in the beans, vinegar, salt, & pepper. Cook uncovered, till the escarole is very tender & the juices have thickened slightly. You need the ultimate dish to have a sauciness but not be soupy. Check the liquid at this level; add more water if the combination is dry, or cook a bit longer if there may be an excessive amount of liquid. Don't stir the beans an excessive amount of, or they may break up & trigger the combination to become a bit pasty. Serve in pasta bowls with some crusty bread.

RED BEANS & RICE

SERVES four
two **tablespoons olive oil**

two **medium onions, finely diced**

two **large garlic cloves, minced**

one **green pepper, finely diced**

one **tablespoon chili powder**

one **teaspoon paprika**

one **cup tomato sauce**

¼ **cup water**

A few dashes hot sauce (such as Tabasco)

two **(15-ounce) cans kidney beans, rinsed well in a strainer**

four cups hot cooked rice (from one cup raw rice)

Sour cream (optional)

1. Heat the oil in a big skillet over medium heat. Add the onions, garlic, & green pepper, & sauté till the pepper is very tender, about 10 minutes.
2. Sprinkle in the chili powder & paprika, & cook 30 seconds. Mix in the tomato sauce, water, hot sauce, & kidney beans, & simmer about 10 minutes, or till the combination is hot & aromatic. Serve over rice with a small spoonful of sour cream on top, if desired.

TIP: To provide the beans a smoky flavor you can add one small chipotle pepper in adobo sauce. Mince it on a small plate with two knives before adding it to the beans. Omit the hot sauce.

VEGETABLE FRIED RICE

SERVES four AS A MAIN COURSE
one **teaspoon plus three tablespoons canola oil**

two **large eggs, well beaten**

eight ounces extra-firm tofu, cut into ½-inch cubes & patted very dry

one **teaspoon minced fresh ginger**

two **celery ribs, thinly sliced**

four scallions, very thinly sliced

six **cups cold, cooked long-grain brown rice (constituted of two cups raw rice & 3¾ cups water)**

¼ **cup tamari soy sauce**

two **tablespoons Asian sesame oil**

two **cups bean sprouts**

1. Heat one teaspoon canola oil in a big, preferably nonstick, skillet over medium-high heat. Pour in the eggs & scramble a couple of minutes. Let the eggs set right into a pancake & cook about 20 seconds, then flip over & cook a few more seconds on this side. Slide onto a big plate & cut into shreds. Put aside.
2. Heat two more tablespoons canola oil in the skillet and, when hot, add the tofu. Stir-fry till golden throughout. Slide onto a plate & put aside.
3. Heat the remaining tablespoon canola oil in the skillet. Add the ginger & celery, & sauté five minutes. Add the scallions & cook 30 seconds.
4. Break up the rice if it's in clumps & add to the skillet. Toss well. Drizzle on the soy sauce & sesame oil, & mix very completely.
5. Stir in the tofu, egg, & bean sprouts. Toss gently & heat through, about five minutes. Serve instantly or let cool & reheat.

CURRIED RICE & VEGETABLE PILAF COOKED IN COCONUT MILK

SERVES four GENEROUSLY
three tablespoons canola oil

one **large onion, minced**

one **large boiling potato (such as red-skinned), peeled & cut into ½-inch dice**

1½ **cups basmati or other long-grain white rice such as transformed rice**

two **carrots, cut into ¼-inch dice**

two **garlic cloves, minced**

one **tablespoon minced fresh ginger**

¼ teaspoon turmeric

½ teaspoon ground cardamom

½ teaspoon ground cumin

⅛ teaspoon ground cloves

⅛ teaspoon cayenne pepper

one **(14-ounce) can coconut milk**

1½ cups water (roughly)

¾ teaspoon salt

½ cup roasted cashews (salted or unsalted)

one **cup frozen peas, thawed**

one **tablespoon finely chopped mint or cilantro (optional)**

1. Heat the oil in a stockpot over medium heat. Add the onion & potato, & sauté 10 minutes, stirring often.
2. Stir in the rice, carrots, & all of the spices, & mix well. Sauté two minutes to toast the spices, stirring constantly.
3. Mix the coconut milk with enough water to make three cups of liquid. Pour into the rice combination & sprinkle in the salt. Cover the pot, bring the combination to a boil, then lower the heat to a delicate simmer. Cook undisturbed till all of the liquid is absorbed, about 25 minutes.
4. Turn off the heat under the pot & gently stir in the cashews & peas. Cover the pot once more & let the rice rest 10 minutes. Serve sprinkled with mint or cilantro.

MUSHROOM & PEPPER BURRITOS

MAKES four LARGE BURRITOS
four large (10-inch) flour tortillas

one **tablespoon olive oil**

one **red bell pepper, halved & thinly sliced**

one **green bell pepper, halved & thinly sliced**

one **pound (6 cups) thinly sliced mushrooms**

¼ teaspoon dried oregano

Salt to taste

Freshly ground black pepper

⅓ cup salsa, either Cooked Tomato-Chipotle Salsa or store-purchased

½ cupsour cream

one **cup grated Monterey Jack cheese with jalapeño peppers**

1. Heat the tortillas utilizing one of many strategies.
2. Heat the oil in a big skillet over medium heat. Add the peppers & cover the pan. Sauté, tossing often, till they become soft & start to brown, about 10 minutes.
3. Mix in the mushrooms, oregano, salt, & pepper, & cook uncovered, till the mushrooms have released their juices they usually have evaporated. When done, the mushrooms might be brown & can start to stay to the pan. Stir in the salsa & take away the pan from the heat. Let cool a bit before filling the burritos.
4. To serve, spoon ¼ of the mushroom combination alongside the middle of the tortilla. Top with ¼ of the sour cream & ¼ of the cheese. Fold in the sides, then roll up the tortilla. Repeat with the remaining ingredients.

LEMON ALMOND CAKE

MAKES sixteen SERVINGS
12 tablespoons (1½ sticks) unsalted butter, very soft, plus extra for greasing

1½ cups sugar

Grated zest of two lemons

three large eggs, at room temperature

½ teaspoon vanilla extract

1½ cups unbleached flour

½ cup finely ground almonds (from ⅓ cup whole almonds)

1½ teaspoons baking powder

½ teaspoon salt

⅔ cup low-fat milk

Lemon Syrup:
⅓ cup lemon juice (1½ lemons)

½ cup sugar

Confectioners' sugar for dusting

1. Preheat the oven to 350 degrees. Butter & flour a 9-inch springform pan.
2. Mix the butter, sugar, & lemon zest in a big bowl. Use an electrical mixer to beat the combination till smooth & well blended. Add the eggs & vanilla, & beat till pale & fluffy, at the very least two minutes.
3. Completely mix the flour, almonds, baking powder, & salt in a medium-size bowl. Add to the butter combination & beat a few seconds, then pour in the milk. Beat 30 seconds or so just till well combined. Scrape the batter into the prepared pan.
4. Bake fifty five minutes, or till a knife inserted in the middle of the cake comes out clean. Cool on a wire rack for 10 minutes, then remove the outer rim of the pan. Invert the cake onto a plate, remove the bottom of the pan, then invert once more, proper side up, onto the rack.
5. To make the syrup, mix the lemon juice & sugar in a small saucepan. Heat, stirring often, just till the syrup is hot & the sugar has dissolved. Don't let it boil.
6. Utilizing a pastry brush, brush the syrup throughout the cake. It should appear as if there's quite a lot of syrup, but the cake will take up all of it. Slide the cake onto an

ornamental plate & let cool completely, a minimum of two hours. Just before serving use a sieve to sprinkle some confectioners' sugar throughout the top of the cake.

UPSIDE-DOWN PEAR GINGERBREAD

SERVES eight

The Topping:
four tablespoons (½ stick) unsalted butter

½ cupfirmly packed light or dark brown sugar

two **ripe but firm pears, preferably Bosc or Anjou**

The Cake:
one **cup unbleached flour**

one **teaspoon baking soda**

¼ teaspoon salt

two **teaspoons cinnamon**

one **teaspoon ground ginger**

½ teaspoon ground cloves

one **egg**

½ cup firmly packed light or dark brown sugar

⅓ cup unsulfured molasses

½ cup sour milk (see Tip)

four tablespoons melted butter

Lightly sweetened whipped cream (preferably spiked with rum)

1. Preheat the oven to 350 degrees. Butter the sides of a 9-inch spherical cake pan (not a spring-form pan).
2. To organize the topping, melt the butter in a small saucepan. Add the brown sugar & stir together till blended. Scrape into the cake pan & spread evenly.
3. Peel & slice each pear into quarters; remove & discard the cores. Slice each quarter into three slices. Arrange the 24 slices evenly across the pan.
4. To make the cake, in a big bowl mix the flour, baking soda, salt, cinnamon, ginger, & cloves. In a separate bowl beat together the egg, brown sugar, molasses, sour milk, & melted butter. Scrape into the flour combination & mix till well blended.
5. Pour the batter over the pears. Bake half-hour, or till a knife inserted in the middle of the cake comes out clean. Cool on a wire rack for 10 minutes, then invert onto a plate. Serve slightly warm or at room temperature with the whipped cream.

UPSIDE-DOWN CARAMELIZED APPLE CAKE

SERVES eight
four tablespoons (½ stick) unsalted butter, plus extra for greasing

½ cupfirmly packed light brown sugar

¼ teaspoon cinnamon

Dash nutmeg

2½ cups thinly sliced apples, such as Cortland, Macintosh, or Macoun (about three small apples)

The Cake:
six **tablespoons unsalted butter, very soft**

one **cup sugar**

two **eggs, at room temperature**

one **teaspoon vanilla extract**

one **cup unbleached flour**

three tablespoons cornmeal

one **teaspoon baking powder**

½ **teaspoon salt**

½ **cupmilk**

1. Preheat the oven to 350 degrees. Lightly butter the sides of a 9-inch cake pan (not a springform pan).
2. Mix the butter, sugar, cinnamon, & nutmeg in a small saucepan & boil 30 seconds. Scrape the combination into the prepared pan & spread evenly. Sprinkle the apples throughout & press them down slightly to degree them.
3. To make the cake, beat the butter & sugar with an electrical mixer till creamy. Add the eggs & vanilla, & beat till very smooth & fluffy, about two minutes.
4. Sprinkle in the flour, cornmeal, baking powder, & salt, & beat 10 seconds. Pour in the milk & beat just till the batter is evenly moistened, about one minute. Spoon the batter over the apples & smooth the top.
5. Bake 50 minutes, or till a knife inserted in the middle of the cake comes out dry. Run a knife alongside the outer fringe of the cake to loosen it from the pan. Place a plate over the cake, then flip it over to invert the cake onto the plate. Let the cake cool completely before serving.

BLUEBERRY CAKE

SERVES eight
two **cups unbleached flour**

two **teaspoons baking powder**

½ **teaspoon salt**

two **cups fresh blueberries, picked over, rinsed, & patted very dry, or** *unthawed* **frozen blueberries (if frozen, preferably small wild berries)**

eight tablespoons (1 stick) unsalted butter, very soft

1¼ **cups sugar**

two **large eggs, at room temperature**

one **teaspoon vanilla extract**

½ teaspoon almond extract

1⅓ cups milk, at room temperature

The Glaze:
¾ cup confectioners' sugar

three—four teaspoons warm water

½ teaspoon almond extract

1. Preheat the oven to 350 degrees. Butter & flour a 9-inch springform pan.
2. Whisk together the flour, baking powder, & salt in a medium-size bowl. With a spoon or rubber spatula gently fold in the blueberries to coat them evenly.
3. Use an electrical mixer in a big bowl to cream the butter & sugar till light & considerably creamy. Add the eggs & the vanilla & almond extracts, & beat till very fluffy, no less than three minutes. Add the milk & beat till blended. (If the milk is cold when added, it is going to in all probability trigger the batter to curdle. This is not going to hurt the cake.)
4. Use a rubber spatula to mix the flour combination & the wet combination till evenly blended. Scrape the batter into the prepared pan.
5. Bake sixty five minutes, or till a knife inserted in the cake comes out clean. Cool the cake on a wire rack for 10 minutes, then remove the skin rim. Place a big plate on top of the cake & invert. Remove the bottom of the pan & invert the cake onto one other plate. Let cool completely, at the least two hours.
6. To make the glaze, mix the confectioners' sugar, three teaspoons water, & the almond extract in a small bowl. Beat completely with a fork till smooth. Add a bit more water if necessary to realize the consistency of honey. Use the tines of the fork to drizzle the glaze throughout the top & a little bit down the sides of the cake. Let harden before cutting the cake, a minimum of 20 minutes. In case you make the cake a day upfront, store covered at room temperature.

LEMON POPPY SEED CAKE

SERVES 12–sixteen

2½ cups unbleached flour

1½ teaspoons baking powder

one **teaspoon baking soda**

¾ teaspoon salt

three tablespoons poppy seeds

sixteen tablespoons (2 sticks) unsalted butter, very soft

1¾ cups sugar

Zest of two lemons

four large eggs

1¼ cups buttermilk, or plain yogurt thinned with a little milk

Confectioners' sugar

1.
   Preheat the oven to 350 degrees. Generously butter & flour a Bundt pan or other 10-cup tube pan.
2. In a medium-size bowl totally mix the flour, baking powder, baking soda, salt, & poppy seeds.
3. In a big mixing bowl beat the butter with an electrical mixer till soft & creamy. Add the sugar & zest, & beat till well blended & smooth, not less than two minutes. Add the eggs & beat till very fluffy, one other two minutes. Beat in half the flour, then half the buttermilk then repeat, beating till the batter is smooth. Scrape down the sides of the bowl as necessary.
4. Pour the batter into the prepared pan & give the pan a thump on the counter to remove any air pockets.
5. Bake forty five–50 minutes, or till a knife inserted in the middle of the cake comes out clean. Cool 10 minutes on a wire rack then invert the cake onto the rack & take away the pan. Let cool completely before utilizing a sieve to cover the cake with a heavy dusting of confectioners' sugar.

COCONUT CAKE

SERVES 6–9
1½ cups unbleached flour

1½ teaspoons baking powder

¼ teaspoon salt

eight tablespoons (1 stick) unsalted butter, very soft, plus extra for greasing

one **cup sugar**

two **large eggs**

1½ teaspoons vanilla extract

¼ teaspoon almond extract

¾ cup milk

1¼ cups sweetened coconut

Coconut Buttercream Icing:
six **tablespoons unsalted butter, very soft**

one **cup confectioners' sugar**

four–5 tablespoons milk

¾ cup sweetened coconut, divided

1. Preheat the oven to 350 degrees. Butter an eight × eight-inch sq. cake pan.
2. Completely mix the flour, baking powder, & salt in a medium-size bowl.
3. Use an electrical mixer in a big bowl to beat the butter & sugar together till thoroughly blended. Add the egg & vanilla & almond extracts, & beat till light & fluffy. Scrape down the sides of the bowl as necessary.

4. Sprinkle in half of the flour combination & pour in half of the milk Beat till blended. Repeat with the remaining flour & milk Stir in the coconut.
5. Scrape the batter into the prepared pan. Bake forty–forty five minutes, or till a knife inserted in the middle of the cake comes out clean. Cool completely on a wire rack at the very least two hours.
6. To make the butter-cream, mix the butter & confectioners' sugar in a big bowl & beat with an electrical mixer till considerably blended; will probably be crumbly. Add the milk & beat just till fluffy, about one minute. (The icing could look a bit curdled, but it is going to look fine once spread on the cake.) Stir in a ½ cup coconut.
7. When the cake is cool, spread the icing on top. Sprinkle the remaining ¼ cup coconut throughout the top.

CHEESECAKE

SERVES 12–sixteen
The Crust:
Butter for greasing

six **whole graham crackers (12 halves)**

¼ teaspoon cinnamon

three tablespoons melted butter

The Filling:
1½ pounds cream cheese (three eight-ounce packages), at room temperature

1¼ cups sugar

one **tablespoon vanilla extract**

three large eggs, at room temperature

The Topping:
one **(sixteen-ounce) container sour cream**

three tablespoons sugar

one **teaspoon vanilla extract**

1. Preheat the oven to 350 degrees. Butter the bottom of a 9-inch springform pan.
2. Place the graham crackers in a plastic bag & seal. Use a rolling pin to roll the crackers till they're crushed into fine crumbs. You need to get nearly ¾ cup crumbs. Pour the crumbs right into a bowl, toss with the cinnamon, then pour on the melted butter. Mix till evenly moistened. Lightly press the crumbs onto the bottom of the springform pan.
3. To make the filling, beat the cream cheese in the bowl of an electrical mixer till smooth. Mix in the sugar & beat once more till smooth. Add the vanilla & one egg. Beat at low speed just till included. Beat in the two remaining eggs one after the other just till mixed. Pour the filling into the prepared pan & give the pan a thump on the counter to remove any air pockets.
4. Place the pan on a baking sheet & bake forty five minutes. The cheesecake will still be considerably jiggly in the middle & lightly golden on top when faraway from the oven.
5. Mix the topping ingredients together & gently spread over the top of the cheesecake. Return the pan to the oven & bake 10 minutes more. Cool the cheesecake on a wire rack till it's room temperature, no less than four hours. Slide a knife across the edges, then remove the sides of the pan. Loosely cover the cheesecake & refrigerate it overnight. Cut into thin wedges & serve.

WHITE CHOCOLATE & RASPBERRY CHEESECAKE

SERVES 12–sixteen
The Crust:
Butter for greasing

six **whole graham crackers (12 halves)**

¼ teaspoon cinnamon

three tablespoons butter, melted

The Filling:
six **ounces white chocolate (either morsels or finely chopped bars)**

259

1½ pounds cream cheese, at room temperature

one **cup sugar**

one **tablespoon unbleached flour**

four eggs, at room temperature

one **teaspoon vanilla extract**

one **cup fresh or partially thawed frozen raspberries, plus extra for garnish**

The Topping:
one **(sixteen-ounce) container sour cream**

two **tablespoons sugar**

½ teaspoon vanilla extract

1. Preheat the oven to 350 degrees. Butter the bottom & sides of a 9-inch springform pan.
2. Place the graham crackers in a plastic bag & seal. Use a rolling pin to roll the crackers till they're crushed into fine crumbs. It's best to get about ¾ cup crumbs. Pour the crumbs right into a bowl, toss with the cinnamon, then pour on the melted butter. Mix till evenly moistened. Lightly press the crumbs onto the bottom of the springform pan.
3. Place the white chocolate in a small heavy-bottomed saucepan over low heat. Stir constantly till about half melted. Remove the pan from the heat & stir till melted & smooth. Be affected person & cautious; white chocolate doesn't like high heat. In the bowl of an electrical mixer beat the cream cheese & sugar till smooth. Add the white chocolate & flour, & beat just till included.
4. Add the eggs one after the other, beating after each addition. Beat in the vanilla.
5. Pour ⅔ of the filling into the prepared pan. Carefully place the raspberries throughout the top. Gently pour on the remaining filling.
6. Place the pan on a baking sheet & bake 50 minutes. It's going to still be jiggly in the middle & a pale golden color on top when faraway from the oven.
7. Mix the topping ingredients together & gently spread over the top of the cheesecake. Return the pan to the oven & bake 10 minutes more. Cool the cheesecake on a wire rack till room temperature, at the least four hours. Slide a knife across the edges, then remove the sides of the pan. Loosely cover the cheesecake & refrigerate it overnight. Cut into thin wedges & serve.

STRAWBERRY-RHUBARB TART

SERVES eight
Walnut Crust:
⅔ **cup walnuts**

three tablespoons sugar

six **tablespoons unsalted butter, very soft**

one **egg yolk**

½ **teaspoon vanilla extract**

one **cup unbleached flour**

The Filling:
one **pound rhubarb, thinly sliced (three cups)**

one **pint strawberries, sliced**

one **cup sugar**

¼ **cup flour**

½ **teaspoon cinnamon**

1. Butter the sides & bottom of a 9-inch tart pan with a detachable bottom or a glass pie plate.
2. Mix the walnuts & sugar in a food processor & process till very fine. Cease the machine & add all of the remaining crust ingredients. Process just till evenly moistened & crumbly. (In case you don't have a food processor, grind the nuts & sugar in a blender till fine. Pour them into a big bowl & use an electrical mixer to combine in the remaining crust ingredients.) Scatter the combination throughout the pie pan & press it into the sides & bottom with your fingers. (It's simpler to do the sides first.) Chill no less than half-hour, or till very firm.
3. Preheat the oven to four hundred degrees.

4. Mix the filling ingredients in a big bowl. Let sit for at the least 20 minutes, stirring often, so the juices can moisten the sugar. Scrape the combination into the chilled crust & smooth over the top.

5. Place the pie pan on a baking sheet & bake forty five minutes, or till the crust is golden & the filling is bubbling hot. Midway through the cooking time use a big spoon to flatten the top of the filling; this may also moisten it for even cooking. In case your tart pan has a detachable rim, cool the pie five minutes before eradicating it. Cool the tart completely on a wire rack no less than three hours, before slicing.

STRAWBERRY & CHOCOLATE PIZZA

SERVES eight–10
The Crust:
eight tablespoons (1 stick) unsalted butter, very soft

one **cup unbleached flour**

½ cup very finely chopped pecans or almonds

¼ cup sugar

two **tablespoons water**

The Topping:
one **cup semisweet chocolate chips**

one **(eight-ounce) package cream cheese (regular or Neufchâtel), at room temperature**

½ cup confectioners' sugar

one **pint fresh strawberries, stems removed & halved**

¼ cup apricot preserves, apple jelly, or red currant jelly

one **teaspoon water**

1. Preheat the oven to 375 degrees. Lightly butter a 10-inch springform pan.

2. To make the crust, place all of the ingredients in a big bowl & use an electrical mixer to beat them together just till blended into even, moist crumbs. Don't overheat. Sprinkle the dough in the springform pan & press it down with your fingers to form a flat crust. Bake 15–20 minutes, or till lightly golden.
3. Instantly scatter the chocolate chips over the hot crust. Let sit five minutes. Use a spatula to spread the melted chocolate throughout the crust & to the outer edges. Remove the outer ring of the pan & let the crust cool completely on a wire rack, about one hour. If the chocolate shouldn't be hard at this level, you can chill the crust for quarter-hour or so. When cool, use a spatula to lift the crust off the pan & place it on a big, flat plate or simply leave it on the bottom.
4. Use an electrical mixer or wire whisk to beat the cream cheese & confectioners' sugar together till blended. Spread throughout the crust, leaving a 1-inch border of chocolate displaying.
5. Place the strawberry halves in concentric circles on the cream cheese.
6. Heat the preserves or jelly with the water in a saucepan till hot, stirring all of the whereas to mix the combination. Use a pastry brush to dab among the glaze on each strawberry half. Chill a minimum of one hour or up to 24 hours before serving. Slide the "pizza" onto a cutting board & cut in half utilizing a very large knife, then cut into wedges. Serve on plates & maintain it in your hands to eat.

LEMON TART

SERVES eight
The Crust:
¼ cup whole almonds

one **cup unbleached flour**

three tablespoons sugar

six **tablespoons unsalted butter, cut into bits**

one **tablespoon canola oil**

three tablespoons ice water

¼ teaspoon almond extract

The Filling:
six **large eggs**

¾ cup sugar

Zest of one lemon

½ cup fresh lemon juice (about three lemons) six tablespoons unsalted butter, cut into bits

1. To make the crust, grind the almonds in a blender or food processor till very fine. Pour right into a medium-size bowl & stir in the flour & sugar. Drop in the butter bits & toss to coat with the flour. Rub the butter into the flour with your fingertips till coarse crumbs form.
2. Mix the oil, water, & almond extract in a small bowl. Drizzle over the flour combination & stir with a fork till moistened. Collect the combination right into a ball & knead one or two times. Form right into a ball once more, then flatten right into a disk. Wrap in plastic & chill 20 minutes.
3. Lightly flour a piece surface. Roll the dough into an eleven-inch circle & use to line a 9-inch tart pan with a detachable bottom. Prick throughout with a fork. Cover with plastic & chill not less than half-hour or freeze 20 minutes.
4. Preheat the oven to four hundred degrees.
5. Line the pastry with aluminum foil & fill with pie weights, dried beans, or rice. Bake 10 minutes. Remove the foil & beans, & bake five minutes more. Let cool. Lower the oven heat to 350 degrees.
6. To make the filling, add about one inch of water to the bottom a part of a double boiler; you don't need the water to the touch the bottom of the top pan. Place over medium heat. Whisk the eggs in a big bowl till very smooth. Whisk in the sugar, lemon zest, & lemon juice. Stir in the butter. Pour into the top of the double boiler and, whisking continually, cook till the combination is the consistency of thick heavy cream, about eight minutes. Don't let the combination boil.
7. Instantly pour the filling into the pie shell. Bake 17–20 minutes, or simply till the edges are slightly set & the middle remains to be jiggly. Cool on a wire rack till room temperature, then chill till prepared to serve. The tart needs to be served cool or cold.

RHUBARB COBBLER

SERVES 6–eight
The Filling:
eight cups diced rhubarb (2¼ pounds)

1¼ cups sugar

two **teaspoons cornstarch**

two **tablespoons unsalted butter**

two **tablespoons orange juice**

½ **teaspoon cinnamon**

¼ **teaspoon ground cloves**

The Biscuit Topping:
¾ **cup unbleached flour**

¼ **cup plus one tablespoon sugar**

1¼ **teaspoons baking powder**

½ **teaspoon salt**

three tablespoons unsalted butter, chilled

one **egg yolk**

¼ **cup milk**

½ **teaspoon vanilla extract**

¼ **teaspoon almond extract**

Vanilla ice cream (optional)

1. Preheat the oven to 375 degrees. Place an eight × eight-inch baking pan or related shallow 2-quart baking dish close by.
2. Mix all of the filling ingredients in a medium-size saucepan & bring to a boil. Lower the heat to a energetic simmer & cook the filling, stirring frequently, for about 10 minutes, or till the rhubarb is very tender. Pour the filling into the baking pan.

3. To make the topping, mix the flour, ¼ cup sugar, baking powder, & salt in a medium-size bowl. Cut the butter into bits & rub it into the flour with your fingertips till little pellets form.
4. In a small bowl stir together the egg yolk, milk, & vanilla & almond extracts. Pour into the flour combination & stir with a fork. Scrape the dough onto a lightly floured work surface & knead a few times. Use a rolling pin to roll the dough the same size because the top of the baking dish. Lightly flour the dough as necessary; it shouldn't be in any respect sticky. Drape the dough onto the rolling pin & unroll it onto the filling. Sprinkle the top with the remaining tablespoon of sugar.
5. Bake 25 minutes, then cool on a wire rack. Serve warm with vanilla ice cream, if desired.

BLUEBERRY CRISP

SERVES four–6
one **quart fresh blueberries, picked over, washed, & well-drained, or 2(12-ounce) packages frozen blueberries, preferably small wild ones**

¼ cupfirmly packed light brown sugar

one **tablespoon Grand Marnier (optional but extremely advisable)**

one **tablespoon unbleached flour for fresh berries or 1½ tablespoons flour for frozen berries**

The Topping:
½ cup unbleached flour

¼ cup quick or regular oats

½ cup firmly packed light brown sugar

½ teaspoon cinnamon

four tablespoons chilled unsalted butter, cut into bits

Vanilla ice cream (optional)

1. Preheat the oven to 375 degrees.

2. Place the blueberries in a shallow 1½-quart baking dish. Sprinkle on the sugar, Grand Marnier, & flour, & toss to coat the berries evenly.
3. To make the topping, mix together the flour, oats, sugar, & cinnamon in a medium-size bowl. Drop in the butter bits, toss, then rub them into the flour combination with your fingertips till a texture resembling coarse crumbs forms. Sprinkle this throughout the berries.
4. Bake forty–forty five minutes for fresh berries, forty five–50 minutes if utilizing frozen berries. When done, the crisp can be golden brown on top & bubbly on the sides. Let cool on a wire rack to room temperature. Serve small parts with a scoop of vanilla ice cream, if desired.

PEACH & RASPBERRY CRISP

SERVES six (eight IF ACCOMPANIED BY VANILLA ICE CREAM)
two ½ **pounds (about 9) barely ripe peaches**

one **cup fresh or unthawed frozen raspberries**

three tablespoons firmly packed light brown sugar

two **tablespoons unbleached flour**

The Topping:
½ **cup unbleached flour**

½ **cup firmly packed light brown sugar**

½ **teaspoon cinnamon**

¼ **teaspoon salt**

four tablespoons (½ stick) chilled unsalted butter, cut into bits

three tablespoons finely chopped pecans

1. Preheat the oven to 375 degrees.
2. Bring a medium-size saucepan stuffed midway with water to a boil. Drop in a few peaches & let sit 10 seconds. Remove instantly & let cool a couple of minutes. With a

small, sharp knife peel off the skin. Repeat with the remaining peaches. Cut the peaches into small chunks & place in an eight × eight-inch pan or other shallow 1½-quart baking dish.

3. Sprinkle the raspberries, brown sugar, & flour over the peaches & toss lightly.
4. To make the topping, mix the flour, brown sugar, cinnamon, & salt in a medium-size bowl. Drop in the butter bits & rub the butter into the combination with your fingertips to form small, moist crumbs. Stir in the pecans. Sprinkle throughout the peaches.
5. Bake forty–forty five minutes, or till the top is golden & the filling boils vigorously. Cool completely on a wire rack before serving.

SEMOLINA PUDDING

SERVES 6–eight
three large navel oranges

two **cups milk**

⅓ cup plus three tablespoons sugar

⅓ cup semolina or farina (see Tip)

two **egg yolks**

½ teaspoon vanilla extract

Oil for greasing

one **cup heavy cream, well chilled**

two **tablespoons Grand Marnier, Triple Sec, or other orange liqueur**

The Sauce:
⅔ cup orange juice (squeezed from the above oranges)

⅓ cup sugar

one **tablespoon cornstarch**

one **tablespoon unsalted butter, cut into bits**

two **tablespoons Grand Marnier, Triple Sec, or other orange liqueur**

1. Grate the zest from one of the oranges & scrape it right into a medium-size heavy-bottomed saucepan. Whisk in the milk & ⅓ cup sugar & bring to a boil, whisking often. Turn the heat to medium-low & slowly whisk in the semolina. Cook whisking continually, for five minutes, or till the combination is like creamy mashed potatoes. Remove the pan from the heat & whisk in the egg yolks & vanilla. Scrape the semolina into a big bowl & cool 20 minutes, whisking often.
2. In the meantime, totally oil a 1-quart ring mould or other 1-quart mildew, deep dish, or bowl.
3. Whip the cream with the remaining three tablespoons sugar till stiff. Whisk the Grand Marnier into the semolina combination till smooth. Carefully mix in half of the whipped cream to lighten the combination, then use a rubber spatula to fold in the remaining cream just till no streaks present.
4. Spoon the pudding into the mildew & smooth the top. Give the mould a few thumps on the counter to be certain there aren't any air pockets. Cover with plastic wrap & chill for not less than two hours or up to eight hours.
5. In the meantime, make the sauce. With a pointy paring knife cut the white pith off the orange that was grated & your complete peel off one of many remaining oranges. Over a bowl cut the sections from the oranges by slicing down on either side of each part, releasing them from the membranes. Let the sections fall into the bowl as every one is freed, then squeeze the juices from the remaining membranes into the bowl.
6. Strain the juice right into a measuring cup; you need ⅔ cup. In case you don't have enough, you can squeeze the juice from *half* of the remaining orange; you will want the opposite half as a garnish. Put aside the orange sections.
7. In a small saucepan totally mix the sugar & cornstarch. Slowly whisk in the orange juice & cook over medium heat, stirring continuously with a rubber spatula, till the sauce is thick & clear, about five minutes. Don't let it boil. Remove from the heat & drop in the bits of butter. Stir till melted, then stir in the Grand Marnier. Pour right into a sauceboat & chill till cold, about one hour. (If the sauce will get too thick to pour easily, thin with a little bit of orange juice.)
8. Run a knife across the outer & inside edges of the pudding mould, place a platter over the mould, & invert the pudding onto the platter. With a slotted spoon remove the orange sections from their bowl & fill the middle of the pudding with them, or place across the outer fringe of the pudding. Cut the remaining orange into thin half-moon slices & enhance the edges of the pudding. Serve the pudding cut into wedges & topped with orange sections & a few sauce.

CHOCOLATE COOKIES

MAKES four DOZEN
two **cups unbleached flour**

one **teaspoon baking soda**

¾ **teaspoon salt**

12 **tablespoons (1½ sticks) unsalted butter, very soft**

one **cup sugar**

½ **cup firmly packed light brown sugar**

two **teaspoons vanilla extract**

two **large eggs**

three tablespoons milk

one **(sixteen-ounce) package (a generous 2½ cups) semisweet chocolate chips**

1. Mix the flour, baking soda, & salt in a medium-size bowl.
2. In a big bowl, utilizing an electrical mixer, beat the butter, sugar, brown sugar, & vanilla till mixed. Add the eggs & milk, & beat till light & fluffy. Pour in the flour combination & beat just till blended. Stir in the chocolate chips. Chill the dough one hour, or cover & chill up to four hours.
3. Preheat the oven to 350 degrees.
4. Scoop up a heaping teaspoonful of dough & roll it between the palms of your hands to form a ball. Place the balls of dough about two inches aside on an ungreased baking sheet & press lightly to flatten. Bake 10–12 minutes, or till lightly browned. Let sit one minute before transferring the cookies to a cooling rack. Cool completely before storing in a covered tin.

TIP: You should utilize this as a primary recipe & mess around with additions, such as white chocolate chips, chocolate chunks, chopped pecans, & walnuts.

GINGER COOKIES

MAKES 18–20 LARGE (3½-INCH) COOKIES
two **cups unbleached flour**

two **teaspoons baking soda**

one **tablespoon ground ginger**

one **teaspoon cinnamon**

½ **teaspoon ground cloves**

½ **teaspoon salt**

12 tablespoons (1½ sticks) unsalted butter, very soft, plus extra for greasing

one **cup firmly packed light brown sugar**

one **large egg**

¼ **cup unsulfiired molasses (such as Grandma's)**

¼ **cup sugar (roughly) for rolling**

1. In a medium-size bowl completely mix the flour, baking soda, ginger, cinnamon, cloves, & salt.
2. In a big bowl, utilizing an electrical mixer, cream the butter & sugar till smooth. Add the egg & molasses, & beat till well blended. Add the dry ingredients & beat just till mixed. (I exploit my hands at this level to knead the dough a few times & get it evenly moistened.) Cover & chill no less than one hour or up to four hours.
3. Preheat the oven to 350 degrees. Make sure that the oven rack is in the middle of the oven. Lightly butter a baking sheet. Place about ¼ cup sugar on a small plate.

4. Collect some dough & roll right into a ball about *1½* inches in diameter. Roll it in the sugar to completely coat it. Continue with more dough, inserting the balls about two inches aside on the baking sheet. It is possible for you to to suit about nine balls on a sheet.

5. Bake 15–17 minutes, or till cracked on top & golden on the edges. Wait two minutes before eradicating the cookies from the sheet. Cool completely on a wire rack. Store the cookies in zippered freezer bags.

CHOCOLATE-GLAZED ALMOND COOKIES

MAKES 1½ DOZEN
eight tablespoons (1 stick) unsalted butter, very soft

¾ cup sugar

one **large egg**

one **teaspoon almond extract**

½ cup finely ground almonds (from about ⅓ cup whole almonds)

¾ cup unbleached flour

½ cup sliced almonds

½ cup semisweet chocolate chips

1. Preheat the oven to 350 degrees. Be certain that the oven rack is in the middle of the oven.

2.In a big bowl, utilizing an electrical mixer, beat the butter & sugar till smooth. Add the egg & almond extract, & beat till well combined. Sprinkle in the ground almonds & flour, & beat just till mixed.

3. Set a cookie sheet in entrance of you. Place the sliced almonds in a small bowl. Use your hands to roll some dough right into a 1½-inch ball. Press it into the sliced almonds in order that one side will get coated with the nuts & flattens out considerably. Place the cookie, nut side up, on the baking sheet. Repeat with the dough to make 12 cookies. They need to be about two inches aside on the baking sheet.

4. Bake quarter-hour, or till golden brown on the edges. Remove the cookies from the baking sheet & cool on a wire rack. Repeat with the remaining dough.

5. To make the glaze: place the chocolate chips in a small zippered freezer bag. Bring a small saucepan of water to a boil. Remove the pan from the heat. Tip the bag diagonally so the chips acquire in a single nook. Dip that nook into the water till the chips melt, just some minutes. Squeeze the nook often to distribute the melted chips. When all of the chocolate is melted, use scissors to trim off the tiniest tip on that nook. Squeeze the chocolate through the outlet & drizzle it throughout the tops of the cookies. I prefer to make "S" strokes. Let the chocolate harden before serving or storing the cookies, about 30–60 minutes, depending on the climate.

CHOCOLATE EARTHQUAKES

MAKES four–5 DOZEN
eight tablespoons (1 stick) unsalted butter

four (1-ounce) squares unsweetened chocolate

four large eggs

two **cups sugar**

two **teaspoons vanilla extract**

two **cups unbleached flour**

two **teaspoons baking powder**

¼ teaspoon salt

one **cup confectioners' sugar**

1. Place the butter in a medium-size heavy-bottomed saucepan & start to melt it over medium-low heat. Add the chocolate & melt it with the butter, stirring frequently. When the chocolate is about eighty % melted, remove the pan from the heat & let the combination continue to melt (you don't want the chocolate to get too hot). Let cool.

2. Whisk the eggs in a big bowl. Whisk in the sugar, vanilla, & melted chocolate combination. Add the flour, baking powder, & salt, & whisk till smooth. Chill the combination till cold & firm, not less than two hours or up to 24 hours.

3. Place an oven rack in the middle of the oven if you'll bake the cookies on one baking sheet, or place one rack on the higher stage & one in the middle in case you are utilizing two baking sheets. Preheat the oven to 350 degrees. Lightly butter one or two baking sheets.
4. Place the confectioners' sugar in a small bowl. Scoop up a heaping teaspoon of cookie dough & roll it between the palms of your hands to form right into a ball. Roll it in the powdered sugar & coat well. Place on the baking sheet. Make a dozen balls for every baking sheet.
5. Bake the cookies for 12 minutes, switching the location of the baking sheets midway through the cooking time in case you are cooking two batches directly. Cool slightly. Use a spatula to maneuver the cookies from the baking sheet to a wire rack to chill. Let the cookies cool completely before storing in a covered tin with a sheet of waxed paper in between the layers.

COCONUT BARS

MAKES 18 BARS

The Crust:
eight tablespoons (1 stick) unsalted butter, very soft

¼ cup sugar

one **large egg**

one **teaspoon vanilla extract**

one **cup unbleached flour**

¼ teaspoon salt

The Topping:
six **ounces Neufchâtel (light cream cheese), very soft**

three tablespoons unsalted butter, very soft

½ cup sugar

one **large egg**

¼ teaspoon almond extract

1½ tablespoons unbleached flour

three cups (about 12 ounces) sweetened coconut

½ cup semisweet chocolate chips

1. Preheat the oven to 350 degrees. Lightly butter a nine × thirteen-inch Pyrex dish or baking pan. (You don't need the baking dish any smaller or the bars will likely be too thick.)
2. In a big bowl, utilizing an electrical mixer, beat the butter & sugar together till blended. Beat in the egg & vanilla till smooth & creamy. Sprinkle in the flour & salt, & beat just till mixed. Scrape the batter into the prepared dish & use a rubber spatula to spread it evenly on the bottom. Will probably be very thin. Bake quarter-hour.
3. In the meantime, make the topping utilizing the same bowl & beaters (you don't have to scrub them). Beat the cream cheese & butter till smooth. Add the sugar, egg, & almond extract, & beat till mixed. Sprinkle in the flour & beat till blended. Stir in the coconut.
4. When the crust is completed, spoon the batter into it. Carefully spread it round to cover the crust evenly. Bake 18–20 minutes, or simply till the top of the batter begins to get a tiny little bit of color. Place on a wire rack to chill.
5. Whereas the bars are still hot, fill a medium-size saucepan midway with water, bring to a boil, & take away the pan from the heat. Place the chocolate chips in a small zippered freezer bag & tilt the bag so the chocolate chips gather in a single nook. Lower the bag into the water, conserving the chips in the nook, & allow them to melt, about two minutes. Squeeze the chips often to see if they're melted. Remove the bag from the water. Retaining the bag tilted, snip off a very tiny piece of the nook. Squirt the chocolate throughout the coconut surface in an summary sample. When everything is completely cooled, cut into small bars.

PECAN CARAMEL BARS

MAKES 24 BARS

Shortbread Crust:

12 tablespoons (1½ sticks) unsalted butter, very soft

½ cup confectioners' sugar

one **egg yolk**

½ teaspoon vanilla extract

1½ cups unbleached flour

Topping:
two **large eggs**

four tablespoons unsalted butter, melted

one **cup firmly packed light brown sugar**

½ teaspoon baking powder

½ teaspoon vanilla extract

two **cups roughly chopped pecans**

1. Preheat the oven to 350 degrees. Set out a 12 × seven × 2-inch baking dish (such as a Pyrex glass dish) or pan.
2. Place the butter & confectioners' sugar in the bowl of an electrical mixer & beat till blended. Add the egg yolk & vanilla, & beat till smooth & integrated. Sprinkle in the flour & beat just till combined but still crumbly; don't overwork the dough.
3. Scrape the dough into the baking dish. Use your fingers or the palm of your hand to press the dough evenly into the baking dish. Bake 20 minutes, or till lightly golden across the edges.
4. Whereas the crust is baking, beat the eggs in a medium-size bowl. Beat in the butter, sugar, baking powder, & vanilla. Stir in the chopped pecans.

5. When the crust comes out of the oven, instantly pour on the pecan combination & ensure it's evenly distributed. Bake quarter-hour, or till the middle is about & never jiggly once you shake the dish. Cool on a wire rack for 10 minutes, then

run a knife across the edges to loosen them. Cool completely, about two hours. Cut into small bars.

PAD THAI WITH CRISPY TOFU

SERVES three–four
The Sauce:
¼ cup tomato paste

⅓ cup firmly packed brown sugar

¼ cup tamari soy sauce

three tablespoons lime juice

½ teaspoon Asian sesame oil

one **garlic clove, minced**

½ teaspoon chili paste with garlic or ¼ teaspoon crushed red pepper flakes

eight ounces dried rice stick noodles (⅛ inch broad)

three tablespoons canola oil

one **pound extra-firm tofu, sliced ½ inch thick, patted *very* dry, & cut into ½-inch cubes**

two **large eggs, well beaten**

⅓ cup chopped roasted peanuts

one **cup bean sprouts**

two **scallions, cut into 2-inch lengths & shredded lengthwise**

1. Mix all of the sauce ingredients together in a small bowl & put aside.
2. Bring a big stockpot of water to a boil. Drop in the rice stick noodles & toss thoroughly with tongs to be sure that they don't stick together. Cook 2–three minutes, or till al dente. Make sure that the noodles are still slightly firm as a result of they are going to

soften additional when stir-fried. Drain completely in a colander & rinse under cold running water. Drain once more.

3. Heat 1½ tablespoons oil in a big nonstick skillet over medium-high heat.
4. When the oil is very popular, add the tofu. Stir-fry till golden throughout. Place the tofu on a platter. Add a half-tablespoon oil to the pan. Pour in the eggs & shortly cook like a pancake. Remove to a plate & cut into bite-size pieces.
5. Pour the remaining tablespoon of oil in the skillet. Add the noodles, tofu, eggs, peanuts, & bean sprouts, & mix with tongs. Pour on the sauce & toss to coat well. Cook till hot all through, about three minutes. Sprinkle on the scallions, toss, & serve.

ROASTED TOFU SATAY

SERVES 6
The Marinade:
two **tablespoons tamari soy sauce**

two **tablespoons Asian sesame oil**

two **tablespoons sherry**

two **pounds extra-firm tofu, sliced one inch thick & patted very dry, then cut into 1-inch cubes & patted once more**

one **red bell pepper, cut into 1-inch squares**

The Sauce:
¾ cup canned coconut milk (see Tip)

½ cup natural-style peanut butter, smooth or chunky

two **garlic cloves, minced**

1½ teaspoons curry powder

1½ tablespoons brown sugar

one **tablespoon lime juice**

one **tablespoon canola oil**

1½ tablespoons tamari soy sauce Dash cayenne pepper

1. Mix the marinade ingredients in a big bowl. Add the dry tofu & red pepper & toss gently with a rubber spatula to coat evenly. Let marinate half-hour or up to eight hours. Refrigerate if longer than one hour.
2. Prepare the grill or preheat the oven to 450 degrees.
3. To make the sauce, place all of the sauce ingredients in a food processor & mix till smooth. Pour into an ornamental serving bowl.
4. Remove about ⅓ cup of the sauce & drizzle it over the tofu. Use the rubber spatula to toss the tofu gently with the sauce. If you're grilling the satay, thread the tofu & red peppers on skewers. (Bamboo skewers have to be soaked for half-hour.) In case you are roasting the tofu in the oven, place it in one layer in a big, shallow baking dish such as a nine X thirteen-inch lasagna pan. Use two pans if one pan isn't large enough.
5. Cook the tofu on the hot grill at the least 20 minutes, turning it often, or roast in the oven for 25 minutes. The tofu is finished when it's a deep golden brown. Let the tofu cool to room temperature before serving. Serve alongside the bowl of sauce for dipping.

ROASTED TOFU SALAD

SERVES four
two **pounds extra-firm tofu**

three tablespoons tamari soy sauce

two **tablespoons Asian sesame oil**

Canola or olive oil for greasing pan

one **celery rib, very thinly sliced**

¼ cup thin red onion slivers

one **carrot, very thinly sliced**

¼ cup finely chopped fresh parsley

The Dressing:
two **tablespoons lemon juice**

one **garlic clove, put through a press or minced**

½ teaspoon Dijon-style mustard

¼ teaspoon salt

Generous seasoning freshly ground pepper

two **½ tablespoons olive oil**

1. Pat the tofu very dry with a linen kitchen towel or paper towels. Slice it into ½-inch-thick slices & lay them on the towel(s). Pat the slices very dry, changing the towels as necessary. Cut the tofu into ½-inch cubes & pat dry once more.

2. Mix the soy sauce & sesame oil in a big bowl. Add the tofu & toss gently with a rubber spatula, till evenly coated. Let marinate at the least half-hour, or up to four hours. Refrigerate if longer than half-hour.

3. Preheat the oven to 450 degrees. Very lightly grease a 17 × eleven × 2-inch baking sheet.
4. Spread the tofu on the baking sheet in one layer. Bake 20–25 minutes, or till the tofu is a deep golden color throughout. Midway through the cooking time use a spatula to flip the tofu over so it browns evenly. Let the tofu cool to room temperature.
5. In the meantime, put the celery, onion slivers, carrot, & parsley in a big serving bowl.
6. Place all of the dressing ingredients in a jar with a decent-fitting lid & shake vigorously.
7. Mix the tofu with the greens, then pour on the dressing & toss. Chill at the very least one hour before serving for the flavors to mix & for the tofu to become firmer.

TIP: Blanched, chilled greens could be a scrumptious & colourful addition to this salad. Attempt broccoli, green beans, asparagus, or red bell peppers, & increase the dressing by half to assist coat the extra greens.

EGGLESS SALAD

MAKES four SANDWICHES
eight ounces extra-firm tofu, patted very dry

¼ teaspoon turmeric

two **tablespoons mayonnaise**

one **scallion, very thinly sliced**

⅛ teaspoon celery seed

¼ teaspoon salt

Freshly ground black pepper to taste

1. Place the tofu on a cotton or linen kitchen towel & collect up the corners. Twist the tofu right into a ball & squeeze out all its liquid. Place the tofu in a medium-size bowl & mash with a fork till it resembles coarse crumbs the size of pine nuts.
2. Mix in all of the remaining ingredients. Cover & chill the combination for at the least half-hour. It's going to become a brighter yellow, & the flavors will meld. Function a sandwich spread with lettuce or sprouts on sliced bread or in pita bread.

ROASTED TOFU SANDWICHES

MAKES four SANDWICHES
one **pound extra-firm tofu**

two **tablespoons tamari soy sauce**

two **tablespoons Asian sesame oil**

¼ cup mayonnaise

eight slices bread

eight slices tomato

four lettuce leaves

1. Preheat the oven to 450 degrees.
2. Slice the tofu into ½-inch-thick slices; it's best to get about 10 slices. Lay them on one finish of a cotton kitchen towel or on paper towels & pat very dry with the remaining half of the towel or more paper towels. For a profitable browning the tofu should be as dry as possible.
3. Place the tofu slices in one layer in a shallow baking dish such as a 12 × seven × 2-inch Pyrex dish.

4. In a small cup mix the soy sauce & sesame oil together. Pour a little of the combination on each slice of tofu & use your fingers to rub it evenly over the surface. Flip the tofu over & repeat on the opposite side.

5. Bake the tofu for 10 minutes. With a spatula flip each slice over & return the dish to the oven. Bake 10 minutes more, or till golden. Let the tofu cool completely, then chill till ice cold.

6. Spread the mayonnaise on the bread slices. Place 2½ slices of tofu on four slices of bread. Top with the tomato, lettuce, & remaining bread to make four sandwiches. Cut each sandwich in half.

Spices Versus Herbs

What ought to they be called, spices or herbs? Well, it relies upon. Spices are fragrant merchandise that come from the seeds, bark, or stems of crops, & they're grown in the tropics. Herbs, however, are the leaves of vegetation, they usually develop in temperate areas.

It's fascinating to ponder how the hunt for tropical spices helped form historical past by stimulating world commerce & exploration. Though spice buying & selling came about as early as 1450 B.C. in Egypt with the importing of cinnamon, it was the Romans' almost insatiable demand for unique spices in the first century A.D. that transformed the pursuit of spices right into a world-shaping power. The attract of the Asian tropics was, in actual fact, instrumental in the invention of America. Christopher Columbus sought a western path to India … & the remaining is historical past. All for a little black pepper.

TEMPEH RAGOUT WITH CORN

SERVES four
¼ cup olive oil

four large garlic cloves, minced

¼ teaspoon crushed red pepper flakes

one **(14-ounce) can prepared-cut diced tomatoes with their juice**

three medium boiling potatoes, peeled & cut into ½-inch dice (no greater)(4½ cups)

one **cup water**

eight ounces tempeh, cut into ½-inch dice

two **medium zucchini, cut into ½-inch cubes 1**

1½ cups frozen corn, thawed

½ teaspoon salt

¼ cup finely chopped fresh basil or ½ teaspoon dried basil & ¼ cup minced fresh parsley

1. Heat the oil in a big skillet or medium-size stockpot over medium heat. Add the garlic & crushed pepper flakes, & cook two minutes. Don't let the garlic get in any respect brown. Pour in the tomatoes & simmer two minutes.
2. Stir in the potatoes & water, & cover the pan. Simmer about quarter-hour, or till the potatoes are almost tender. Remove the cover & stir the combination often to prevent sticking.
3. Mix in the tempeh & zucchini, & cover the pot. Simmer the ragout till the zucchini & potatoes are tender, about quarter-hour. Check the liquid during this era. If the ragout appears dry relatively than stewlike, add a bit more water. Add the corn, salt, & basil, & simmer two minutes. Serve without delay.

TEMPEH SANDWICH SPREAD

MAKES three SANDWICHES
one **tablespoon canola oil**

one **(eight-ounce) package tempeh, very finely chopped**

¼ cup minced red onion

I celery rib, very thinly sliced

¼ cup mayonnaise

1. Heat the oil in a medium-size, preferably nonstick, skillet over medium heat. Add the tempeh & sauté till lightly golden, about five minutes. Scrape it right into a medium-size bowl & let cool.
2. Mix in all of the remaining ingredients. Cover & chill till prepared to make use of.

GOLDEN TEMPEH SANDWICHES

MAKES four SANDWICHES
eight ounces tempeh

two **tablespoons canola oil**

two **tablespoons tamari soy sauce**

The Dressing:
⅓ **cup plain yogurt or mayonnaise, or a mix of each**

1½ **tablespoons Dijon-style mustard**

one **tablespoon honey**

eight slices bread or four spherical sandwich rolls cut in half

eight pieces red leaf lettuce

1. Cut the tempeh in half crosswise (vertically), then cut each bit in half horizontally to make four thin cutlets.
2. Heat the oil in a big nonstick skillet over medium heat. When it's hot, fry the cutlets till golden brown on either side, about seven minutes. Remove the tempeh to a platter. Drizzle ½ tablespoon soy sauce on each slice & rub it in with your fingers (the tempeh will readily soak up it). Let cool to warm or room temperature.
3. To make the dressing, mix the yogurt (or mayonnaise), mustard, & honey together in a small bowl. Spread the dressing on all of the bread slices, top with the tempeh & lettuce, & shut the sandwich.

TIP: Toasted bread is particularly good for these sandwiches.

BARBECUED TEMPEH CUTLETS FOR SANDWICHES

MAKES four SANDWICHES
Barbecue Sauce:
½ **cup ketchup**

two **tablespoons firmly packed brown sugar**

two **teaspoons apple cider vinegar**

one **tablespoon lemon juice**

two **teaspoons chili powder**

one **teaspoon dry mustard powder**

¼ teaspoon salt A few dashes Tabasco

eight ounces tempeh

one **tablespoon canola oil (roughly)**

Sandwich additions: mayonnaise, lettuce, tomato, thinly sliced onion, bread

1. To make the barbecue sauce, place all of the sauce ingredients in a small bowl & mix well.
2. Slice the tempeh in half vertically. Cut each bit in half horizontally to make four thin cutlets.
3. Heat the oil in a big nonstick skillet over medium heat. Brush some barbecue sauce on each side of every tempeh piece & place in the hot skillet. Sauté on either side till a deep golden brown, about 10 minutes total. Remove to a plate & brush some more sauce on one side of every cutlet. You'll most likely have some leftover sauce. Let the tempeh cool to room temperature. To make sandwiches, lightly spread some mayonnaise on some bread. Top with the tempeh, lettuce, tomato, & onion.

SPAGHETTI PUTTANESCA

SERVES four
¼ cup olive oil

six **garlic cloves, minced**

¼ teaspoon crushed red pepper flakes, or more for an additional-spicy model two **cups canned crushed tomatoes or tomato puree**

one **teaspoon oregano**

Generous seasoning freshly ground black pepper

½ cup pitted, coarsely chopped black & green olives, such as Kalamata, Niçoise, & Picholine (see Tip)

two **teaspoons drained capers**

½ cup finely chopped fresh parsley

one **pound spaghetti**

1. Bring a big stockpot of water to a boil for the spaghetti.
2. To make the sauce, heat the oil in a three-quart (or bigger) saucepan over medium heat. (The sauce wants a whole lot of room to cook as a result of it would splatter.) Add the garlic & red pepper flakes, & cook one minute. Don't let the garlic get in any respect coloured. Add the tomatoes, oregano, pepper, olives, & capers, & simmer, partially covered to prevent splattering, for 20 minutes. Stir in the parsley & keep warm whereas the pasta cooks.
3. Cook the spaghetti till al dente. Drain totally & return to the pot. Spoon on the sauce & toss well. Function is; it actually doesn't need any cheese.

TIP: Pit olives just the best way you'd crush garlic—that's, lay the flat side of a giant knife on an olive & give it a thump. The flesh will release itself from the pit. Discard the pits & chop the flesh.

SPAGHETTINI WITH SPINACH IN GARLIC-CREAM SAUCE

SERVES four
one **pound spaghettini**

one **(10-ounce) bag triple-washed fresh spinach, stems discarded & leaves torn, or one (10-ounce) package frozen chopped spinach**

three tablespoons olive oil

three large garlic cloves, put through a press or minced

½ cup heavy cream

½ cup milk

Pinch nutmeg

½ teaspoon salt

Generous seasoning freshly ground black pepper

Grated Romano or Parmesan cheese to taste

1. Bring a big stockpot of water to a boil over high heat. Drop in the spaghettini & cook till barely done—that's, with about two minutes more to go till al dente.
2. Add the fresh or frozen spinach to the pasta & stir till wilted (if fresh) or thawed (if frozen), about two minutes. Drain everything in a colander & leave undisturbed.
3. Heat the oil in the same stockpot over medium-high heat. Add the garlic & cook one minute. Pour in the cream & milk then stir in the drained pasta & spinach. Sprinkle on the nutmeg, salt, & pepper. Heat everything for one minute. Serve with Romano or Parmesan cheese on each serving.

SPAGHETTINI WITH CRISPY BROILED EGGPLANT

SERVES four
¼ cup plus two tablespoons olive oil

one **medium-large (1¼ pounds) eggplant, peeled & sliced ½ inch thick**

six **garlic cloves, minced**

¼ teaspoon crushed red pepper flakes

two **cups canned crushed tomatoes (preferably) or tomato puree**

½ teaspoon dried oregano

¼ cup minced fresh parsley

½ teaspoon salt

one **pound spaghettini**

three tablespoons grated Parmesan cheese

1. Preheat the broiler. Bring a big amount of water to a boil in a stockpot. Lightly brush ¼ cup oil on either side of the eggplant slices & lay them on a baking sheet.
2. Broil till a deep golden brown, flip over, & broil once more till very brown. Let cool. Cut the slices into 1-inch-huge strips.
3. To make the sauce, heat the remaining two tablespoons oil in a medium-size saucepan. Gently cook the garlic & red pepper flakes till they sizzle but aren't coloured in any respect, about one minute. Stir in the crushed tomatoes, oregano, parsley, & salt. Simmer, partially covered to prevent splattering, for 20 minutes.
4. Cook the spaghettini till al dente, about eight minutes. Drain completely in a colander.
5. Stir half of the eggplant into the sauce. Return the pasta to its pot, pour on the sauce, & sprinkle on the cheese. Toss gently. Serve with the remaining eggplant mounded on each portion.

PASTA WITH TOASTED PINE NUTS

SERVES four
three tablespoons pine nuts

½ cup Basic Pesto

½ cup light cream or ¼ cup heavy cream & ¼ cup milk

½ teaspoon salt

Generous seasoning freshly ground black pepper

one **pound pasta, such as spaghetti, vermicelli, or linguine**

Pasta

We've all heard the story of how Marco Polo brought noodles to Italy from China, or at the very least the concept for making noodles. It appears, nonetheless, that this legend has lingered due to its shock worth slightly than its accuracy. Upon a better studying of Marco Polo's writings, food historians have found that when he mentioned he "found" pasta in China, he went on to say "that are like ours." So let's just say that the

Chinese & Italians loved pasta concurrently (and, by the way, together with the Indians & Arabs).

At the moment the typical Italian eats about sixty five pounds of pasta a yr, most of it industrial dried pasta produced from only semolina & water, which is then dried in ovens & packaged. Occasional forays to the fresh pasta store are often to buy stuffed pastas, such as ravioli & tortellini, & in addition fresh fettuccine & tagliatelle, that are all made with an egg-primarily based dough.

1. Bring a big stockpot of water to a boil for the pasta.
2. Place the pine nuts in a small skillet over medium heat & toast, stirring consistently, till lightly golden, about five minutes. Place on a small plate & let cool.
3. In a small bowl mix the pesto, cream, salt, & pepper.
4. Cook the pasta in the boiling water till al dente. Drain in a colander & leave undisturbed.
5. Instantly pour the pesto-cream sauce into the stockpot & heat 30 seconds. Place the pasta back in the pot & rapidly toss to coat it completely. Serve without delay, preferably in pasta bowls, with some pine nuts sprinkled on each portion.

LINGUINE WITH SPICY MUSHROOM RAGU

SERVES four
three tablespoons olive oil

four garlic cloves, minced

¼ teaspoon crushed red pepper flakes

one **pound typical white mushrooms, thinly sliced**

1½ cups canned crushed tomatoes or tomato puree

⅛ teaspoon dried rosemary, crumbled

½ teaspoon salt

one **pound linguine**

Grated Parmesan cheese to taste

1. Bring a big amount of water to a boil in a stockpot.

2. To make the sauce, heat the olive oil in a medium-size saucepan over medium heat. Add the garlic & crushed pepper flakes, & cook 30 seconds. Stir in the mushrooms & cook till brown & juicy, about 10 minutes. Mix in the tomatoes, rosemary, & salt, & cook stirring often, for 10 minutes. If the sauce begins to splatter during cooking, lower the heat to medium-low. Keep the sauce warm whereas cooking the linguine.

3. Drop the linguine into the boiling water & cook till al dente. Taste one alongside the way in which to avoid overcooking it. Drain completely in a colander & return to the pot. Pour on the sauce & toss. Serve with a light-weight sprinkling of Parmesan cheese.

FRESH LINGUINE WITH VEGETABLES

SERVES four
¼ cup pine nuts

one **tablespoon olive oil**

eight ounces sliced mushrooms (three cups)

one **medium zucchini, quartered lengthwise & thinly sliced**

four garlic cloves, minced

one **cup canned tomato puree**

½ cup heavy cream

½ teaspoon salt

Generous seasoning freshly ground pepper

1¼ pounds fresh linguine or fettuccine (see Tip)

½ cup shredded fresh basil

Grated Parmesan cheese to taste

1. Bring a big amount of water to a boil in a stockpot.
2. Place the pine nuts in a big skillet. Toast them over medium heat, tossing constantly, till they start to get golden. Watch out not to burn them. Drop them right into a small dish & let cool.

3. Pour the oil into the skillet. Add the mushrooms & sauté just till they start to melt & render a few of their juices. Mix in the zucchini & garlic, & sauté till the zucchini begins to get tender. Don't cook it an excessive amount of at this level as a result of it can cook more in the sauce.
4. Stir in the tomato puree, cream, salt, & pepper, & mix totally. Bring the sauce to a boil, then lower the heat to maintain it warm.
5. Drop the fresh pasta into the boiling water & cook just till al dente, about five minutes. Taste it a minute or so before you anticipate its being done to avoid overcooking it. Drain completely in a colander & return it to the pot.
6. Pour on the sauce, mix in the basil, & toss in a small handful of Parmesan cheese. Serve in individual pasta bowls or on large plates with some pine nuts on each serving. Cross more Parmesan cheese on the table.

.

STUFFED BABY PUMPKIN WITH WILD RICE & MUSHROOMS

SERVES four–6
one **(3½-pound) sugar or pie pumpkin**

two **tablespoons unsalted butter, softened**

Salt

Freshly ground pepper

¾ cup very finely diced celery

½ cup finely diced onion

one **½ cups (four ounces) sliced mushrooms**

1½ cups vegetable broth/stock, store-purchased or home made

two **tablespoons sliced almonds**

two **tablespoons Asian sesame oil two tablespoons sherry**

¼ teaspoon salt

¼ cup wild rice

¼ cup brown rice

1. Preheat the oven to 350 degrees.
2. Slice the replenish the pumpkin, reserving the lid. With a spoon scoop out & discard all of the seeds & fibrous inside. (Watch out not to make any holes in the pumpkin, particularly on the bottom. Leave the little "level" on the middle of the bottom.) Slather one tablespoon butter in the inside of the pumpkin, then season with salt & pepper. Cover the pumpkin with its lid & place on a baking sheet. Bake 20 minutes.
3. In the meantime, melt the remaining tablespoon of butter in a medium-size saucepan. Add the celery, onion, & mushrooms, & sauté 10 minutes, or till the mushrooms are juicy. Stir in the vegetable broth/stock & bring to a boil. Add all of the remaining ingredients & cook at a energetic simmer for 10 minutes.
4. Remove the pumpkin from the oven. Carefully ladle in the boiling rice combination & cover with the lid. Return to the oven & bake 1–1½ hours more, or till all of the broth/stock is absorbed & the rice is cooked. Place the pumpkin on an ornamental platter & encompass with some leafy greens such as kale. Let sit 10 minutes before cutting the pumpkin into wedges.

CURRY

SERVES four–6
1¾ cups dried unsweetened coconut (accessible at well being food stores)

2½ cups extremely popular water

¼ cup tomato paste

three tablespoons unsalted butter one large onion, minced

one **tablespoon minced fresh ginger**

four large garlic cloves, minced

two **teaspoons turmeric**

1½ teaspoons ground cumin

one **tablespoon ground coriander**

½ teaspoon ground cardamom

⅛ teaspoon cayenne pepper (or more to taste)

two **medium red-skinned potatoes, cut into ½-inch dice (no greater)**

four cups very small cauliflower florets (from one small cauliflower)

one **carrot, thinly sliced**

1½ cups frozen peas, thawed

1½ tablespoons minced cilantro

½ teaspoon salt

1. To make the coconut milk, mix the coconut & hot water in the container of a blender (preferably) or food processor & process two minutes. Place a strainer over a big bowl & pour in half the coconut combination. With the back of a giant spoon press the coconut to extract as much liquid as possible. Discard the pressed coconut & repeat with the remaining combination. It's best to have ⅔ cups coconut milk.
2. Place the tomato paste in a small bowl & stir in about ½ cup coconut milk to dilute the tomato paste & make a smooth combination. Pour this into the remaining coconut milk & put aside.
3. Melt the butter in a stockpot over medium heat. Add the onion, ginger, & garlic, & sauté, stirring often, till the onions are golden brown, about 10 minutes.
4. Stir in the turmeric, cumin, coriander, cardamom, & cayenne, & "toast" the spices for two minutes, stirring frequently. Pour in the coconut milk combination & bring to a boil. five * Stir in the potatoes, tightly cover the pan, & cook five minutes.
5. Carefully mix in the cauliflower & carrots, & stir to coat the greens evenly. Cover the pan tightly once more & cook over medium heat till the potatoes are tender, about quarter-hour. Often remove the cover & stir the greens for even cooking. (The curry may be made a few hours prematurely so far. Reheat before continuing with step **7.** If the sauce has become very thick, thin with a little water.)
6. Stir in the peas, cilantro, & salt. Cover once more & cook 1–2 minutes, or simply till the peas are heated through.

VEGETABLE & CASHEW CURRY

SERVES four
¼ cup canola oil

one **onion, finely diced**

four garlic cloves, minced

one **tablespoon minced fresh ginger**

1½ tablespoons curry powder

one **teaspoon ground cumin**

one **(14-ounce) can prepared-cut diced tomatoes with their juice**

½ teaspoon salt

2½ cups peeled & finely diced (½-inch) boiling potatoes

three small to medium zucchini, quartered lengthwise & thinly sliced

¾ cup dry-roasted (preferably unsalted) cashews

one **tablespoon lemon juice**

four cups hot cooked basmati rice (constructed from one cup raw rice)

Plain yogurt

1. Heat the oil in a big skillet over medium heat. Add the onion, garlic, & ginger, & sauté five minutes. Mix in the curry powder & cumin, & cook two minutes to toast the spices.
2. Add the tomatoes & one cup water, & bring to a boil. Stir in the potatoes & cover the pan. Cook at a delicate simmer till the potatoes are tender, about 20 minutes. Stir often to prevent sticking.

3. Remove the cover of the pan & add the zucchini & cashews. Cook, uncovered, till the zucchini are tender, about 10 minutes. Mix in the lemon juice. Serve the curry over rice with a spoonful of yogurt on top.

VEGETABLE STOCK

MAKES seven cups
one **tablespoon olive oil**
six **garlic cloves, chopped**
two **onions, roughly chopped**
one **bunch scallions, roughly chopped**
three celery ribs, roughly chopped
three unpeeled carrots, roughly chopped
six **mushrooms, chopped**
½ bunch parsley with stems, roughly chopped
two **bay leaves**
two **tablespoons tamari soy sauce**
10 cups water
Dash nutmeg
Freshly ground pepper to taste

1. Heat the oil in a big stockpot over medium heat. Add the garlic, onions, & scallions, & sauté 10 minutes, stirring often.
2. Mix in all of the remaining ingredients & bring the broth/stock to a boil. Lower the heat to a mild simmer & cook one hour, stirring often. Strain the broth/stock through a big strainer or a colander set over a big bowl. With the back of a giant spoon, press out as much liquid as possible from the greens. Discard the greens. Let the broth/stock cool to room temperature. Refrigerate the refill to one week or freeze up to three months.

CLASSIC PESTO

MAKES one ⅓ cups
two **cups reasonably well packed fresh basil leaves, well washed & spun**

dry

½ cup olive oil (preferably mild-flavored)
four medium-size garlic cloves, chopped
two **tablespoons pine nuts (optional)**
½ cup grated Parmesan cheese

two **tablespoons unsalted butter, very soft**

Mix the basil, oil, garlic, & pine nuts (if you're utilizing them) in a blender (preferably) or food processor & process till it's a smooth puree. Scrape the pesto right into a container & stir in the cheese. Use a fork to stir in the soft butter. Chill till prepared to make use of. When utilizing as a sauce for pasta, thin with a few tablespoons of boiling pasta water before utilizing. This pesto will keep about one month if covered with a thin movie of olive oil & refrigerated.

WINTER PESTO

MAKES two cups
2½ **cups tightly packed triple-washed fresh spinach, stems removed**
½ cup chopped fresh parsley
one **tablespoon dried basil three garlic cloves, chopped ¼ teaspoon salt**
¼ cup walnuts (optional)
⅔ cup olive oil
½ cup grated Parmesan cheese
two **tablespoons unsalted butter, very soft**

1. Mix the spinach, parsley, basil, garlic, salt, walnuts, & oil in a blender (preferably) or food processor & process till it's a smooth puree. Turn off the machine & scrape down the sides as necessary.

2. Pour the pesto right into a container with a good-fitting lid & stir in the cheese & butter by hand till well blended. If the pesto is for use as a sauce for pasta, stir in a few tablespoons of boiling pasta water to thin it out before utilizing. This pesto will keep for a few weeks if covered with a tablespoon of olive oil & refrigerated.

SUN-DRIED TOMATO PESTO

MAKES one cup
(ENOUGH FOR one POUND PASTA)
½ cup packed loose sun-dried tomatoes (about 18)
two **garlic cloves, chopped**
½ cup chopped fresh parsley
¼ cup chopped fresh basil, or two teaspoons dried
½ teaspoon salt (see Tip)
Freshly ground pepper to taste
⅔ cup olive oil
two **tablespoons pine nuts**
¼ cup grated Parmesan cheese

1. Place the tomatoes in a vegetable steamer in a saucepan with about one inch of water. Cook covered, over medium heat for 10 minutes. Remove the steamer from the pot & let the tomatoes cool 10 minutes. (Alternatively, you can place the tomatoes in a small bowl & cover them with boiling water. Cover the bowl with a plate & let sit 10 minutes. Drain & cool the tomatoes.)
2. In a food processor or blender mix the tomatoes, garlic, parsley, basil, salt, & pepper, & process till finely ground. Slowly pour in the oil & process till smooth. Scrape the pesto right into a bowl & stir in the pine nuts & cheese. If you're utilizing the pesto on pasta, stir in ½ cup boiling pasta water to thin it out.

ROASTED RED PEPPER & WALNUT PESTO

MAKES ¾ cup
(ENOUGH FOR one POUND PASTA)
one **(7-ounce) jar roasted red peppers, well drained**
¼ cup walnuts
three garlic cloves, minced
¼ cup olive oil
½ teaspoon salt (use only ¼ **teaspoon if not for pasta)**
Freshly ground pepper to taste
⅓ cup grated Parmesan cheese

Collect the peppers between your hands & gently squeeze out all of the moisture you can. Place the peppers & all of the remaining ingredients besides the cheese in the container of a food processor & process till very smooth. Scrape the pesto right into a bowl & stir in the cheese by hand.

PIE CRUST

MAKES one 9-OR 10-INCH CRUST
Water
1¼ cups unbleached flour
¼ teaspoon salt (for a savory crust)*or*
two **teaspoons sugar (for a sweet crust)**
six **tablespoons chilled unsalted butter**
two **tablespoons canola oil**
1½ teaspoons lemon juice or apple cider vinegar

1. Fill a glass midway with water & drop in an ice cube. Put aside.

2. In a big bowl mix the flour & salt or sugar. Cut the butter into bits & drop them in the flour. Toss to evenly coat them. With your fingertips, a pastry cutter, or two knives, rub the butter into the flour till they're flattened & the size of dimes. You don't need the pieces to be too small, or they may melt too shortly in the crust & never create flakes.

3. In a small bowl or glass mix three tablespoons of the ice water, the oil, & lemon juice or vinegar. Drizzle this over the flour combination & stir with a fork to distribute it. Collect the dough right into a ball & knead three or four times to make it pliable. (If the dough is very dry & crumbly, add a few more teaspoons of ice water.) Collect right into a ball once more, then flatten right into a disk. Wrap in plastic wrap & chill for a minimum of 20 minutes, or up to forty eight hours.

4. To roll out the dough, let it come to a cool temperature. It is going to be too firm & crumbly if rolled when it's too cold. It have to be cool but not at room temperature as a result of the butter bits should stay firm & never melt into the dough. Lightly flour the work surface, rolling pin, & the surface of the dough. Roll the dough right into a circle about two inches bigger than the pie plate. Keep turning the dough as you roll it to maintain it an ideal circle. Lightly flour beneath & on top if it sticks. Pinch together any areas that break.

5. Place the rolling pin in the middle of the dough & fold half of the pastry over it. Unfold the dough onto the tart pan or pie plate. Press it into the edges & trim any extra. Place the tart pan or pie plate in a plastic bag or cover with foil. Chill for at the least half-hour or up to 24 hours before baking. You can too freeze the crust if it's totally wrapped.

STORE-BOUGHT TOMATO SAUCE

MAKES 3¼ CUPS
one **(28-or 32-ounce) can or jar store-purchased**
tomato sauce
three tablespoons dry red wine
two **garlic cloves, put through a press (preferably) or minced**
one **teaspoon dried oregano**
½ cup minced fresh parsley
Generous seasoning freshly ground pepper
Mix all of the ingredients & mix well. Store any unused portion in the fridge.

MARINARA SAUCE

MAKES ABOUT three CUPS
½ cup olive oil

four garlic cloves, put through a press or minced
one **(28-ounce) can tomato puree** three **tablespoons dry red wine**
one **teaspoon sugar or honey**
two **teaspoons dried oregano one teaspoon dried basil**
¼ **teaspoon salt**
Generous seasoning freshly ground pepper

Add the oil to a big stockpot (which helps to avoid splattering) & warm it over medium-low heat. Add the garlic & cook 30-60 seconds, or simply till it sizzles a bit but doesn't become in any respect coloured. Stir in all of the remaining ingredients & lift the heat to medium. Simmer the sauce for 20 minutes, stirring often.

PERFECT BROWN RICE

MAKES 2½ TO three CUPS RICE SERVES four AS A SIDE DISH
one **cup long-grain brown rice**
two **cups water or vegetable broth/stock, store-purchased or home made**
½ **teaspoon salt**
one **teaspoon canola oil**

1. Place the rice in a strainer & rinse under cold running water. Place in a 1½-quart saucepan. Add all of the remaining ingredients.
2. Cover the pan & bring the combination to a boil. Lower the heat to a simmer & cook undisturbed for forty-forty five minutes, or till all of the liquid has been absorbed. Use a knife to make a separation in the rice to make sure that there is no such thing as a liquid left. Remove the rice from the heat & let sit, covered, for at the least five minutes, or up to twenty minutes before serving. Serve without delay or scoop the rice right into a covered baking dish & keep warm in a 325-diploma oven.

GREEN SALSA

MAKES 1⅔ cups
12 ounces tomatillos (about 18 small-golf-ball size, or 10 medium)
one **very small onion, chopped**
one **garlic clove, chopped**
two **jalapeño peppers, seeded & chopped**
(put on rubber gloves)
one **tablespoon lime juice**
¼ **teaspoon sugar**
¼ **teaspoon salt**
two **tablespoons minced cilantro**

1. Remove the husks from the tomatillos, then rinse under cold running water to wash off any sticky residue. Place in a medium-size saucepan & cover with water. Bring to a boil, lower the heat to a energetic simmer, & cook 10 minutes, or till softened. Drain totally & let cool.
2. Place the onion, garlic, jalapeños, & lime juice in the container of a food processor & pulse a few times till coarsely chopped. Add the tomatillos & process till finely chopped but not completely smooth. Scrape the combination right into a bowl.
3. Stir in the sugar, salt, & cilantro. Serve at room temperature.

CLASSIC HUMMUS

MAKES two ½ CUPS

one (19-ounce) can (2 cups) chickpeas, rinsed well in a strainer, or two cups freshly cooked chickpeas

three garlic cloves, minced

½ cup fresh lemon juice (about three lemons)

one cup tahini (stirred well before measuring)

½ teaspoon salt

½—1 cup water

Paprika for garnish

Place the chickpeas & garlic in a food processor & process a few seconds, till the chickpeas are ground. Cease the machine & add the lemon juice, tahini, salt, & ½ cup water. Process till the combination is very creamy, a minimum of two minutes. Check the consistency. For a sandwich spread it ought to be slightly firmer than for a dip. Add a bit more water if necessary & process till very smooth.

ROASTED RED PEPPER HUMMUS

MAKES 2½ CUPS

⅔ cup diced roasted red peppers (home made, or store-purchased), patted very dry

three garlic cloves, minced

one (19-ounce) can (2 cups) chickpeas, rinsed well in a strainer

½ cup fresh lemon juice

½ cup tahini, stirred well before measuring

½ teaspoon ground cumin

½ teaspoon salt

⅓–⅔ cup water

Minced fresh parsley for garnish

Mix the red peppers & garlic in a food processor & process till liquefied. Cease the machine & add the chickpeas, lemon juice, tahini, cumin, salt, & a ⅓ cup water. Process till very smooth & creamy, no less than two minutes. Check the consistency; if the hummus is just too thick, beat in a little more water. Top with fresh parsley.

WHITE BEAN & ROASTED RED PEPPER SPREAD

MAKES ABOUT 1½ CUPS
one **(15-ounce) can white beans (such as**
Nice Northern, cannelini, or navy), rinsed completely & drained, or 1½
cups freshly cooked white beans
¼ **cup diced roasted red peppers, patted very dry (selfmade, or store-**
purchased)
two **medium garlic cloves, minced two tablespoons fruity olive oil**
¼ **teaspoon good-quality paprika**
Salt to taste
two **tablespoons minced fresh basil, or ½ teaspoon dried**

1. Mix all of the ingredients besides the basil in a food processor & process till very smooth & creamy, no less than three minutes.
2. Scrape the combination right into a bowl & stir in the basil. Cover & chill not less than one hour. Bring almost to room temperature before serving.

WHITE BEAN SPREAD WITH LEMON & MINT

MAKES ABOUT 1½ CUPS
one **(15-ounce) can white beans (such as**
navy, Nice Northern, or cannelini), rinsed & well drained
three tablespoons lemon juice
three tablespoons olive oil
two **garlic cloves, minced ¼ teaspoon salt**
Freshly ground pepper to taste
two **tablespoons chopped fresh mint**
two **tablespoons chopped fresh parsley**

1. In the container of a food processor mix the beans, lemon juice, oil, garlic, salt, & pepper, & process till smooth, a least one minute.
2. Cease the processor & add the mint & parsley. Process just till the herbs are minced & blended. Scrape the combination right into a serving bowl; it will likely be a little soupy but will get firmer upon chilling. Cover with plastic wrap & chill

no less than one hour or overnight. Bring almost to room temperature before serving.

PORTOBELLO MUSHROOM PÂTÉ

MAKES ABOUT one CUP
four medium-large Portobello mushrooms (with caps four to five inches in diameter)
one **tablespoon unsalted butter**
four garlic cloves, put through a press or minced
one **teaspoon fresh thyme, or ¼ teaspoon dried**
Salt to taste
Freshly ground pepper to taste
Sour cream for garnish (optional)
Italian flat-leaf parsley leaves for garnish (optional)

1. Remove & discard the stems of the mushrooms. Wipe the mushroom caps clean with a humid paper towel. Use a spoon to scrape off among the bottom gills of the mushrooms; this may reduce moisture in the spread. Cut the mushroom caps into quarters & place in a food processor. Pulse a few times till the mushrooms are evenly ground & resemble coarse bread crumbs. Don't over process them. It's greater to process them in two batches if the bowl of the processor appears too crowded.

2. Heat the butter in a medium-size skillet over medium heat. Add the garlic & cook one minute. Don't let it get brown. Stir in the mushrooms & thyme, & sauté about five minutes, or till the juices have evaporated & the mushrooms are cooked through. Season with salt & pepper.

3. Scrape the combination right into a bowl & let cool to room temperature. Serve on toast factors or crostini with a garnish of sour cream & parsley, if desired.

ROASTED EGGPLANT CAVIAR

SERVES 6
Olive oil for greasing plus two tablespoons
one medium-large (1½–2 pounds) eggplant,
halved lengthwise
two tomatoes, cored, cut horizontally in half,
& seeded
one green pepper, cored & halved lengthwise
two onions, quartered
four garlic cloves, minced ½ teaspoon salt ½ teaspoon sugar

Liberal seasoning freshly ground pepper

1. Preheat the oven to four hundred degrees.
2. Oil a baking sheet that has sides or a big roasting pan. Place the eggplant, tomatoes, green pepper, & onions, cut-side down, on the pan. Bake forty five minutes. Let cool about quarter-hour, then peel the skin from the pepper & tomatoes with your fingers. Remove no matter slips off easily; it doesn't must be good.
3. Scrape the eggplant out of its skin & place in a big bowl. Discard the skin. Add the pepper, tomatoes, & onions. Use two knives in a crisscross vogue to finely chop all of the greens.
4. Heat the two tablespoons oil in a medium-size skillet. Add the garlic & sauté 1-2 minutes. Stir in the greens, salt, sugar, & pepper, & cook till thick & the combination begins to stay to the pan, about quarter-hour.
5. Puree half the combination in a food processor, then place in a bowl. Stir in the remaining combination. Chill several hours before serving.

SMOKED CHEESE & SUN-DRIED TOMATO SPREAD

MAKES 1¼ CUPS
five **loose sun-dried tomatoes**
eight ounces Neufchâtel (light cream cheese), at room temperature
½ cup grated smoked Gouda

1. Place the tomatoes in a small bowl & cover with boiling water. Let sit half-hour. Remove them with your hands & squeeze out all their liquid.
2. **2**. Place the tomatoes in a food processor & process till pureed. Add the cream cheese & smoked cheese, & process till very smooth & fluffy at the least three minutes. Scrape the combination right into a bowl. This spread will keep, covered & refrigerated, up to five days.

CREAMY RICOTTA BASIL SPREAD

MAKES 1¼ CUPS
one cup ricotta cheese, preferably whole milk
¼ cup cream cheese, preferably Neufchâtel (light cream cheese)
one garlic clove, minced
two tablespoons grated Parmesan cheese Dash salt
three tablespoons minced fresh basil, plus a
little extra for garnish

1. Mix all of the ingredients besides the basil in a food processor & process till smooth.

2. Scrape right into a bowl & stir in the basil by hand. Cover & chill a minimum of one hour for the flavors to meld. Serve with some basil sprinkled on top.

SPICY BLACK BEAN DIP

MAKES ABOUT 1½ CUPS
one (15-ounce) can black beans, rinsed in a
strainer & drained thoroughly, or 1½ cups freshly cooked black beans
two tablespoons lime juice
three tablespoons olive oil
one chipotle pepper in adobo sauce, or dried chipotle soaked in boiling water
half-hour
one very small garlic clove, minced
one tablespoon sour cream for garnish (optional)
Minced fresh parsley for garnish

1. Mix all of the ingredients besides the sour cream & parsley in a food processor & process till fluffy.
2. Scrape the dip right into a serving bowl. Place the sour cream in the middle in case you are utilizing it & sprinkle the dip with some minced parsley.

CLASSIC TZATZIKI

MAKES ABOUT 1½ CUPS
two **cups low-fat or whole milk yogurt (not nonfat)**
one **cucumber, peeled, seeded, & grated**
one **garlic clove, put through a press or minced**
1½ teaspoons minced fresh dill one tablespoon minced fresh parsley one tablespoon olive oil ¼ teaspoon salt
Generous seasoning freshly ground pepper

1. Line a strainer with a single layer of cheesecloth, letting the fabric dangle over the sides. Spoon the yogurt into the strainer & place it over a medium-large bowl to permit the drippings (whey) to gather. Cover the strainer with plastic wrap & place it & the bowl in the fridge for twenty-four hours. (You need to pour out the liquid no less than once during this time as a result of so much will accumulate & also you don't need the bottom of the strainer to sit in it.)
2. Place the grated cucumber in a cotton kitchen towel & collect right into a ball. Squeeze out all of the juices. Drop the ball of grated cucumber onto a cutting board & mince it with a big knife.

3. Put the yogurt in a medium-size bowl & discard the accrued liquid. Mix in the cucumber & all of the remaining ingredients. Chill no less than two hours so the flavors can mingle.

CLASSIC GUACAMOLE

SERVES four
two **ripe Haas (dark pebbly-skinned) avocados**
four teaspoons fresh lime juice
two **tablespoons minced red or white onion**
¼ cup minced tomato
¼ teaspoon salt

1. To open the avocado slice it lengthwise across the pit. Twist each halves to separate them & discard the pit. Slip the tip of a teaspoon handle between the skin & flesh of the avocado & slide it throughout to separate the avocado half from its skin.
2. Place the avocado halves & lime juice in a food processor & process till smooth & fluffy. Scrape the combination right into a bowl. Stir in the remaining ingredients. Serve instantly or cover & chill up to 24 hours, then bring to room temperature before serving.

GARLIC & OIL DIPPING SAUCE

MAKES ⅓ CUP, ENOUGH FOR four PEOPLE
⅓ cup fruity, extra-virgin olive oil
one large garlic clove, put through a press or minced
⅓ teaspoon crushed red pepper flakes one long strip orange peel, 3X1 inch
Tuscan-style bread pieces for dipping

1. Place the oil, garlic, & red pepper flakes in a small saucepan. Heat just till the garlic begins to sizzle. You don't need it to get in any respect coloured. Instantly drop in the orange peel.
2. Pour the combination right into a shallow medium-size bowl. Let sit at the very least 20 minutes. Discard the orange peel. Serve surrounded by pieces of bread. (I like to chop the bread into triangles.)

CLASSIC FRESH SALSA

MAKES ABOUT two CUPS
two **large ripe tomatoes or five ripe plum tomatoes, seeded & finely diced**
¼ cup minced red onion

¼ **cup finely chopped cilantro**

one **jalapeño pepper, or more to taste, seeded & minced (put on gloves)**

one **garlic clove, put through a press or**
minced

two **tablespoons lime juice**

¼ **teaspoon salt**

Mix all of the ingredients in a medium-size bowl. Serve instantly.

COOKED TOMATO-CHIPOTLE SALSA

MAKES two CUPS

one **tablespoon olive oil**

one **small onion, minced**

two **garlic cloves, minced**

½ **green bell pepper, minced**

one **(14-ounce) can diced tomatoes**

one **tablespoon tomato paste**

½ **chipotle pepper in adobo sauce, minced**

one **teaspoon sugar**

Salt to taste

one **tablespoon minced fresh cilantro**

two **tablespoons lime juice**

1. Warm the oil in a medium-size saucepan over medium heat. Add the onion, garlic, & green pepper, & sauté 10 minutes.
2. Mix in the tomatoes with their juice, tomato paste, chipotle, sugar, & salt, & simmer 20 minutes, or till the green pepper is soft.
3. Pour the salsa right into a food processor & pulse eight times, or till it's finely minced but not pureed. Scrape right into a bowl & let cool. Stir in the cilantro & lime juice. Serve at room temperature.

BASIC CROSTINI

MAKES ABOUT forty TOASTS

one baguette (1 pound) French bread or four grinder (submarine) rolls

½ cup olive oil

1. Preheat the oven to 350 degrees. Thinly slice the bread with a serrated knife into ¼-inch-thick slices.
2. Place the oil in a small bowl. Utilizing a pastry brush very lightly coat either side of the bread slices with the oil. Place in one layer on the baking sheet. You'll have

to do that in two batches or use two sheets. Bake five minutes, turn the toasts over, & bake 5-7 minutes more, or till golden throughout. Let cool completely before storing in plastic bags.

GARLIC PITA CHIPS

MAKES sixty four CHIPS

four tablespoons olive oil
two garlic cloves, put through a press (preferably) or minced
four (6-inch) pita breads

1. Mix the oil & garlic in a small bowl & let sit half-hour.
2. Preheat the oven to 300 degrees.
3. Cut one pita bread in half to make two pockets. Use kitchen shears to snip the outer fringe of one pocket to separate it into two single layers. Repeat with the opposite pocket. Utilizing a pastry brush lightly coat the tough side of every piece with the garlic oil, scooping up bits of garlic if you do that. With a pointy knife cut every bit into four triangles. Place on a baking sheet, tough side up. Repeat with the remaining pita breads. You'll have to make use of a few baking sheets
4. Bake 12–quarter-hour, or till golden & cooked all over. Cool completely before storing in plastic bags.

MARINATED OLIVES

SERVES four-6
four cups assorted olives (such as Niçoise, Kalamata, & green Picholine)
¼ cup olive oil
one **teaspoon grated orange zest (from about**
⅓ of an orange)
two **garlic cloves, pressed or minced**
A few dashes cayenne pepper
two **teaspoons minced fresh rosemary, or one teaspoon dried, crumbled**
Mix all of the ingredients in a glass or ceramic bowl & marinate at the least one hour at room temperature or up to one week in the fridge. Bring to room temperature before serving.

EDAMAME

SERVES four
one **(12-ounce) bag frozen edamame**
Salt to taste
Bring a medium-size saucepan crammed with lightly salted water to a boil. Drop in the edamame & let the water return to a boil. Cook about five minutes. Drain, place in a big bowl, & let cool to warm or room temperature. Sprinkle with salt & serve. Each individual can break up the pods open & pop the beans into his or her mouth. Discard the pods.

CLASSIC LENTIL SOUP

SERVES four-6 AS A MAIN COURSE
¼ cup olive oil
three large onions, finely diced
four large garlic cloves, minced
10 cups water
1¼ cups lentils, picked over & rinsed
one **green bell pepper, finely diced**
four carrots, finely diced
two **celery ribs, thinly sliced**
⅓ cup tomato paste combined with ½ cup water
two **tablespoons tamari soy sauce**
one **teaspoon salt**
Freshly ground pepper to taste
one **tablespoon red wine vinegar**
two **tablespoons unsalted butter**

1. Pour the oil in a big stockpot & heat over medium-high heat. Add the onions & garlic, & sauté till the onions start to brown, about 10 minutes.
2. Stir in all of the remaining ingredients besides the vinegar & butter. Bring to a boil, lower the heat to a simmer, & cook, stirring frequently, for forty five minutes. When done, the soup can be thick & the greens tender. Stir in the vinegar & butter just before serving.

CURRIED RED LENTIL SOUP

SERVES four AS A MAIN COURSE

1½ **cups red lentils, picked over for stones & rinsed in a strainer**
six **cups water**
one **tablespoon canola oil**
¾ **teaspoon salt**
two **medium-size boiling potatoes (such as red-skinned), peeled & cut into** ½-**inch dice**
three tablespoons unsalted butter
one **medium onion, finely diced**
one **teaspoon minced gingerroot**
two **garlic cloves, minced**
one **teaspoon turmeric**
two **teaspoons ground cumin**
1½ **teaspoons ground coriander**
⅛ **teaspoon cayenne pepper**
¾ **cup finely diced canned tomatoes**
two **tablespoons lemon juice (about ½ lemon)**
Minced cilantro for garnish (optional)

1. Mix the lentils, water, oil, & salt in a three-quart saucepan & bring to a boil over medium-high heat, stirring often. With a big spoon skim off any foam that rises to the surface & discard it. Lower the heat & cook 20 minutes, stirring often.
2. Stir in the diced potatoes.
3. Melt the butter in a medium-size skillet over medium heat. Add the onion, ginger, & garlic, & cook two minutes. Sprinkle on the turmeric, cumin, coriander, & cayenne, & brown these spices two minutes, stirring consistently. Mix in the diced tomatoes & cook one minute more.
4. Scrape the combination into the soup & stir well. Cook the soup 20 minutes more, or till the potatoes are tender. Stir frequently from this level on to prevent the soup from sticking. When done, the soup ought to be considerably smooth & the consistency of thick cream. If it's thick & pasty, thin with a little water. Mix in the lemon juice. Serve with a sprinkling of cilantro, if desired.

CORN & RED PEPPER CHOWDER

SERVES four AS A MAIN COURSE
two **tablespoons unsalted butter**
one **tablespoon olive oil**
two **medium onions, finely diced**
two **garlic cloves, minced**
four cups vegetable broth/stock, store-purchased or home made
two **large potatoes, peeled & finely diced (about 2½ cups)**
two **medium-size red bell peppers, finely diced**

one **celery rib, very thinly sliced**
one **bay leaf**
two **tablespoons finely chopped fresh basil,**
or ½ teaspoon dried
¾ teaspoon salt
one **tablespoon sugar**
Freshly ground pepper to taste
four cups frozen or fresh corn kernels
six **scallions, very thinly sliced**
½ cup milk
½ cup heavy cream

1. Mix the butter & oil in a big broth/stock-pot & place over medium heat. Add the onions & garlic, & sauté till the onions are tender but not brown, about 10 minutes.
2. Stir in the broth/stock & bring to a boil. Add the potatoes, red peppers, celery, bay leaf, basil, salt, sugar, & pepper, & bring to a boil. Lower the heat to a energetic simmer, partially cover the pan, & cook till the potatoes are tender, about quarter-hour. Stir in the corn & scallions, & cook two minutes more if utilizing frozen corn, eight minutes more if utilizing fresh corn. Remove the bay leaf.
3. Remove three cups of the soup & puree in a blender. Return to the pot. Stir in the milk & cream, & heat a minute or so before serving.

VEGETABLE CHOWDER

SERVES four AS A MAIN COURSE
two **leeks**
two **tablespoons olive oil**
four garlic cloves, minced
eight ounces mushrooms, quartered & thinly sliced
five **cups vegetable broth/stock, store-purchased or selfmade**
one **red bell pepper, cut into ¼-inch dice**
three medium boiling potatoes (such as red-skinned), peeled & cut into ½-inch dice
one **medium sweet potato, peeled & cut into ½-inch dice**
one **cup frozen corn**
three cups milk
½ cup heavy cream
¾ teaspoon salt
Generous seasoning freshly ground pepper
two **tablespoons minced fresh dill, or one ½ teaspoons dried**

1. To wash the leeks slice off their root ends & the robust green leaves besides about two inches above the white base. Slice the leeks in half lengthwise. Wash the leeks under cold running water, flipping through their leaves to dislodge any hidden dust. Pat the leeks dry. Thinly slice the leeks, discarding any dark green pieces & saving only white & pale green ones.
2. Heat the oil in a big stockpot over medium heat. Add the leeks & garlic, & sauté five minutes, stirring often. Mix in the mushrooms & sauté the combination till the mushrooms are juicy & start to brown, about seven minutes.
3. Stir in the broth/stock, red pepper, potatoes, & sweet potato, & bring the soup to a boil. Lower the heat to a full of life simmer & cook half-hour,
4. Add the corn, milk, cream, salt, & pepper, & heat to almost a boil. Remove three cups of the soup & puree in a blender or food processor. Return it to the pot & stir in the dill.

KALE SOUP

SERVES six AS A MAIN COURSE
½ cup olive oil
three large onions, finely diced
four garlic cloves, minced
two **bay leaves**
10 cups vegetable broth/stock, store-purchased or selfmade
one **(sixteen-ounce) can prepared-cut diced tomatoes**
one **(15-ounce) can kidney beans, drained & rinsed well, or 1½ cups freshly cooked beans**
one **pound kale, leaves torn from stems & finely chopped (10 cups leaves)**
three medium-size red-skinned potatoes, unpeeled & cut into ½-inch dice
2teaspoons good-quality (sweet) paprika
Dash cayenne pepper
one **teaspoon salt**
Liberal seasoning freshly ground pepper

1. Heat the oil in a big stockpot over medium heat. Stir in the onions & garlic, & sauté till the onions are golden & tender, about 10 minutes.
2. Elevate the heat to high, stir in all of the remaining ingredients, & bring the soup to a boil. Lower the heat to a full of life simmer & cook about half-hour, or till the potatoes are tender & the soup has thickened.
3. Discard the bay leaves. Remove about two cups of the soup & puree in a blender or food processor. Return it to the soup & stir to mix. This soup's flavor will intensify with time, so don't hesitate to make it a few days prematurely.

CLASSIC BARLEY MUSHROOM SOUP

SERVES four AS A MAIN COURSE
three tablespoons olive oil
two **medium onions, finely diced**
four garlic cloves, minced
one **pound mushrooms, coarsely chopped into small pieces (see Tip)**
10 cups vegetable broth/stock, store-purchased or selfmade
one **celery rib, very thinly sliced**
two **carrots, finely chopped**
½ cup barley, rinsed in a strainer two tablespoons tamari soy sauce
one **teaspoon fresh thyme, or ½ teaspoon dried**
½ teaspoon salt
Generous seasoning freshly ground pepper
two **tablespoons minced fresh parsley**

1. Heat the oil in a big stockpot over medium heat. Stir in the onions & garlic, & cook till tender & golden, about 10 minutes. Add the mushrooms & sauté, stirring often, till they release their juices & start to brown, about 10 minutes.
2. Stir in all of the remaining ingredients besides the parsley & bring to a boil. Cover the pot, lower the heat to a vigorous simmer, & cook forty five-60 minutes, or till the barley is very tender. Stir in the parsley just before serving.

BARLEY YOGURT SOUP

SERVES four AS A MAIN COURSE
two **tablespoons unsalted butter**
one **tablespoon olive oil**
one **large onion, minced**
two **garlic cloves, minced**
six **cups vegetable broth/stock, store-purchased or selfmade**
½ cup barley, rinsed in a strainer
one **large egg**
two **cups plain yogurt**
½ cup finely chopped fresh parsley
three tablespoons finely chopped fresh mint, or one tablespoon dried
two **scallions, very thinly sliced**
¼ teaspoon salt

1. Heat the butter & oil in a three-quart saucepan over medium heat. Add the onion & sauté till golden & soft (but by no means brown), about five minutes. Stir in the broth/stock & barley, & bring to a boil. Lower the heat to a full of life simmer, partially cover the pan, & cook forty minutes, or till tender. Stir often.

2. In the meantime, beat the egg in a medium-size bowl. Beat in the yogurt, parsley, mint, scallions, & salt. When the barley is tender, stir in the yogurt combination. Instantly remove the pot from the heat & stir the soup a couple of minutes. You don't need to boil the soup at this level, or the yogurt will curdle. Serve instantly or at a later time. In case you chill the soup & wish to reheat it, do so over low heat without boiling it.

BUTTERNUT SQUASH & CIDER SOUP

SERVES four AS A MAIN COURSE
three tablespoons olive oil
two **large leeks, thinly sliced (together with two inches of light green top)**
three garlic cloves, minced
1½ teaspoons curry powder
three cups water
three cups apple cider
three pounds (1 large) butternut squash, peeled, cored, & cut into 1-inch cubes (about seven cups)
⅓ cup white rice, preferably transformed, basmati, or jasmine
one **teaspoon salt**
Minced parsley or chives for garnish

one Heat the oil in a big stockpot over medium heat. Add the leeks & garlic, & sauté till the leeks are tender, about eight minutes. Sprinkle on the curry powder, toss, & cook one minute.

2. Pour in the water & cider, then stir in the butternut squash, rice, & salt.

3. Cover the pot & bring the soup to a boil. Lower the heat to a simmer & cook till the squash is very soft, about 20 minutes. Let cool a couple of minutes, then puree the soup in batches in a food processor & place in a smaller pot, if desired. Check the consistency. If necessary, thin with a little water & cider till creamy like heavy cream. Serve garnished with parsley or chives, if desired.

CURRIED BUTTERNUT SQUASH SOUP

SERVES four AS A MAIN COURSE
two **tablespoons olive oil**
two **onions, finely diced**

three garlic cloves, minced
one **tablespoon minced gingerroot**
one **tablespoon curry powder**
four cups water
7-eight cups diced butternut squash (1 large three-pound squash)
two **teaspoons sugar**
1¼ teaspoons salt
one **(14-ounce) can coconut milk**
two **tablespoons lemon juice**

1. Warm the oil in a big stockpot over medium heat. Stir in the onions, garlic, & gingerroot, & cook five minutes. Sprinkle on the curry powder & cook one minute, tossing repeatedly.

2. Pour in the water & bring to a boil. Mix in the squash, sugar, & salt, & lower the heat to a energetic simmer. Cook half-hour, or till the squash is very tender. Pour in the coconut milk & simmer five minutes. Stir in the lemon juice

3. Puree the soup in batches in a blender & return to a smaller pot, if desired. Reheat the soup before serving, if necessary.

THICK CORN & VEGETABLE SOUP

SERVES 6-eight
¼ cup olive oil
two **tablespoons butter**
two **medium onions, diced**
four garlic cloves, minced
two **bay leaves**
four cloves
Dash cayenne pepper
12 cups vegetable broth/stock, store-purchased or selfmade
one **teaspoon salt**
Generous seasoning freshly ground pepper
one **(28-ounce) can prepared-cut diced tomatoes**
15-ounce can pinto or small white beans, rinsed well & drained, or 1½ cups freshly cooked beans
two **medium carrots, halved lengthwise & thinly sliced**
two **medium potatoes, cut into ½-inch dice**
one **cup diced (½-inch) butternut squash (see Tip)**
one **cup finely chopped fresh parsley, divided**
two **cups frozen corn**

Herb Dumplings:
one **cup unbleached flour**
two **tablespoons cornmeal**
two **teaspoons baking powder**
one **teaspoon sugar**
½ **teaspoon salt**
two **tablespoons minced fresh parsley**
½ **teaspoon freshly minced dill, or one teaspoon dried**
one **tablespoon chilled butter**
⅔ **cup cold milk**

1. **1**. Heat the oil & butter in a big stockpot over medium heat. Add the onions & garlic, & sauté till tender, about 10 minutes. Stir in the cloves, bay leaves, cayenne, vegetable broth/stock, salt, pepper, & tomatoes, & bring to a boil.

2. **2**. Add the beans, carrots, potatoes, butternut squash, & half the parsley, & return to a boil. Lower the heat & cook at a full of life simmer for half-hour, or till the greens are tender. Stir the soup often. Mix in the corn & the remaining ½ cup parsley, & cook five minutes. Discard the bay leaves. (The soup may be prepared so far up to three days upfront & refrigerated. Reheat before continuing with the next step.)

3. To make the dumplings: mix the flour, cornmeal, baking powder, sugar, salt, parsley, & dill in a medium-size bowl. Cut the butter into bits & drop into the combination. Rub the butter into the flour with your fingertips till small crumbs form. Stir in the milk just till evenly moistened; don't overmix. Cover & chill till prepared to make use of, up to eight hours.

4. To cook the dumplings, keep the soup at a vigorous simmer. Maintain one tablespoon in each hand, scoop out about ⅛ of the batter, & utilizing the spoons, shortly form right into a ball. Place the dumpling in. the soup & repeat with the remaining batter. Cover the pot & cook at a full of life simmer, not a violent boil, for quarter-hour. Don't uncover the pot during this time. When done, the dumplings shall be fat & puffy. Serve the soup with one dumpling in each bowl.

Made in the USA
Lexington, KY
11 December 2017